That He Might Be Revealed

That He Might Be Revealed

Water Imagery and the Identity of Jesus
in the Gospel of John

RHONDA G. CRUTCHER

◆PICKWICK *Publications* • Eugene, Oregon

THAT HE MIGHT BE REVEALED
Water Imagery and the Identity of Jesus in the Gospel of John

Copyright © 2015 Rhonda G. Crutcher. All rights reserved. Except for brief quotations in critical publications or reviews, no part of this book may be reproduced in any manner without prior written permission from the publisher. Write: Permissions, Wipf and Stock Publishers, 199 W. 8th Ave., Suite 3, Eugene, OR 97401.

Pickwick Publications
An Imprint of Wipf and Stock Publishers
199 W. 8th Ave., Suite 3
Eugene, OR 97401

www.wipfandstock.com

ISBN 13: 978-1-62564-435-0

Cataloging-in-Publication data:

Crutcher, Rhonda G.

That he might be revealed : water imagery and the identity of Jesus in the Gospel of John / Rhonda G. Crutcher.

x + 176 p. ; 23 cm. —Includes bibliographical references and index(es).

ISBN 13: 978-1-62564-435-0

1. Bible. John—Criticism, interpretation, etc. 2. Bible. John—Theology. 3. Jesus Christ—Person and offices—Biblical teaching. 4. Water in the Bible. I. Title.

BS2615.2 C73 2015

Manufactured in the U.S.A. 08/11/2015

All Scripture quotations, unless otherwise indicated, are taken from the Holy Bible, New International Version®, NIV®. Copyright ©1973, 1978, 1984, 2011 by Biblica, Inc.™ Used by permission of Zondervan. All rights reserved worldwide. www.zondervan.com The "NIV" and "New International Version" are trademarks registered in the United States Patent and Trademark Office by Biblica, Inc.™

For my mother
Mary DeMart Olson
Who never got to realize her dream

And my father
Ronald H. DeMart
(1942–2007)
Who didn't understand the dream,
but supported it anyway

Also for my children
Andrew, my miracle baby
Alex, my European baby
and Elizabeth, my thesis baby

As much as I did this for myself
I was also doing it for you
Someday I hope you'll understand

Contents

Acknowledgments | ix

CHAPTER 1
Prolegomena | 1

CHAPTER 2
Water and Yahweh's Identity in the Old Testament Tradition | 34

CHAPTER 3
Setting Up the Motif: Water and Identity in John 1 & 3 | 65

CHAPTER 4
Weddings and Waterpots: Water and Identity in John 2 & 4 | 88

CHAPTER 5
Bethesda and Siloam: Water and Identity in John 5 & 9 | 114

CHAPTER 6
The Water from Jesus' Side: Water and Identity in John 7 & 19 | 133

CHAPTER 7
Summary and Conclusions | 158

Bibliography | 167

Acknowledgments

I must acknowledge two people in particular who each in their own way awakened me to study of the Bible. First, Dr. Peggy Poteet, Chair of the Department of English and the Communication Arts Division at Southern Nazarene University. As an undergraduate student in English I discovered the literary study of the Bible in her class, and I was fascinated.

Secondly, Dr. Roger Hahn, Dean of the Faculty and Professor of New Testament at Nazarene Theological Seminary (Kansas City, Missouri, USA) who was my first Bible professor and under whose tutelage I heard the Lord calling me to the scholarly study of the Bible. He is forever to me the model of what a Christian scholar should be. If I can teach my students even a fraction of what he taught me, I will be a success.

Pertaining to the production of this particular work I must thank the following for giving me much more than I could ever give back:

My doctoral advisor, Dr. Kent Brower, Nazarene Theological College, Manchester, UK, who demonstrated extreme patience in guiding me through many crises of indecision and uncertainty. Few would have stuck with me for as long or with as much grace, and for that alone I am forever grateful.

The rest of the administration, faculty, and staff of NTC Manchester. In particular I must mention the always cheerful and helpful support of Rita Stuart and Alison Yarwood, two of my very favorite genuine British persons. Partly as a result of their efforts the NTC campus has become a second home to me.

Director(s) and staff of the R. T. Williams Library at Southern Nazarene University (Bethany, Oklahoma, USA) for granting me access to the library at odd days and times and patiently processing hundreds of interlibrary loan requests.

ACKNOWLEDGMENTS

Dr. Gwen Ladd Hackler, former Vice-Provost for Academic Administration at Southern Nazarene University, who was a great support and very generous with work arrangements allowing me to have the necessary time to complete the project.

And finally, to my husband Tim, my biggest fan, most vocal supporter, my head cheerleader. Thank you for not letting me give up on myself.

CHAPTER 1

Prolegomena

INTRODUCTION

Jesus' gradual revelation of his "true" identity as the Son of God is a prominent theme of the Gospel of John. While occasionally encountered in the Synoptics, this motif is developed much more deliberately and deeply by the Fourth Evangelist. This is not surprising in light of the author's self-stated goal of engendering belief in Jesus as the "Christ, the Son of God" (20:31). Since this theme is a significant component of the Gospel it naturally interacts with many of the motifs, metaphors and images employed by the author. One of the most important of these is the recurring water imagery that has been long noted and discussed.

Water imagery is widely acknowledged as pervading the Gospel, especially the first nine chapters, and interacts with many of the larger themes of the work including that of the revelation of Jesus as the Christ, and the subject of identity in general. However, while each of the motifs of water, revelation, and identity has received due attention and examination individually, to date there has not been a specific and thorough exploration of the inter-connections of the water motif and the revelation of Jesus' identity in the Gospel. That is the purpose of this study: to show how the water imagery of the Gospel interacts with the theme of Jesus' self-revelation, and to uncover how this relationship serves the author's purpose of stimulating belief in his audience.

PRELIMINARY DISCUSSION

Water is a powerful and pervasive image in the Hebrew Scriptures and other ancient Jewish literature. It appears significantly at crucial moments in Israel's history—the creation of the world (Gen 1:1–2), the Flood (Gen.7:6ff), crossing the Sea of Reeds as part of the Exodus (Ex 14:21ff) and the provision of water in the wilderness (Num 20:9ff) being the most important. It is also a frequent metaphor in poetic and wisdom literature, and figures significantly in the writings of the prophets. This preoccupation reflects the crucial place of water in the arid climate of Palestine and the lands surrounding it,[1] while the abundance of water metaphors, flood stories, and water rituals in the ancient world at large is a testament to the universal significance of water in day to day life.[2]

Many of these water images from the Hebrew Scriptures are reused by the writers of the New Testament, particularly in the Gospels and the book of Revelation. But nowhere do we find water imagery exercised with such frequency, breadth and theological importance as in the Gospel of John, as has been well-noted.[3] Some of the most memorable stories in the Gospel involve water: the changing of the water into wine (2:1–11); Jesus' conversation with the Samaritan woman at the well (4:7–15); the healing of the man at the Pool of Bethesda (5:2–9); Jesus walking on the Sea of Galilee (6:16–21); Jesus washing the disciples' feet (13:3–11); and the reinstatement of Peter beside the Sea of Galilee (21:1–19). In addition, water plays a prominent part in Jesus' discussion with Nicodemus in 3:3–5; Jesus' speech at the Feast of Tabernacles in 7:37–39; the healing of the blind man in 9:1–12; and in the crucifixion scene, where water mingles with the blood flowing from Jesus' side (19:34).

---

1. As L. Goppelt puts it: "There is no assurance of water for either men or plants in Palestine. Water supply is always threatened. Hence bread and water are given equal emphasis in the OT as vital necessities.... [and] the technique of providing water lies behind many OT stories [e.g. the digging of wells or drawing water from them]." Goppelt, "ὕδωρ," 318.

2. Cf. ibid., 314–17, who distinguishes three basic categories of water usage in the literature of the ancient Oriental and Greek-Hellenistic world: 1) Flood stories; 2) Water as Dispenser of Life; 3) and Cleansing by Water. The large majority of Old and New Testament water references would fit into one of these three categories, with larger bodies of water being related to flood imagery and smaller bodies (rivers, lakes, streams, fountains, etc.) fitting into either of the final two categories.

3. Barrett, *Gospel*, 195–96; T. Brown, *Spirit*, 121–22; Culpepper, *Anatomy*, 195–96; Keener, *Gospel*, 440; Koester, *Symbolism*, 155–84; Lightfoot, *St. John's*, 121.

Water imagery and metaphors are so embedded in daily language and life that one is not surprised that they are commonly found in literature. However, so many prominent instances within a particular piece of literature can scarcely be attributed to simple coincidence. John's Gospel contains the most references to water of any book of the New Testament except Revelation, and nearly as many as the Synoptic Gospels combined. Of the 118 instances of the various forms of the words ὕδωρ (water), λίμνη (lake), πηγή (spring or well), κολυμβήθρα (pool), and ποταμός (river) in the New Testament, nine are found in Matthew, seven in Mark, fourteen in Luke and twenty-eight in John. Revelation has 38. The Johannine writings combined (Gospel, 1 John and Revelation) account for 70 instances of these water terms, over half the total in the New Testament.

This invites the question, then, of the significance of this particular image to the tradition behind the Gospel and to the person or people who were responsible for its final form.[4] What point, or points, were intended by such deliberate employment of water imagery? There are many ways in which to approach an answer to this question. To date the majority of those who have delved into the issue have done so from a historical-critical viewpoint—studying the significance of water in cultures and literature of the ANE in general and Israel in specific as a clue to the author's purpose. These scholars turn most often to the Hebrew Scriptures and other ancient Jewish writings, which, indeed, are the most helpful context for understanding John's water usage. However, this work is often lacking. First of all, to most it seems as if a mere mention of this background is sufficient, as if the connections are obvious without further comment. One frequently finds commentators who simply rattle off a list of Old Testament passages which stand in the background of a particular water image with little if any attempt to explicate the significance of this background for the particular text at hand.[5] Furthermore, few see Johannine water imagery as a specific continuation of the imagery related to God in the Old Testament, and even those who do often fail to use such observation to assist in interpreting the author's purpose and message.

Additionally, although the Exodus imagery and structure in the Fourth Gospel has long been acknowledged and discussed, there has been

---

4. See my discussion of authorship below under "Assumptions and Rationale."

5 To be fair, some commentators do show interest in this subject, but are limited by the commentary form from exploring too deeply. Cf. Barrett, *Gospel*, 195; Lightfoot, *St. John's*, 100, 184; Beasley-Murray, *John*, 60; Bernard, *Critical*, 138–40; Bruce, *Gospel*, 71, 84, 105; Morris, *Gospel*, 260–61.

no serious attempt to use the water events of the Exodus narratives to help explicate relevant Johannine water passages. This is somewhat surprising since water figures so prominently in two pivotal Exodus events, the crossing of the Sea of Reeds and the water from the rock in the wilderness, and since so many other connections between John's Gospel and the Exodus narratives have been posited.[6]

Therefore, this study proposes to examine the relationship of the water imagery in the Fourth Gospel and water events and imagery in ancient Jewish literature with the goal of illuminating the interpretation of the Johannine passages in question. Through this investigation we will show that John appropriated water images from previous and contemporary Jewish literature and history to serve as an agent, both actual and metaphorical, for the revelation of Jesus as the Christ. He accomplishes this by playing on the memory of water experiences in Israel's Exodus history (echoed through their poetry and prophets) and making clear connections between Jesus and the coming eschatological "Exodus" in which figurative water so often played a part. By recalling the association made by the OT writers between Yahweh's control of the waters and his identity as creator, king, and God, the Fourth Evangelist connects Jesus both to the Yahweh of Israel's past and the triumphant king of Israel's future hope, and so cements his argument that Jesus was the Son of God.

REVIEW OF RELATED LITERATURE

Water Imagery in John

Scholars have long recognized and commented on the water images in the Gospel of John. Some have made more of them than others, however. For example, many authors, especially those deeply rooted in the methods of historical criticism, barely comment on the undercurrent of water symbolism flowing through the Gospel, if they notice it at all.[7] These interpreters

---

6. For a discussion of the motif of Jesus as the new Moses in John cf. Glasson, *Moses*; Harstine, *Moses*, 40–75; Keener, *Gospel*, 1.291; Schapdick, "Religious Authority," 181–210. For other work on Exodus imagery in the Gospel see Brunson, *Psalm 118*; Enz, "Exodus," 208–15; Glasson, "Typology," 329–42; Lierman, "Mosaic Pattern," 210–32; Schnackenburg, *Gospel*, 2.14. For specific discussion of the Exodus imagery in John 6 including a review of the history of the issue see Hylen, *Allusion*, 1–40; also Dennis, *Jesus' Death*, 188–98; Kim, "Christological," 307–22.

7. Some of these authors include Beasley-Murray, *John*; Bernard, *Gospel*; R.E. Brown,

sometimes examine the meaning of water in passages where discussing it is unavoidable (e.g., 3:5; 4:4–14; 7:38–39; 19:34), but there is rarely any attempt to make connections between these instances, with the exception of 7:38–39 and 19:34, where most scholars find a relationship.[8]

There are others who identify the overarching water symbol in the Gospel and make attempts to bring the individual instances into a larger whole, but the confines of the commentary form often limit their discussion of the subject.[9] These include R. H. Lightfoot, who notes most poetically: "the theme of water runs like a silver thread through the early chapters of this Gospel."[10] Lightfoot draws connections between the water imagery in chapters 2, 3 and 4, shows the important theological and thematic connections between the water motif and the Temple motif (2:13–22), and sees these two symbols as coming together in 4:1–26.[11] His comments are quite helpful, but unfortunately he does not continue this work to cover other instances of water imagery in the Gospel. Also, it is somewhat curious that Lightfoot makes no connection between the temple symbolism and the water symbolism in 19:34, when the water flows from Jesus' side since a reference here to the water flowing from the temple in Ezekiel 47:1ff. seems intended, and especially in light of his insightful discussion on the many stylistic and thematic similarities between ch. 4 and the Johannine passion narrative.[12]

As we have demonstrated, a number of authors in the middle part of the 20th century raised awareness to the symbolic water motif of John. This trend was concurrent with the renewed concern during those years for the use of more literary methods in the examination of the Bible. Soon other scholars began to delve even more deeply into the study of Johannine symbolism, and Johannine water symbolism in particular. The first scholar of note in this area is C.H. Dodd who argued that John's use of

---

Gospel, (who generally limits his water-related comments to discussion of possible baptismal motifs in various passages); Bruce, *Gospel* (who does recognize connections between some of the water passages, but does not elaborate on them); Morris, *Gospel*; Painter, *Witness* (Painter includes some very helpful discussion on symbolism in John in general, but little on the symbol of water in specific); Talbert, *Reading*.

8. Beasley-Murray (*John*, 116; 356) is one of the few who does not.

9. Barrett, *Gospel*; Bultmann, *Gospel*; Schnackenburg, *Gospel*.

10. Lightfoot, *St. John's*, 121.

11. Ibid., 120–24.

12. Cf. ibid., 319–20 where he comes very close to this connection, but does not state it explicitly.

extended symbols, or "allegories," differs from the use of parables in the Synoptic Gospels.[13] Using the Parable of the Good Shepherd as an example, he maintains that while complex examination of the details of a parable is not required for understanding,[14] in John's extended symbolism the details of the "allegory" have particular and separate significance with the result that "long before the allegory is at an end, the figure of the shepherd is fused with that of Jesus Himself." The details of the allegory are significant, then, because "they aptly symbolize aspects of [Jesus'] work."[15] Dodd goes on to use the "allegory" of the vine as an example of:

> a kind of symbolism in which the images or figures employed, although they are taken from workaday experience, derive relatively little of their significance from the part they play in such experience. The symbol is almost absorbed into the thing signified. The meaning of the 'allegory' is only to a slight extent to be understood from a knowledge of what vines are as they grown in a vineyard; it is chiefly to be understood out of a rich background of associations which the vine-symbol had already acquired.[16]

Water and bread are just such kinds of symbols in that they "retire behind the realities for which they stand, and derive their significance from a background of thought in which they had already served as symbols for religious conceptions."[17]

Dodd was well ahead of his time in thinking about the Gospel symbolically. Indeed, most subsequent discussion of Johannine symbolism has reacted in some way to Dodd's ideas. Among his most significant contributions for our study is his recognition of the importance of a symbol's past literary and cultural use. Dodd emphasized that a symbol, particularly one with such universal significance as water, cannot be completely divorced from the previous connotations that it has been given in religious thought: "While water as a simple natural phenomenon, especially running water . . .

---

13. Dodd, *Interpretation*, 133–43. Indeed, he includes an entire chapter on symbolism under the section "Leading Ideas." The fact that it is the first chapter in the section (and precedes such important Johannine concepts as "eternal life," "truth," "faith," "Spirit," "Son of God," and "Logos") would seem to indicate the importance, in Dodd's mind, of understanding John's use of symbolism in order to properly interpret the ideas propounded in the Gospel.

14. Ibid., 134.

15. Ibid., 135.

16. Ibid., 137.

17. Ibid.

provides in itself a suggestive figure, it is the rich accumulation of symbolical meaning about the figure that gives its main significance to the water-symbol in the gospel."[18] Therefore, an author can use a symbol from the past to create new meaning, but that new meaning will always have some relationship to the way the symbol was used in the past.

The seeds planted by Dodd's work produced small shoots here and there for the next 30 years, but it wasn't until the publication of R.A. Culpepper's enormously important work *Anatomy of the Fourth Gospel*[19] that John's use of symbolism was examined again in a specific and comprehensive way. In this work Culpepper sees the symbols of the Gospel as the things which "carry the principal burden of the narrative and provide implicit commentary and directional signals for the reader."[20] These symbols are the primary means by which both the characters in the story and the later readers of the narrative are introduced to the "upper sphere of reality and meaning"[21] or spiritual things, as opposed to the lower, or earthly, sphere. "Consequently," Culpepper says, symbols "are often the ladder on which readers, like the angels of Jacob's dream, may ascend and descend while moving to and from the heaven opened by the story."[22]

Culpepper rightly recognizes that symbolism occurs in the Gospel with varying levels of frequency and importance. The symbols which appear most often and in the most important places he calls "core" symbols. For John these are light, water and bread. Subordinate to these are symbols which are related to them and which will evoke the idea of the core symbol.[23] For the core symbol of water the subordinate symbols would include lakes, seas, streams, rivers, springs, wells, pools, and water jars as well as references to baptism. This division is very helpful. Keeping this distinction in mind when interpreting the use of water in John may help the interpreter avoid placing more importance on a "peripheral" symbol than may have been intended by the author.[24] The nature of Culpepper's work,

18. Ibid., 138.
19. Culpepper, *Anatomy*, 180–202.
20. Ibid., 181.
21. Ibid., 180.
22. Ibid., 181.
23. Ibid., 189.
24. For example, the water jars that appear at the feast at Cana (2:6) have often been understood as symbols themselves. They may well be, but are probably best understood as subordinate, or peripheral, symbols that help develop the idea of the main symbol—water—and its meaning in the passage.

however, only allows him to comment briefly on the various instances of water throughout the Gospel, and he admits the there is plenty of work still to be undertaken on this subject, including the linking together of all the occurrences of water into one coherent symbolic whole.[25]

C. R. Koester continues this effort to interpret Johannine symbolism in his work *Symbolism in the Fourth Gospel*.[26] He begins with a recognition of the diverse background of the usage of water as a symbol. Because water is basic to all human existence everywhere, it can call forth a wide range of "different and even contradictory associations on both the cognitive and affective levels."[27] These "contradictory associations" are both positive and negative: "A glass of cool water is refreshing on the tongue, but waves surging over one's head bring the threat of drowning. The gentle rains that spatter on parched earth awaken the seeds within it to life, but the torrents that wash down the hillsides wreak destruction. Paradoxically, water brings both life and death."[28]

Koester points out that all symbols in the Gospel, including water, are to be understood christologically. With other major symbols Jesus makes a direct connection to himself by use of the "I am" statements: "I am the bread of life" (6:35); "I am the light of the world" (9:5); "I am the Good Shepherd" (10:11); "I am the true vine" (15:1). Only in the instance of water does Jesus not make such a direct statement. However, Koester maintains, this connection is implied when Jesus is shown as the source of living waters (4:10; 7:37–39; 19:34) and when water is used to reveal who Jesus is (2:1–11; 5:1–9).[29]

Even so, for Koester, water doesn't represent Jesus himself, but rather, "revelation and the Spirit." There is an "interplay" between Spirit and revelation that is due to the fact that the Gospel is speaking within two different contexts: that of the ministry of Jesus on earth, and that of the early church. Koester concludes: "If living water is the revelation Jesus offered people during his ministry, this revelation is extended through the Spirit to readers living after Jesus' departure to the Father."[30] Koester's work, based on this principle, is important in that it is the first to examine, with any kind

25. Culpepper, *Anatomy*, 188–89.
26. Koester, *Symbolism*.
27. Koester, *Symbolism*, 155.
28. Ibid.
29. Ibid., 176.
30. Ibid.

of depth, each of the individual water references in the Gospel and attempt to connect them into a coherent theological and literary whole.[31]

However, it was not until 1997 that the first monograph on the specific subject of Johannine water symbolism was published by L. P. Jones.[32] In it Jones presents a comprehensive review of each passage which contains a reference to water to determine what the meaning is and, on the basis of Culpepper's concept of "expanding symbols,"[33] demonstrates how that meaning develops and grows throughout the Gospel. He concludes that "above all, water symbolizes the Spirit."[34] But most importantly for Jones, water "calls for a decision." He demonstrates that in every instance of water in the Gospel there is a call to faith in Christ—an opportunity for a decision either for or against him. This choice is sometimes starkly presented, for example, in 13:8 when Peter is told he "will have no part" in Jesus unless he allows him to wash his feet. But in most cases the call to decision is much softer and more open-ended.[35]

Jones continues that while the Johannine symbols which have overt opposites (e.g.—light-darkness) often represent the division of the world into two camps—those for God and those against him—the symbol of water, which has no explicit opposite in the Gospel, functions differently. It unites rather than divides; by calling people to a decision for Christ, it brings together people from diverse backgrounds and understandings. He states it this way:

> Because water is an archetypal symbol, readers of the Fourth Gospel (or members of the Johannine community) from a variety of backgrounds could have been familiar with its symbolic function. The narrator invites all of them to add their previous understandings of water to its meanings and functions in the Gospel. Unlike symbols that function as a dividing line, water serves as a bridge linking the new identity believers receive when they come to faith in Jesus through the traditions from which they came.[36]

---

31. Ibid., 155–84.
32. Jones, *Symbol*.
33. Culpepper, *Anatomy*, 189–90.
34. Jones, *Symbol*, 229.
35. Cf. ibid., 230. He lists several examples including the steward at the wedding feast who did not know what the miracle meant (or even that a miracle had taken place!), the lame man at the pool of Bethesda, Nicodemus, and the man born blind.
36. Ibid., 231.

This recognition that the symbol may have a variety of different meanings depending on the background of the particular reader is a significant one. Symbols, unlike signs, have not one fixed meaning, but a range of possible meanings which is influenced by, among other things, the previous understandings of the symbol which the reader brings to the reading of the Gospel. That previous understanding will be influenced and formed by the cultural, linguistic and literary world which the reader inhabits. Therefore, the use of the symbol in these contexts is extremely important to comprehend in order to determine what understandings a reader from a particular group would be expected to bring to the text.

The most recent extensive treatment of Johannine water symbolism was produced by Wai-Yee Ng in 2001.[37] In it Ng finds the water symbol in John to be, at its most basic, eschatological in nature in that it is constantly pointing forward toward God's ultimate purpose in the universe. She says: "Whenever 'water' alludes to the Old Testament, a christological point is made in one way or another, and the perspective is always eschatological."[38] She also points out that of all the themes and concepts contained within the Gospel "it is only with eschatology that water symbolism in John continuously interacts."[39] We will show this to be an inaccurate generalization—the water motif continuously and consistently interacts with several themes of the Gospel, particularly the revelation of Christ's identity—but Ng's refocusing of the discussion on the importance of water imagery to the Gospel's eschatology is noteworthy.

Of importance to our study is Ng's contention that John's interpretive method is the idea of salvation history: God's working through history to bring about the fulfillment of his kingdom. Johannine symbolism points forward to this coming kingdom and yet, at the same time, draws significance from its past usage in Jewish writing and thought. Therefore, a general understanding of the past uses of the water symbol in the Old Testament is important for interpretation, and Ng includes a section which examines in a general way many of the OT allusions which are important to the understanding of water in the Gospel. She points out that the symbol of water is a natural choice for the author of John because of its previous well-established connections in Jewish writings and thought with both the end-times (seen in the prophets especially) and its connection with the

37. Ng, *Water*.
38. Ibid., 161.
39. Ibid., 95.

Spirit and wisdom, all of which are important themes in Johannine theology. She also does a good job of outlining the basic uses of the water image as it recurs in the different sections of the Old and New Testaments.

In 2003 C. S. Keener published his two-volume commentary on the Gospel of John.[40] In it he presents the most comprehensive examination of Johannine water symbolism found in any commentary on the Gospel to date. He suggests that most references to water in John are related in some way with the theme of the superiority of Christ and his gifts over Jewish ritual and law.[41] In explicating the specific instances of water in the Gospel Keener significantly includes water references in 5:1ff., 9:1ff.,[42] and 13:1ff.,[43] instances which most authors either gloss over or ignore completely.

However, that is not to say that Keener is indiscriminate in his inclusion of water references into the overall motif. He recognizes instances when the water symbol functions in the background rather than as the main symbol of the passage,[44] and does not try to force a connection to the larger motif where it does not seem to be warranted.[45] He also brings together as clearly as anyone the connections between the symbols of water and temple and their implications for the water flowing from Jesus' side in 19:34.[46] Finally, he sees this flux of blood and water at the cross as the thematic and theological climax of the water symbol in the Gospel.[47] Keener's work on the water symbol will helpfully inform the present study.

In conclusion, although several authors have pointed in the past to the importance of the cultural and literary background for the understanding of biblical symbols in general, only Ng has seriously attempted to use this principle to help interpret the water symbolism in John. There is still much work to be done in this area. To date there has been no detailed attempt to connect the understanding of previous Jewish water symbolism to the water symbolism in a specific passage or passages in the Gospel of John.

---

40. Keener, *Gospel*.

41. Ibid., 1.548.

42. Ibid., 1.638.

43. Ibid., 2.902.

44. Such as the references to the Pool of Bethesda in 5:1ff. (ibid., 1.638), and the water with which Jesus washes the disciples' feet in 13:1ff. (ibid., 2.902).

45. As with the reference to the Sea of Galilee in the story of Jesus walking on the water in 6:16ff. (ibid., 1.673), a water reference which most scholars do not see as part of the overarching theme.

46. Ibid., 1.730.

47. Ibid., 2.1153.

Many scholars have commented on the connection, but none has gone further and examined the implications of that connection for interpretation of specific water passages in the Gospel. This is an area which could yield fruitful results, and is one of the goals of this study

Identity and Johannine Christology

Much scholarly attention has been paid to the Christology of the Fourth Gospel,[48] and in particular there has recently been something of a renaissance in the study of Jesus' identity in John.[49] Of course, Jesus appropriates a specific identity to himself in all of the Gospels, but the way this identity is presented in the Gospel of John is unique and distinctive. We have not the space here to review all the major theories and issues concerning the Christology of the Fourth Gospel, and we will not attempt to do so. However, a study purporting to look at one of the major images of the Gospel and how it interplays with the self-identification of Jesus necessitates the delineation of a specific approach toward the issues of the Christology in the book.

First of all, it should be clarified that our concern will be primarily with the interaction between Old Testament water imagery and Christ's identity claims in the Fourth Gospel. While other issues in Johannine Christology certainly warrant scholarly attention, we shall bracket them out as topics of explicit discussion in this study. We shall not, for instance, engage the vigorous debate over the historical Jesus and how he is best understood in his social-cultural context. Neither will we spend time on the question of the relationship between the Jesus of history and the Jesus of the Gospel narratives, or the historical, theological and sociological forces that drove the development of the one into the other.[50] These are admittedly interesting issues and discussions, but they will impact our study only to the extent

---

48. Surveys of significant works and theories in on this subject can be found in Anderson, *Christology*; Culpepper, "Theology," 417–32; Menken, "Christology," 292–320 as well as in most commentaries on the Gospel.

49. Lincoln, *Gospel*, 39–49; O'Day and Hylen, *John*, 16–17; Thompson, "Word of God," 166–79.

50. The following are some of the major works on the subject of the historical Jesus and the Jesus of the Gospels in the last 20 years and represent a wide variety of viewpoints on the issue: Allison, *Jesus of Nazareth*; Borg, *New Vision*; Crossan, *Historical Jesus*; Dunn, *Jesus Remembered*; Funk, *Credible*; Meir, *Marginal*; Theissen and Mertz, *Historical Jesus*; Sanders, *Historical Figure*; Schüssler Fiorenza, *Politics*; Vermes, *Authentic Gospel*; Witherington, *Jesus Quest*; Wright, *Victory*.

that they touch on the relationship of Jewish theology and history to the interpretation of Christ's purpose and identity in the Gospel of John.

Some of the best recent work on the issue of Christ's self-identification in the Gospels and its connection with Jewish theological precedents has been done by Richard Bauckham. In *God Crucified: Monotheism and Christology in the New Testament* Bauckham presents what he terms "a Christology of divine identity."[51] In attempting to define the process by which the historical Jesus came to be understood as divine, Bauckham rejects two of the most popular prevailing theories on the subject. The first is that the Jesus of history couldn't possibly have been understood as divine while on earth because strict Jewish monotheism would not have allowed for another figure to be considered on equal footing with Yahweh. Jesus' deification could only have come about, then, as the result of a radical break with traditional Jewish monotheism and, therefore, was a later development of the early Christian community after the time of Christ. An alternate theory proposes that Jewish thought did allow for the concept of intermediary or demi-god-type figures who shared some qualities of divinity but were still not Yahweh's equal. These figures were often used by Yahweh as messengers or agents throughout Jewish history, literature and theology. Therefore, it would not be impossible for a devout Jew to view Jesus as another such being and Christ may well have been understood in this way by some even during his earthly life.

Both of these theories are unsatisfactory to Bauckham. He believes it would have been possible for a 1st century Palestinian Jew to incorporate the person of Jesus into the identity of Yahweh and still maintain a clear distinction between Yahweh and all other reality. Furthermore, he does not find the category of "intermediary figure" helpful in the discussion because these beings were "not ambiguous semi-divinities straddling the boundary between God and creation."[52] While some were understood to share aspects of Yahweh's unique identity, "most were regarded as unambiguously creatures, exalted servants of God whom the literature often takes pains to distinguish clearly from the truly divine reality of the one and only God."[53] Instead, he maintains that "[a] high Christology was possible within a

51. Bauckham, *God Crucified*, 41. This book derived from the 1996 Didsbury Lectures given by Bauckham at Nazarene Theological College (then British Isles Nazarene College) in Didsbury, Manchester, UK; reprinted as part 1 of *Jesus and the God of Israel*, 1–59.

52. Ibid., 3–4.

53. Ibid., 4.

Jewish monotheistic context, not by applying to Jesus a Jewish category of semi-divine intermediary status, but by identifying Jesus directly with the one God of Israel, including Jesus in the unique identity of this one God."[54]

Bauckham argues the necessity of a better understanding of how Jews of the Second Temple period would have understood Yahweh. That Yahweh was considered unique and unequalled in Jewish thought is clear. This distinction from all else requires and implies that he is also "significantly identifiable.... the God of Israel had a unique identity."[55] This concept of God's identity is not to be confused with his nature. Nature describes *what* Yahweh is as a deity; identity is concerned with *who* Yahweh is as distinguishable from anyone and anything else. As to what constitutes this divine identity, Bauckham suggests two major components found in Second Temple literature: Yahweh is the sole *creator* of all things, and the sole *ruler* of all things.[56] Through playing on these two distinctive characteristics of the Hebrew God the New Testament authors were able to "include Jesus in the unique divine identity as Jewish monotheism understood it."[57] Bauckham elaborates:

> The writers do this deliberately and comprehensively by using precisely those characteristics of the divine identity on which Jewish monotheism focused in characterizing God as unique. They include Jesus in the unique divine sovereignty over all things, they include him in the unique divine creation of all things, they identity him by the divine name which names the unique divine identity, and they portray him as accorded the worship which, for Jewish monotheists, is recognition of the unique divine identity. In this way they develop a kind of christological monotheism which is fully continuous with early Jewish monotheism but distinctive in the way it sees Jesus Christ himself as intrinsic to the identity of the unique God.[58]

---

54. Ibid.

55. Ibid., 7.

56. Ibid., 10. For evidence of God's identity as sole creator cf. Isa. 40:26, 28; 42:5; 44:24; 45:12, 18; 48:13; 51:16; Neh 9:6; Hos 13:4 LXX; 2 Macc. 1:24; Sir 43:33; *Jub.* 12:3–5; *SibOr* 3:20–35; 8:375–376; *2 En* 47:3–4; 66:4; *Apoc. Ab* 7:10; *Jos.Asen.* 12:1–2; *T. Job* 2:4. For evidence of his identity as sole ruler cf. Dan 4:34–35; Add. Est. 13:9–11; 16:18, 21; 3 Macc. 2:2–3; 6:2; Wis 12:13; Sir 18:1–3; *SibOr* 3:10, 19; *1 En* 9:5; 84:3; *2 En* 33:7; *2 Bar* 54:13.

57. Bauckham, *God Crucified*, 26.

58. Ibid., 26–27.

In making his case for this point of view Bauckham examines how certain New Testament authors interpreted Old Testament texts concerning Yahweh's creative abilities and sovereignty as pertaining to Jesus, thereby including Jesus in the unique divine identity. In particular he demonstrates how various texts from Deutero-Isaiah are read in Philippians, Revelation and John.[59] The nature of his study, which was first presented as a series of lectures, does not allow him to explore these observations in depth, nor does it provide room for a full treatment of the many wider passages outside Deutero-Isaiah which could also be used in support of his argument.[60] However, his theory and methodology are particularly well-suited to an examination like ours, which will explore the relationship between Old Testament water imagery in the Gospel of John and the way the author presents Jesus' identity as the Son of God.

Therefore, we propose to take Bauckham's thesis and apply it specifically to one particular recurring image of Yahweh's creative and sovereign powers in the Jewish mindset of the Second Temple period: his control and command of the waters of the universe both in creation and in his rule over the earth.

METHODOLOGY

The examination of the use of Old Testament imagery by New Testament authors raises some intriguing questions. Not the least of these is the issue of how the newly created text relates to the previous or "precursor" text and the role of the author's intentionality in this relationship. We begin this study with the assumption that the Hebrew Scriptures accurately reflect at least a part of Jewish thought and belief and were one of the main sources of religious imagery and language. If this is the case, then it would be expected that this previous Jewish literature would have influenced the thought, language and imagery of the New Testament authors, all of whom were steeped (in some cases deeply so) in the religious beliefs and traditions of Judaism.

---

59. Ibid., 45–69.

60. Bauckham is currently working on such a study, tentatively titled *Jesus and the Identity of God: Early Jewish Monotheism and New Testament Christology*. A book of Bauckham's essays and other writings on this topic was published in 2008 which constitutes "working papers on the way to that book"(*Jesus*, xi) and also includes the majority of the material contained in *God Crucified* called *Jesus and the God of Israel: God Crucified and Other Studies on the New Testament's Christology of Divine Identity* (Grand Rapids: Eerdmans, 2008).

It would be natural, then, to expect to find in the New Testament many direct references back to the theology, words and images of the Old Testament, which is indeed readily observable. However, it is equally natural that these authors would have also unconsciously tinged their writing with words, images, ideas and symbols deeply embedded in their cultural memory, which are at the same time established by and preserved in the texts of the Old Testament. Therefore, examining the links between New Testament passages and Old Testament precursors, both bold and subtle, is a fundamental part of New Testament studies. There are a number of different approaches that could be applied. The one which will be most useful to us in this study is the intertextual method of Richard B. Hays, which we will outline below. However, we will first begin with a brief definition of intertextual methodology.

Intertextuality

Intertextuality has been described as "the imbedding of fragments of an earlier text within a later one."[61] By this definition an intertextual method is one which examines the way in which one text interacts with another. Intertextuality may be found in any type of expression where words, structures, forms or symbols refer in some way to an outside idea or concept which the audience has previously experienced and attached significance to, which means that nearly all forms of communication are open to intertextual analysis.[62] We will confine our discussion here to the intertextual relationships between certain biblical texts, but that is not to imply that Intertextuality is a phenomenon limited to written communication.

These intertextual relationships are not found only in instances in which the author specifically quotes a previous text. Indeed, an intertextual method recognizes that texts interact with each other quite apart from the agency or intentionality of the author. This means that an intertextual method will go beyond simply examining an author's citing of earlier texts and try to tease out other texts that interplay with the text in question in more subtle, and perhaps unwitting, ways. This referencing of the previously experienced "text" by another work is a sort of shorthand which evokes

---

61. Hays, *Echoes*, 14.

62. As Hays says, "All discourse, in this view, is necessarily intertextual in the sense that its conditions of intelligibility are given by and in relation to a previously given body of discourse" (ibid., 15).

the emotions, images, concepts or experiences related to the original text. An intertextual method of examination concerns itself with how the later text builds on these inherent connections created by the earlier text to make new meaning or to analyze or critique the earlier text.

John Hollander and Richard B. Hays

In formulating his intertextual method Hays relies heavily on the writings of the literary critic John Hollander in *The Figure of Echo: A Mode of Allusion in Milton and After*[63] so we will briefly review that work before discussing Hays's contribution to the discussion.

Hollander seizes upon the acoustical phenomena of an echo and uses it as a metaphor to describe the relationship between one text and another. He prefers the idea of "echo" over the more traditional "allusion" because it is "poetic rather than expository" and "makes new metaphor rather than learned gestures." The usage of this term also acknowledges that authors may reuse earlier texts with "suppressed consciousness that, and of how, they are doing so, by accident or by plan, but with the same shaping spirit that gives form to tropes of thought and feeling."[64]

Hollander clarifies from the outset that his intertextual method will not "take up problems of actual or putative audience, or of the degree of the self-awareness, of conscious design" on the part of the author. He is "content to observe that poems seem to echo prior ones for the personal aural benefit of the poet, and of whichever poetic followers can overhear the reverberations."[65] This phenomenon occurs not only because old voices are overhead in new settings, but also because "the rebounds of intertextual echo generally . . . distort the original voice" (in much the same way that a sound is distorted when it is reflected off a surface) "in order to interpret it."[66] Holland concludes by delineating the "two-fold task" of a methodology based on these observations: (a) to make others aware of these echoes within a text so that they can hear as an original audience would have heard; and (b) to examine the result, on the later text, of the acoustical "distortions" that inevitably happen in figurative echo.[67]

63. Hollander, *Figure*.
64. Ibid., ix.
65. Ibid.
66. Ibid., 19.
67. Ibid.

It is this idea of metaphorical "echo" which Richard B. Hays picks up and applies to biblical texts, specifically to the Apostle Paul's use of earlier Jewish texts. However, while Hollander goes on to completely develop the acoustical metaphor Hays focuses simply on the elements of a methodology which has the goal of "overhearing" such echoes. Hays recognizes that intertextual echoes may have variable levels of volume determined by the "semantic distance between the source and the reflecting surface." Quotation, allusion, and echo, then, are not conflicting concepts, but exist together as points along a spectrum of intertextual reference, moving from the explicit to the subliminal:

> As we move farther away from overt citation, the source recedes into the discursive distance, the intertextual relations become less determinate, and the demand placed on the reader's listening powers grows greater. As we near the vanishing point of the echo, it inevitably becomes difficult to decide whether we are really hearing an echo at all, or whether we are only conjuring things out of the murmurings of our own imaginations.[68]

Hays also appropriates Hollander's term "transumption" or "metalepsis" to describe what happens in the dialogical space between texts. By this Hollander and Hays recognize that the effect of an echo on a text may actually come from points of resonance that are unstated by the later text ("transumed text") rather than from the actual use in the text itself. In order to understand the effect of the echo on the later text one must "recover the transumed material."[69] In order to do this, Hays argues, "text B should be understood in light of a broad interplay with text A, encompassing aspects of A beyond those explicitly echoed."[70]

With this Hays makes clear that his intertextual methodology will focus on trying to "hear" the echoes of earlier texts in later ones by, as much as possible, recovering this transumed material. In the case of Paul (and, we will argue, the author of the Gospel of John as well) the transumed material will come largely from "the symbolic field created by a single great textual precursor: Israel's Scripture."[71] He elaborates:

---

68. Hays, *Echoes*, 23.
69. Hollander, *Figure*, 115.
70. Hays, *Echoes*, 20.
71. Ibid., 15.

The vocabulary and cadences of Scripture—particularly the LXX—are imprinted deeply on Paul's mind, and the great stories of Israel continue to serve his as a fund of symbols and metaphors that condition his perception of the world, of God's promised deliverance of his people, and of his own identity and calling. His faith, in short, is one whose articulation is inevitably intertextual in character.[72]

Hays insists that these intertextual echoes from Israel's past history and literature are not merely decorative literary devices. Instead, they have the effect of "reactivat[ing] past revelation under new conditions."[73] Hays discusses the reuse of precursor texts largely on the level of the language of the text, but texts may also echo the form, genre, setting and plot of precursor texts; this will especially be significant for our study of the water "echoes" in the Gospel of John.

In this study we propose to follow Hays's approach to intertextual echoes within Scripture, particularly focusing on the water passages within the Gospel of John. But first we will briefly engage critics of this method.

Criticism of Hays's Method

One of the more scathing repudiations of Hays's method comes from George Aichele and Gary A. Phillips. They name Hays along with Draisma and Buchanan as representative of a group of scholars who use the language of intertextuality "as a restrictive tool for nailing down authorial intent and literary influence" and contend that "thinly veiled in such efforts are conservative ideological and theological interests in maintaining the primacy of certain (usually Christian) texts over against secondary (usually Jewish) precursors."[74] They claim that the use of the concepts of allusion and citation are really just ways to disguise a search for authorial intent and influence in the text. Moreover, they believe this method relies on a "linear, agentive" notion of influence which has long been prevalent in biblical studies but is no longer valid.[75]

---

72. Ibid., 15–16.
73. Ibid., 14.
74. Aichele and Phillips, "Introduction, 7."
75. Ibid., 11–12: "Intertextuality poses a challenge to a unidirectional and linear understanding of literary history, indeed to a 'flat' understanding of history altogether."

Aichele and Phillips declare that true intertextuality requires a new way of thinking about "the privileged notions of authorial consciousness and intentionality." They also challenge the advisability (or possibility) of attempting to "isolate meaning at a safe distance 'inside' the text."[76] They believe "true" intertextuality poses a challenge to the view of the relationship between the text and material outside the text that is popular with traditional biblical critics. In this practice, which they maintain is still regnant among most biblical scholars, there is a vast gap between what is inside and what is outside the text. Good biblical scholarship has been understood as that which "preserves the integrity of the inside and the outside by ensuring that the one does not contaminate the other. Hence, the rigid dichotomy between exegesis and eisegesis, between text and reading, between author and text, between text and reader." They continue:

> In a non-interference view the text is set apart from reality—a material reality that lies outside of the text (the extratextual)—which grounds the proper meaning of the text. At a distance too stands that self-sufficient, technically trained, expert reader who operates on the text. At a further remove yet is the question of responsibility and accountability.[77]

However, they maintain, this division is unnatural since in reality there is (often significant) "interference" between outside and inside.[78] This view of a text as a separate entity from other things around it is not acceptable to such critics precisely because for them the meaning of a text (or an intertext) arises as a result of the interaction of the text with all the other "texts" surrounding it. Partitioning a text off from the surrounding landscape, in their view, makes it impossible for the creation of meaning to occur.

The issue in dispute here between Aichele, Phillips and their ilk, and Hays and those like him, is more one of angle of approach rather than actual theoretical disparity, although one might argue a difference of philosophical opinion is involved in determining which "angle" is the best vantage point from which to view the interaction of texts. Hays et al. simply choose a different vantage point than that of more philosophical (and one might say ideological) textual critics. These critics of Hays's approach focus on a *synchronic* approach to textual relationships—examining, for example,

---

76. Ibid., 13–14.
77. Ibid., 14.
78. Ibid.

how one text's structures may have been imposed on that of another text. This requires placing the texts, figuratively, beside each other within the same space and time, to examine them. Hays and his school, however, approach texts *diachronically*, that is, with a concern to how texts interact with each other *through time*. Therefore, while texts are compared side-by-side to a certain extent, there is always an awareness of the historical and chronological gap between the two texts. That "gap" is often the place in which the meaning of the textual reusage will be found (Hollander's idea of "transumption").

Aichele and Phillips are not justified in accusing proponents of Hays's methodology of hiding behind intertextual terminology while still adhering to traditional methods which seek authorial intention or awareness. Hays, et al. are merely recognizing that while texts can interact on their own we can never divorce a text completely from its author or its original context. There will always be contextual residue left behind no matter how hard we try to clean up afterwards. All language is contextual, and therefore all text must be contextual as well. Whether we know anything about the author or historical background of a text, that author and context have imprinted themselves upon the text to the point that the two can never be said to be completely distinct. Critics who choose to ignore context and treat texts as if they exist independently in some nebulous space "out there" where they meet and interact misrepresent the fundamental nature of a text. A text cannot have any meaning at all apart from a context. Hays et al. are right to recognize this.

This is a crucial point because it is precisely this "contextual residue" which will guide the reader in understanding the "bank of literary patterns"[79] from which the author draws to form new meaning. We may never be able to confidently reconstruct the identity and personal information of the author of the Gospel of John. However, we can know something of his mindset and his worldview *from the text itself* without relying on outside speculation. Hays is simply proposing that readers of a text naturally pick up on such contextual clues and use them to make sense of the text, just as the writer used previous texts to make sense of the "text" of his own experience. Examining the interaction of Scriptural texts with earlier texts in a diachronic manner, then, is not an attempt to reconstruct the original

---

79. Kristeva, "Word." It was translated into English in Roudiez (ed.), *Desire and Language* and can now be found in Moi (ed.), *Kristeva Reader*. The quotation is taken from Moi (ed.), *Kristeva Reader*, 36.

author or his intentionality so much as an effort to understand the text *as it stands* including its inherent contextual structures. It attempts to understand the author only to the extent that the author's context is crucial to the understanding of the text and, indeed, imbedded within the text itself.

To the second point of contention between Hays and his critics: we believe a diachronic approach to textual echoes is completely justified for those dealing with biblical Scripture. This is because of the nature of Scripture itself and how Scriptural writers viewed their task. For the biblical authors, both Jewish and Christian, the great bank of textual patterns they were pulling from was not just any cultural reservoir, but one with great personal and communal significance—previous Scripture. The arena of textual interaction for the authors was earlier revelation and history; they saw themselves as playing a small part in the larger continuing drama of God's interaction with the world and, therefore, they grounded themselves and their work within this larger context.

Therefore, it is only natural that the primary text with which biblical texts are interacting is the previous salvific acts of Yahweh on behalf of the people of Israel, and, for the writers of the Christian Scriptures, God's revelation of Himself through Jesus Christ. These are the two grounding points for all of Scripture. This worldview, then, demands a diachronic approach to intertextual echoes; what is happening here and now (for the biblical writers) only makes sense in light of what has happened in the past. These authors would have seen their texts as firmly grounded in a particular historical context. And while it is possible to use these earlier texts to help interpret their own experiences, the original context is still very important, whether the author is aware of this context or not. Indeed, as Hollander and Hays would agree, often the significance of an intertextual connection is found in the intersection of the two *contexts* as much as between the two *texts* themselves.

Therefore, Hays's method, through criticized by some, is quite appropriate for dealing with Scriptural texts. It is possible that a synchronic intertextual approach may at times be useful, particularly for texts which do not originate in such a historically conscious arena as the biblical canon. But for the purposes of our study of the intertextual relationships of water imagery in the Gospel of John, Hays's methodology will prove very helpful and we will consider it our primary method of operation.

While we will utilize much of Hays's approach described in the last paragraph in regards to the water language and imagery in the Gospel of

John, we believe that when dealing with a document as allusion-rich as the Fourth Gospel, some methodological tweaking is required. We agree that, like Paul, the author of the Fourth Gospel pulled from a vast cultural bank of images, language and events, in this case involving water, to tell his story. We also believe that these watery "echoes" are part of his overall strategy to reach his goal of revealing Jesus as the Christ, the Son of God. However, recognizing that John's use of metaphor and symbol is more complex and synthetic than figurative language found in the writings of Paul, or really anywhere else in the Scriptures, we must make a few adjustments in methodological approach.

Application of Intertextuality to Johannine Language

One of the primary elements that distinguishes John among the Gospels, and, indeed, from the entire body of Scripture, is its unique use of language and imagery. This allusive language has been a subject of intense study, particularly in recent years. Specifically it has been noted that the Gospel's author often uses words or phrases that can have more than one specific meaning within its literary context.[80] When this "ambiguity" appears in dialogues between Jesus and individuals, it is often the cause of "misunderstandings," another much-studied phenomenon in the Gospel.[81]

After years of applying historical-critical methods to such texts to determine "the correct" understanding of such ambiguous figures, scholars have come to understand that an ambiguous term may appear in the Gospel precisely because it evokes more than one idea or image; both meanings are to be read at the same time, not one at the expense of the other. Therefore, attempting to discover the "one" correct interpretation of such words or phrases leads to either oversimplification or complete misinterpretation. Instead, in such instances the multiple meanings must be held in tension with one another. The significance of the reference is found in the interplay between the two (or more) possible meanings of the word not within the meaning of one or the other.

---

80. For an excellent survey on the study of the "ambiguous," "ironic," or "dual-levelled" language of the Gospel cf. Hamid-Khani, *Revelation*, 4–16; see also the seminal article which started the modern discussion on the topic: Cullmann, "Johanneische Gebrauch," 360–72.

81. Carson, "Understanding," 59–92; Richard, "Expressions," 96–112; Pyle, "Understanding," 26–47.

Johannine language, then, leaves room for the possibility that more than one "text" may be echoed by a particular word or figure. If this is true, then a particular allusion may well have more than one textual reference. And, indeed, we will argue that this is precisely what is happening in many instances of Johannine metaphor and imagery. It is intertextuality of a slightly different type, one which may not be best explained by conventional intertextual approaches. Traditional intertextual methodology is based on the assumption of a specific reference in the NT text to one or two specific and identifiable passages in the OT, with the connection usually being made through language—specific words or phrases that are identical or similar.

This certainly happens numerous times in the Synoptics and is not impossible to be found in John, even in an occasional water passage (e.g., 19:34 is specifically linked to OT passages cited in vv. 36–37 through the word "pierce"). However, this is not John's only (or even typical) mode of allusion. Instead of intending to evoke a particular passage from the OT and all the context that surrounds it, the Gospel of John often uses imagery and language that calls up larger themes or motifs from the OT without specifically referencing one instance of the figuration. The Evangelist is often more concerned with the cultural and connotative associations that have attached themselves to the entire motif, rather than the connections to a specific precursor text.

These ambiguous words and phrases, therefore, create "braids" of meaning where related words and images from a variety of different texts are intertwined to the point where it becomes impossible to extricate one from the other. This results in one large metaphor that is more connotative than denotative and therefore has no "one" origin. This is not to say that these evocative "braids" have no "meaning" or no relation to specific Scriptures and theological concepts in the OT. But it does mean that we have to find a different way to look for and at the various strands that have come together to form the braid, and this is what requires us to look to more than one intertext behind the reading of any Johannine water passage (or indeed, any symbolic usage in the Gospel).

Indeed, we contend that when it comes to the water imagery of the Gospel of John, the author is actually borrowing already braided together strands of water tradition, particularly from the Pentateuchal stories of Creation, Flood and Exodus. The water imagery of these narratives was intertwined together from very early in the Jewish tradition in such a way that one cannot be read without reference to the other. For example, the Flood narrative is directly related to the narrative of God's creation of the universe, particularly to its description of the parting of the waters to make room for the earth in Gen 1:2ff, and the destruction of these restrictions in Gen 6–7 to allow for the great deluge to occur. The narrative and poetic interpretations of the Sea of Reeds incident borrow language and imagery from both the Flood and the Creation narrative. Likewise, the crossing of the Jordan later in Joshua 3 clearly borrows language from the earlier Sea of Reeds incident, which, since it is saturated with imagery and language form the Creation and Flood narrative, in turn means that the Joshua 3 narrative is also inextricably linked to all of these earlier water events. Additionally, Cross has argued persuasively that the water imagery of the Exodus event has actually retroactively shaped the water imagery of the Creation narrative in Gen 1.[82] We shall examine these premises in more depth in chapter two of this work.

Given this phenomenon, then, we suggest that through the use of water imagery the Gospel deliberately recalls the comprehensive compilation of the water motif in the OT, rather than individual references to particular instances of the image. Indeed, as noted above, it may be impossible to speak of "only" the Crossing of the Sea of Reeds or "only" the Flood narrative, because these events were so linked together in language and imagery. An intertextual examination of Johannine water imagery, then, requires a slightly revised methodology, one which recognizes possible intertexts between "braids" of images in the precursor text and anterior texts. This necessitates an understanding of the "expanding" (to use Culpepper's terminology) of the water image throughout both the OT and the Gospel text—the changing relationship between later occurrences of an image and earlier ones which require one to look at the entire "string" of usages in order to come to a nuanced understanding of any one particular reference. This study will apply such a methodology to the water imagery within the Gospel of John for the purpose of deepening our understanding of John's message, particularly as it relates to the revelation of Jesus as the Christ, the Son of God.

---

82. Cross, *Canaanite Myth*, 112–44.

DEFINITIONS, DELIMITATIONS, AND ASSUMPTIONS

Methodological Definitions

Intertextual terms

The problem of definition when it comes to terms like quotation, allusion, and echo is a long-standing one. Intertextual critics have sometimes failed to be explicit in their distinctions which has led to confusion.[83] In general it is best to think of quotation, allusion and echo as points on a spectrum going from the stronger and more intentional usage (quotation) to the least discernible and possibly even unintended reference (echo).

Moyise helpfully distinguishes between these three, and we will appropriate his definitions. He sees a quotation as a reference which involves "a self-conscious break from the author's style to introduce words from another context." A quotation is generally preceded by some type of introductory formula ("as it is written" or "as Moses said") or a grammatical clue such as the word ὅτι. An allusion is distinguished from a quotation in that it is "usually woven into the text rather than 'quoted' and often rather less precise in terms of wording." Finally, Moyise defines echoes as "faint traces of texts that are probably quite unconscious but emerge from minds soaked in the scriptural heritage of Israel."[84]

Of course, these definitions leave plenty of room for debate over how much verbal agreement is necessary to establish something as an allusion rather than an echo, and whether or not an audience can be expected to pick up on any given allusion or echo, but these are discussions for another place. For our purposes the above definitions will suffice. We are more concerned with the cumulative effect of the quotations, allusions and echoes of water in the Gospel, and therefore will not quibble over the exact definition of individual instances.

Literary terms

The words "symbol" and "symbolism" are often used in a casual sense to mean anything from a metaphor to a motif to a sign. But for the following study it will be important to establish a definition of the word "symbol" and

---

83. See Porter's survey of works that have attempted to nail down definitions for these terms and wrestled with the issues inherent in doing so—Porter, "Use," 79–96.

84. Moyise, "Intertextuality," 18–19.

how it distinguishes itself from the related concepts of "metaphor," "sign," "motif," and "imagery."

For the definition of a symbol we will turn to literary critic Philip Wheelwright who writes that "a symbol, in general, is a relatively stable and repeatable element of perceptual experience, standing for some larger meaning or set of meanings which cannot be given, or not fully given, in perceptual experience itself."[85] C. Chadwick elaborates on the last part of this definition when he says that symbolism "is not the mere substitution of one object for another . . . . but the use of concrete imagery to express abstract ideas and emotions."[86] Tillich echoes this idea when he says that in symbolism "something which is intrinsically invisible, ideal, or transcendent is made perceptible" and "is in this way given objectivity."[87] This ability of a symbol to make tangible something which is normally intangible is why symbols were so important to the biblical authors, and especially to the creator the Gospel of John. These authors were attempting to express eternal truths which could not be completely apprehended through the five senses; the concepts were true, but could not be empirically proven or demonstrated. Therefore, the authors came to use symbols in an attempt to express the inexpressible.

While these definitions help us toward an understanding of what a symbol is, we may actually learn as much, if not more, by discussing what a symbol is *not*. The first term which needs to be distinguished from "symbol" is "sign." A sign, in its most basic meaning is simply something that points to or indicates something else. This is a very broad category which would include many things, including all language, "mathematical symbols, musical notation, road signs and knitting patterns."[88]

In each of these systems, a particular letter, shape, or figure is used as shorthand for a much longer or bigger idea. The meanings of each "sign" are fixed; they cannot be altered. Likewise they require that the person reading them has already been taught the proper meaning of each sign. The Greek letter π is a good example from mathematical notation. The mathematical equivalent of π is far too long to be written down in figures (and

---

85. Wheelwright, *Metaphor*, 92.
86. Chadwick, *Symbolism*, 1.
87. Tillich, "Symbol," 75.
88. Caird, *Language*, 148. Caird actually refers to these types of signs as "codes" but his definitions make it clear that his "codes" would be the same as our "signs." Ibid., 148–49.

has an infinite number of decimal places in any case), so in its place the scientist uses the Greek letter. Everyone in the scientific and mathematical community knows what the Greek letter π stands for. In this sense, then, π is a "sign" because it points or refers to something else and its meaning is always the same; it does not vary from equation to equation. A sign can have one, and only one exact meaning.[89]

This, however, is very different from the way a symbol works. Culpepper says, "The meaning of a sign must be learned, and whereas a symbol may point to many things, to be effective, a sign can point to only one."[90] A sign ceases to be useful if its referent is unclear. If a note of musical notation is not written clearly, or if its tonal value is in question, then there can be disastrous consequences for the musician. However, a symbol may have more than one meaning depending upon its context and usage by the author. This point will be illuminated more when we discuss the use and function of a symbol.

The next difference between a sign and a symbol which should be noted is that a sign may represent another thing, but it doesn't necessarily tell us anything about that other thing. We may learn, for example, that a "k" in a knitting pattern represents a "knit" stitch, and a "p" represents a "purl" stitch. However, these signs themselves do not give us any information about how to make these stitches or how they differ from one another. Conversely, the entire purpose of a symbol is for us to learn something about the thing(s) being symbolized, as our initial definitions of "symbol" imply.

A sign also doesn't share in the reality of the thing it represents. There is no inherent relationship between the Greek letter π and the number 3.1412, etc. π was chosen because it is the first letter in the Greek word περίμετρος and therefore was a convenient sign to represent it; from a mathematical standpoint any other Greek letter would have done just as well, assuming it had not already been assigned another meaning. A symbol, however, shares in the reality of, and tells us something about, that which it represents. Culpepper makes the point: "Unlike a sign, a symbol is not arbitrary but bears some inherent analogical relationship to that which it symbolizes. The reader understands that the symbol means or expresses something more or something else than its plain or superficial meaning."[91]

---

89. Wheelwright, *Metaphor*, 93–94

90. Culpepper, *Anatomy*, 182.

91. Ibid., 182.

A symbol also is not the same as a metaphor, although these two concepts are very closely related. A metaphor has two components: a thing being compared and the thing it is compared to. In literary studies these are often referred to as the "tenor" (the thing being compared) and the "vehicle" (the thing it is compared to). Exactly what the vehicle tells us about the tenor is left to the reader to determine.[92] Culpepper uses this illustration of a metaphor from the Gospel of John: "When Jesus says, 'I am the bread of life' (6:35) in the context of a discourse on the true bread, the reader is given both the tenor ("I") and the vehicle ("the bread of life"). Our task is to infer the relationship between the tenor and the vehicle and in doing so to understand those features of the identity of Jesus which led the author to use the metaphor."[93]

A symbol serves a similar purpose—finding a relationship between two seemingly unrelated things—but with a symbol the vehicle is presented alone and the reader is left to discover exactly what the tenor is as well as what the vehicle says about the tenor.[94] So, for example, when Jesus refers to the water that he gives as "a spring of water gushing up to eternal life" (John 4:14), he is giving the vehicle (the gushing well) and leaving the Samaritan woman, as well as the Gospel's audience, to discover the tenor (the thing is that Jesus is offering which is like a gushing well), as well as how this offered thing is like a gushing well. This, then, is a symbol, not a metaphor.

Another point about the nature of symbols should be noted: A true symbol is one which is repeatable. Wheelwright says: "when an image is employed as metaphor only once, in a unique flash of insight, it cannot be accurately be said to function symbolically. It acquires a symbolic nature when, with whatever modifications, it undergoes or is considered capable of undergoing recurrence."[95] This is true because a symbol only comes to represent something else as the end result of the whole process of metaphor creation. Only after a particular metaphor has become well-established in a particular community can an abridgment of that metaphor, in the form of a symbol, come to have meaning in that community.[96] Therefore, repetition is a very important element in the symbolic process.

---

92. Ibid., 181; Wheelwright, *Metaphor*, 73.
93. Culpepper, *Anatomy*, 181.
94. Ibid., 182.
95. Wheelwright, *Metaphor*, 93.
96. Wead, *Devices*, 73–74; see also Tillich, *Symbol*, 76–77.

But how is a symbol related to the literary concept of a motif? This is a bit more difficult because in this case the two terms are not mutually exclusive. A motif may be a symbol, and a symbol may compose a motif. A motif is something within the narrative which is "necessarily recurrent and its effect cumulative."[97] It may be a character, a word, an item, or a place which recurs consistently and deliberately throughout the narrative. A motif may be symbolic in nature, in that it may be composed of a symbol, or many symbols, which persist throughout the story. So while symbols may, through their recurrence, form a motif, not all elements of a motif are necessarily symbolic in nature. Based on these definitions, one could argue that the water symbolism throughout the Gospel of John is a motif because it is "recurrent" and it has a "cumulative effect." Simultaneously the motif itself becomes a symbol in the Gospel as our study will demonstrate.

Finally, symbolism should be distinguished from "imagery." At times, the two words are used interchangeably, but they are not identical. Caird explains imagery as "The full stock of a book's non-literal language, and more particularly its comparative language."[98] While symbolism is a type of comparative language, it is not the only type. The imagery of a work may also contain metaphors, allusions, and other devices. Thus, "imagery" is a much broader term than "symbolism"; the imagery of a work includes, but is not limited to, its symbolism.

Other Definitions and Delimitations

We shall use the terms "Jewish literature" or "ancient Jewish literature" to refer to the body of literature that would have been commonly known to the Jewish community throughout the Ancient Near East at the end of the 1st century CE. For our purposes this literature will include the Hebrew canonical scriptures (or "Jewish canon"),[99] the Old Testament Apocrypha, and those writings of the Pseudepigrapha which pre-date the Gospel of John.[100] We will also at times use the term "Old Testament" when referring

---

97. Freedman, "Motif," 124.

98. Caird, Language, 149.

99. Although we will use the term "Hebrew canon" at times, it is nevertheless understood that the majority of Jews by the 1st century CE would have accessed their canon through the Greek translation (LXX) rather than the original Hebrew.

100. For the purposes of this study we will define the "Pseudepigrapha" as the works contained in the two volumes by Charlesworth that are not also contained in the Old

to the Hebrew canon for the sake of convenience and familiarity without intending any judgment on the collection's content or significance. Of course there are other ancient Jewish writings that might be considered, but the literature in these three collections was arguably the most well-known in the ANE and therefore was the most likely to influence the thought and imagery of 1st century Judaism.

Likewise, we recognize that "Judaism" in the 1st-century was by no means monolithic in either belief or practice. But just as we must limit our examination to the most major pieces of Jewish literature, we also must limit our discussion of Jewish groups to those who would have been formed by and who adhered to the three sections of Jewish literature mentioned above. These writings were created by different groups and sects within the same religion who managed to co-exist peacefully (for the most part), and, likewise, our study will hold the many factions in tension—by keeping our focus on the written texts in which all the groups come together. Indeed, one might make the argument that water imagery, language and ritual were one of the few constants across all branches of Judaism during the 1st century and before. Although actual practices would have varied depending on climate and other factors, water (both physical and metaphorical) was crucial to the identity and the functioning of all Jews everywhere.

This study will not spend significant time on the influence on John's symbolism that might have come from the Hellenistic culture which surrounded him or from the literature and imagery of other Semitic cultures of the ANE. This is no doubt an interesting and productive area of investigation, but is outside the purpose of this study. We may occasionally mention water language or ritual that was present in other cultures outside 1st-century Judaism, but only as it helps illuminate our understanding of the water imagery of ancient Judaism.

This study will also be looking "back" at the Hebrew culture and writings from the standpoint of the Gospel of John, rather than looking from the Hebrew writings "forward" to the Gospel of John. It will not be a study of the development of the theme throughout all of the Hebrew writings, for that would be an impossibility in such a short work. The objective is to determine how an understanding of the Jewish background of the symbol influences a modern reader's interpretation of the texts in which John uses

---

Testament Apocrypha. Some of the works in Charlesworth's Pseudepigrapha post-date the Gospel of John. We will confine our exploration to those works which can plausibly be ascribed to a date earlier than the assumed writing of the Gospel of John (i.e., 90 CE).

the image, and development will be dealt with only to the point necessary to reach this objective.

Finally, this study will, for convenience and clarity, refer to the Christian canonical books as the "New Testament." However, this is not intended to imply its superiority over the Hebrew canon. We will use the term "Johannine literature" to refer to the Christian canonical works traditionally attributed to the Apostle John (the Gospel of John; 1, 2 and 3 John; and Revelation) without implying any conclusion about the actual identity of the author or authors of these works.

Assumptions

We will work from the understanding of the Gospel as a narrative whole, despite the fact that it may have been pieced together, or at least edited, after its original writing. Technical issues of authorship and source will not be examined. Instead, the assumption will be maintained that all parts of the Gospel are intended to make a coherent whole and therefore water images from all parts of the Gospel will be considered, regardless of theories of origin or authorship.

We will operate under the theory that the written Gospel, while originating in the preaching of one person (who may be equated with the Apostle John and/or the Beloved Disciple) is the work of more than one hand. At the very least two different people appear to have worked on it, with at least one editorial stage in the process. Therefore, we will use the word "author" to refer to the unified mind behind the content and general form of the Gospel. This person was probably a follower of Jesus (possibly one of the "twelve") who preserved the Lord's words and disseminated them through his preaching. Later, the "shaped" narratives and discourses were written down and formed into a coherent whole by someone, perhaps the source of the material, perhaps someone else. We will use the title "editor" to refer to the person who was responsible for some or all of the obvious editorial comments and possible format and sequence revisions. In reality the editing may have been the work of more than one person, possibly in more than one time-period, but since this distinction has little bearing on this study we will not spend time on it.

Another obvious assumption, but one worth mentioning, is that the author of John was actually influenced in some way by his Jewish background. Although it may not be possible to prove to a certainty, it is a fairly safe assumption that a person will be influenced by the culture in which he or she is raised to such an extent that he or she may not even be aware of the cultural conditioning of symbolism. One does not develop understanding of such things in a vacuum, and therefore must be influenced by cultural understandings, even if it results in a rejection of those understandings.

Of course, this assumes that the author of the Gospel of John actually does come from a Jewish background. We will hold to the belief that the unified mind behind the Gospel, while possibly thoroughly Hellenized, is still Jewish in background. The understanding of Jewish customs and religion demonstrated in the Gospel, as well as the narrator's intimate knowledge of Palestine in general and Galilee in particular, make it most likely that the Gospel originated with one who was born a Jew. The instances in the Gospel where the text seems to explain Jewish customs to non-Jews was either added by the author because he knew that many in his audience would not be Jewish, or were the addition of a later editor for the same reason.

Finally, this study will work at the level of the author and the text, not so much with the audience. We certainly recognize that the audience of a work is involved to a certain extent in its interpretation, and therefore its creation of meaning. But we will maintain that the text itself sets limits for this interpretation. The locus of meaning comes from within the text itself and while there may be a range of possible interpretations supported by the text, there is not an unlimited number of them; a reader is not justified in ignoring the clues within the text which lead him or her to an appropriate interpretation. There may be times when the influence of the symbol on the audience will be discussed, but this will assume that the audience of that day would interpret the symbol in a way that is consistent with the traditional Jewish usage and within the limits set by the text.

CHAPTER 2

Water and Yahweh's Identity in the Old Testament Tradition

INTRODUCTION

Chad Bird begins his series of Bible studies on water in the Scriptures by saying: "Almost every page of the Old Testament is wet."[1] While this perhaps overstates the case, it rightly recognizes the importance of water in many of the formative events in Israelite history and the subsequent references to these events: Yahweh mastered and molded the waters in Genesis 1 to bring about his "good" creation for the sustenance and pleasure of his people; he used the waters of the flood to lift up the ark to carry Noah and his family to safety; he controlled the waters of the Sea of Reeds to rescue his people from the murderous pursuit of Pharaoh, and he later brought water out of a rock in the wilderness to sustain those same people. While water does appear centrally in some other narratives (e.g., the water miracles of Elisha), the water events of the Creation, Flood and Exodus are the most significant in terms of Israel's history, for these are the stories that are most often hearkened back to in later Scriptures when remembering Yahweh's faithfulness or when chastising Israel's failures.

The definition of Yahweh as the one true God and the description of his unique characteristics is also, naturally, one of the foremost concerns of

---

1. Bird, *Water*, 5.

the Jewish Scriptures.[2] In delineating Yahweh's character, the water events of Israel's history play a central role in the praise of his unique characteristics and distinctive identity. These two motif strands—water and Yahweh's identity—are significantly and inextricably linked throughout much of OT history, literature and thought to the extent that Yahweh's ability to control the waters became a hallmark of his deity and kingship. Yahweh is uniquely identified as the one who controls the waters of the universe and the earth and this is one of the primary abilities which separates him from all other gods.

In this chapter we propose to examine each of the four major water events in Israel's history focusing particularly on the issues of Yahweh's unique identity raised in each. Then we will proceed with some observations on the use and reuse of this water-identity motif in Israelite poetry and prophecy. The goal of this chapter is to construct a possible background to help us understand John's use of the connection between Jesus' identity and the water motif in the Fourth Gospel.

We will consider the historical events in chronological order as they are presented in the canon: Creation first (Gen 1:1ff), followed by Flood (Gen 6–8),[3] and then the two central water events in the Exodus narrative: the Sea of Reeds and the water from the rock at Meribah (Exod 14–15; Exod 17; Num 20). Then we will proceed to an examination of poetic and prophetic passages which reference and interpret these events. Voluminous amounts have been written on the mythic background of the waters of creation, the flood, the Sea of Reeds, and the ancient embodiment of the rebellious sea in the form of a dragon or serpent. We shall not have space here to review all of this literature or to enter into the many intriguing background debates. Suffice it to say that much groundwork has been laid by earlier scholars, to whom we are greatly indebted.

---

2. Labuschagne, *Incomparability*, says "The distinctiveness of Old Testament religion can be explained solely by the distinctiveness of the God of the Old Testament" (3).

3. I include Creation and Flood here under the category of "historical" events not intending to imply anything about the historicity of these events; they should clearly be understood as part of Israel's mythical pre-history and as such have no specific grounding in time or place. However, as we shall see, the images, motifs and language of these two primeval events have become so intertwined with the retellings of the more concrete historical events that they must be treated alongside them.

WATER AND YAHWEH'S IDENTITY AT CREATION: GENESIS 1 AND 2

We will begin with the most fundamental of water references in the Hebrew scriptures—the waters of creation. In the cosmology of much of the ancient world the waters of creation were believed to be eternal. They were used to create the universe or, at least, certain parts of the universe—the "foundations" on which the earth sat and the sky or heavens above it. The priestly Hebrew creation narrative of Gen 1:1–10 likewise accords these primordial waters a central place and, therefore, we also find them interwoven into a number of later expressions of Yahweh's greatness and power.

The opening image of the Hebrew Scriptures is one of a dark, formless mass of heaving, chaotic water (Gen 1:2). This watery *tĕhôm* (Heb. תהום) becomes an important element in God's formation of the heavens and the earth (Gen 1:6–10). This most basic role in one of the foundational Israelite stories simultaneously accounts for and reflects water's importance in the history, thought and writings of the Jewish people.[4] However, water as a part of creation was not a uniquely Jewish idea: the creation narratives of many other societies of the ANE also featured water as a central element. More specifically, these myths often involved a *Chaoskampf*–the motif of a god defeating the personified forces of water in order to create the universe.

It was common for biblical scholars to use this *Chaoskampf* motif as the model for understanding Yahweh's relationship to the primordial waters in Gen 1:1–2 for at least a century, mostly due to the influence of Hermann Gunkel in *Schöpfung und Chaos in Urzeit und Endzeit*.[5] In this work Gunkel connected the word תהום in Gen 1:2 to the name of the Babylonian water goddess Tiamat.[6] But this equation has been shown to be problematic,[7] and it is more likely that both words go back to a common Semitic root, *t-h-m*, which means "the ocean" or "the deep." Even if the word did have mythical

---

4. Tsumura in *Creation* affirms: "The 'watery beginning' of Gen 1:2 could well be a reflection of the universal understanding of water as a basic element of the cosmos" (130).

5. Gunkel and Zimmern, *Schöpfung und Chaos*; an English translation was published in 2006, *Creation and Chaos*.

6. Gunkel, *Creation and Chaos*, 78ff.

7. Heidel (*Babylonian*, 98–101) has shown that it is grammatically impossible to derive the word תהום from the name Tiamat; also Gunkel's theory that Gen 1 is a reworking of the older Babylonian myth has had to be reexamined in light of the discovery of the Ugaritic texts which included the Baal and Anat cycle, probably a closer parallel to Genesis 1 than the *Enuma Elish*. For various other arguments against this theory see Hamilton, *Genesis*, 110–11.

WATER AND YAHWEH'S IDENTITY IN THE OLD TESTAMENT TRADITION

connotations at one time, it appears that the association had died out by the time of the writing of Gen. 1. If תהום in this passage did allude to a personified water deity it would seem rather odd to speak of the wind or spirit of God hovering over its face or surface (1:2b). Most recent scholars, therefore, have concluded that תהום does not have mythological meaning in Gen. 1.[8]

Furthermore, there is no evidence of an actual *Chaoskampf* in Gen 1.[9] The primordial waters in Gen. 1:2 may be intended to represent chaos, but at no point in this passage is the תהום portrayed as being in conflict with Yahweh. Instead it is depicted as mere putty in the hands of the creative deity (vv. 6–10). Rather than being rebellious, the תהום is passive; the struggle, if there ever was one, was over before creation began.[10] Also note that God's "spirit," "wind" or "breath" (Heb. רוח) blows or sweeps over the face of the waters in 1:2b. There is not the slightest hint of rebellion here; indeed, God "hovers" (מרחפת) over the waters like a bird, exercising his authority and sovereignty over the subjugated תהום.[11] This idea would surely have appealed to the ancient Israelites who were concerned with demonstrating their God's superiority over those of the other nations around them. Other gods may have distinguished themselves through their ability to defeat chaos at creation; Yahweh is unique in that this archetypal rebellious force never even challenged him.

This is not to say that the ancient Israelites were not familiar with the common cultural myths of a god's battle with the sea or sea creatures (called Lotan in Canaanite myth; Rahab or Leviathan in the Hebrew writings), or with the story of a god's control over the watery deep which represents chaos; there are many allusions to these ideas in other parts of the Old Testament.[12] But there is simply no reference to such a battle in the first chapter

---

8. Westermann, *Genesis*, 105; cf. Also Wenham, *Genesis 1–15*, 16.

9. Tsumura, *Creation*, 143.

10. Even Gunkel admits that in Gen 1 the myth has been so attenuated that "no more than allusion is made" to the battle with chaos (*Creation and Chaos*, 82; cf. also 59).

11. Wensinck, *Ocean*, notes a difference between mythological and monotheistic creation narratives in that "in the former class of passages the ocean bears the character of being hostile to the creating god; in the latter class it has become the one god's instrument, or his resting place" (1).

12. Cf. Job 7:12; 26:12; 38:8–11; 40:19–41:26; Ps 18:15–18; 33:6–8; 44:20; 74:12–14; 77:17; 89:10–11; 93:3–4; 104:5–9; Prov 8:22–31; Isa 27:1; 50:2–3; 51:9–10; Jer 5:22; 31:35; Ezek 29:3–6; 32:2–7; Nah 1:4; Hab 3:8ff; cf. also *I Enoch* 60:7–9; *4 Ezra* 6:49–52; *Pr Man* 2–4. (See Gunkel's discussion of each of these passages, *Creation and Chaos*, 21–77). Cf. the comment by Westermann, *Genesis*, 29.

of Genesis. Indeed, the fact that ancient Jewish society was clearly familiar with such legends makes it even more noteworthy that the authors of Genesis chose not to include allusions to such a battle in Genesis 1, where one might expect to find the myth in its fullest form.[13] Instead, by hinting that the waters usually associated with chaos were completely under Yahweh's control from the very beginning, the authors send a clear message about the superiority and absolute authority of their God.[14]

Genesis 1:2 describes the state of things before God's creative activity began: "the earth was a formless void and darkness covered the face of the deep, while a wind from God swept over the face of the waters."[15] These two phrases "a formless void" (Heb. תהו ובהו) and "darkness covered the face of the deep" (תהום) stand in parallel to one another as different ways of describing the cosmic primordial condition.[16] Therefore, we cannot attempt to understand the meaning and significance of the waters of creation (תהום) without also investigating the complex meaning of תהו ובהו. There is little question that (תהום) here means "the deep" or "waters of the deep." This word occurs 36 times in the OT and always refers to a flood of water or the "deep."[17] The etymology and meaning of the phrase תהו ובהו is much more complex. The literal translation of these words is actually "waste and void," two nouns working together as a hendiadys.[18] So although the words

---

13. Propp, following Talmon, credits the restriction of the myth to biblical poetry alone to the "Canaanite roots" of biblical poetry, which, he contends, is not shared by "the historiographic tradition" (cf. Propp, *Exodus*, 558).

14. It is possible that the omission of a *Chaoskampf* motif from the Creation account of Gen 1 was not an intentional polemic. Walton argues that the *Chaoskampf* motif, which was assumed by Gunkel to be a standard feature of creation narratives from the ANE, is not actually present in most of them. Therefore, it was not a common enough motif that its absence from the Genesis narrative would make a statement one way or another. Cf. Walton, "Creation," 48–63. This does not affect our argument, though, as later Hebrew writings contain clear references to the *Chaoskampf* motif at Creation, indicating that it was known in the Israelite tradition regardless of how common it may or may not have been in other ancient societies.

15. All translations are from the New Revised Standard Version unless otherwise indicated.

16. Wenham, *Genesis*, 15–16.

17. Cf. Gen 7:11; 8:2; 49:25; Ex 15:5, 8; Deut 8:7; 33:13; Job 28:14; 38:16; 38:30; Pss 33:7; 36:6; 42:7; 71:20; 77:16; 78:15; 104:6; 106:9; 107:26; 135:6; 148:7; Prov 3:20; 8:24, 27–28; Isa 51:10; 63:13; Ezek 26:19; 31:4, 15; Amos 7:4; Jon 2:5; Hab 3:10.

18. Wenham, *Genesis*, 15. For a more detailed definition of *hendiadys* cf. Watson, *Poetry*, 324–25.

Water and Yahweh's Identity in the Old Testament Tradition

are literally descriptions ("unformed and void") as a unit they become concrete ("a formless waste").

The meaning of תהו is relatively straight-forward. Usually translated as "waste" or "nothingness," it is related to the Ugaritic word *thw* ("desert")[19] and is used with this meaning in several OT passages.[20] The word ובהו is more problematic,[21] but it is probably best taken as "nonce word," one with no independent meaning but which is created to rhyme with and reinforce the meaning of its companion word.[22] Or it could be an intentional case of rhyme indicating that the verse is, or was at some point, poetic in nature.[23] Therefore, a translation of תהו ובהו as "a desert wasteland" or something similar does perhaps a better job of conjuring up the intended image than the traditional "formless and void." The primordial landscape before creation was an empty nothingness similar to an endless stretch of uninhabited wilderness. This is an image that certainly would have been understandable to the ancient Hebrews, for whom land travel either east or west out of their country required long and perilous journeys through the unmarked desert.

Tsumura mounts a compelling argument for תהו ובהו to be understood in this way. He suggests that תהו ובהו refers not to a state of chaos or even to ephemeral emptiness, but rather to "an unproductive and uninhabited place."[24] He believes this emphasis on the earth as an uninhabitable wasteland is set up as an intentional contrast to the coming creative work of Yahweh, who, as one of the main acts in creation, brings forth both plants and humans to fill the formerly lifeless space.[25] He therefore argues that תהו ובהו refers to a state of "aridness or unproductiveness" or "desolation"[26]

---

19. For the best modern discussion of the Ugaritic parallel see Tsumura, *Earth*, 17–19.

20. Sailhamer, *Pentateuch*, 84n8; also note Hamilton's attempt to capture this nuanced meaning with the translation "a desert and a wasteland" (*Genesis*, 108).

21. It is only found two other times in the OT and always in conjunction with תהו (Is. 34:11; Jer. 4:23); it is likely that both of these references borrow the phrase from Genesis 1. ובהו (often translated "void") is never used on its own.

22. Alter, *Genesis*, 3n2; Hamilton, *Genesis*, 108n15. However, Tsumura postulates a connection between ובהו and the Arabic word *bahiya* which refers to the "empty or vacant state of a tent or house which contains nothing or little furniture or goods" (*Earth*, 21).

23. Westermann, *Genesis*, 103; Hamilton, *Genesis*, 108; Gunkel, *Creation and Chaos*, 81.

24. Tsumura, *Earth*, 43.

25. Ibid., 42–43. Cf. Gen 2:5, where the lack of vegetation before Yahweh's creative acts is emphasized.

26. Ibid., 41.

and that in Gen 1:2 it "has nothing to do with 'chaos' and simply means 'emptiness' and refers to the earth which is an empty place." He concludes: "The main reason for the author's mentioning the earth as תהו ובהו in this setting is to inform the audience that the earth is 'not yet' the earth as it was known to them."[27]

There is not space here to discuss Tsumura's theory thoroughly, although his analysis of the linguistic evidence from various Semitic languages is very detailed and helpful. However, even though this explanation does seem to harmonize somewhat better with the rest of the creation narrative in Gen 1 as well as that in Gen 2, this does not appear to be the way the ancient Israelites as a whole interpreted God's control of the waters of creation, at least not in the Scriptural tradition. In the Scriptural passages which remember this event (some of which we examine below) it is impossible to ignore that the Creation image called on again and again is that of Yahweh controlling the rebellious, chaotic waters of the תהום. This image was so firmly lodged in the Israelite imagination that it became fused to the descriptions of other water events in Israelite history, bringing the two into intricate relationship (as we shall see below).[28]

Therefore, we are not comfortable with fully accepting Tsumura's thesis. While it is completely plausible that the words תהו ובהו may be interpreted as he suggests, and it certainly seems compatible with the rest of the creation narratives, it does not seem to be the way it was understood in the traditions that produced the other ancient Jewish writings outside of Genesis 1. In the rest of the OT whenever Yahweh is praised as Creator it is rarely for his ability to bring forth life out of a barren land, or for making plants grow or even for creating humanity. What is most often lauded is Yahweh's supremacy over the waters of chaos at creation.

The important thing for our study is an understanding of how Yahweh's characteristics exhibited in Gen 1 and 2 compare to the attributes of other deities of the ANE. In Gen 1, Yahweh is portrayed as the master of the waters of the cosmos, particularly the "deep" (תהום), the subterranean waters. In Gen 2, he also has control of waters, but this time they are the waters of the earth: rivers, springs and even the rain (2:5–6; 10–14). The division of the waters of the universe into these two categories was quite common in the worldview of peoples of the ANE. The Babylonian myths

---

27. Ibid., 43.

28. Cross deals thoroughly and decisively with this issue, cf. *Canaanite Myth*, 79–90. See discussion below.

Water and Yahweh's Identity in the Old Testament Tradition

pictured two types of water represented by two different goddesses: Tiamat, the goddess of the earthly waters (the sea) and Apsu, the goddess of the subterranean waters (the "deep"). Similarly, the Ugarits distinguished between the cosmic waters below the earth (*thmtm*) and the waters of the earth (*ym*). These would be roughly equivalent with the Hebrew concepts of תהום ("the deep") and ים ("sea") or מים ("earthly waters").[29]

Furthermore, in both Babylonian and Ugaritic traditions each of these types of water were controlled or ruled over by a separate deity. The Babylonian Enuma Elish tells the story of Marduk's triumphant victory over Tiamat, the earthly waters, but makes it clear that this occurs only after the god Ea has already tamed the subterranean abyss Apsu. Likewise, the Ugaritic myths purport that the waters of the earth (*ym*) were controlled by Baal, but the "deep" (*thmtm*) was the domain of El.[30] The closest these myths come to portraying one god as supreme over all the waters of the cosmos is found in Ugaritic thought, where El was believed to have made his abode at the source of both of these waters, possibly on a mountain.[31] This may be seen as a reference to a point at the farthest horizon where 'heaven' (the waters of the cosmos) and 'ocean' (the waters of the earth) meet. This reference to El sitting, as it were, at the source of the cosmic waters which flowed in two different streams is deemed by some to represent a more primitive form of the myth before Baal came on the scene.[32]

In this context, then, the portrayal of Yahweh (or Elohim) as the sole master of both the waters of the abyss (תהום) in Gen 1 and the waters of the earth (Gen 2) represents something of a departure from traditional ANE thought. This sovereignty over all the waters in all their various forms would indeed make Yahweh unique among the gods of the ANE—even El, who, while in some traditions seen as the ruler over both the deep and the earthly waters, is not portrayed as having control of the rain; that power belonged to the storm god Baal.[33] Yahweh, by contrast, controls the waters of the תהום (Gen 1), those of the earth (Gen 2)[34] and is pointedly identified as the one who directs the rains (Gen 2:5).

---

29. Tsumura, *Creation*, 130–35.

30. Ibid.

31. Although this is disputed and the source of vigorous debate; see the summary of the positions and arguments in ibid., 137.

32. Cross, *Canaanite Myth*, 36–39; Tsumura, *Creation*, 136–39.

33. Tsumura, *Creation*, 128–29.

34. For discussion of the translation of the notoriously difficult word אד (spring,

In summary, then, the subdued waters of Gen 1, are a foreshadowing of what will come in the rest of Israelite history. Yahweh, the one whom the seas of chaos at creation didn't dare challenge, will always be the victor over the watery forces of chaos and destruction, whether in the form of a devastating flood, an uncrossable sea, or a raging river. The outcome of these later events is telegraphed to us through the very first image of the Scriptures. Additionally, Yahweh, like other deities of the Ancient Near East, controls the waters of the universe, both those below the earth (the "deep") and the surface waters that brings life to plants and humans. However, Yahweh is unique in the fact that in the Hebrew creation accounts he is the *sole* master of these waters; his power is not shared with any other deity. This alone marks him as distinctive from all other gods. Yahweh's ability to control the waters is one of the foremost markers of his unique status as God in ancient Hebrew thought.

WATER AND YAHWEH'S IDENTITY IN THE FLOOD: GENESIS 6–9

In the biblical account of the great Flood we find much consonance with the creation narrative in Gen 1. In many ways, both literal and figurative, the Flood event can be seen as the antithesis of creation—the "undoing" of all of Yahweh's work at the beginning of time. Indeed, the Flood story derives much of its meaning in the biblical narrative from its relationship to the creation story. And much of that relationship has to do with Yahweh's control of the waters, both primordial and earthly.

The description of the flooding of the world in Genesis 7 must have been terrifying for the people of Israel. Verses 11–12 describe the source of the deluge, "all the fountains of the great deep burst forth, and the windows of the heavens were opened. The rain fell on the earth for forty days and forty nights." What is described here is nothing short of a complete cosmic cataclysm. The primordial waters, which were driven back by God at creation to make a place for the earth, once again envelop the earth and destroy it completely. The "fountains of the great deep" refers to the channels through which water flowed to irrigate the earth. In ancient cosmologies these were believed to be connected directly to the waters of the great "deep" (תהום) itself. "The windows of heaven" refers to similar conduits

---

stream, mist) cf. Hamilton, *Genesis*, 154–56; Westermann, *Genesis*, 200–201; also Hasel and Hasel, "Hebrew Term," 321–40.

Water and Yahweh's Identity in the Old Testament Tradition

from the heavens to the earth through which the rain was channeled. These two poetic expressions are intended to recall the "waters above and below" of Gen 1:6–7. The Flood un-creates, and returns the earth to its primordial state when there was only water (Gen 1:2).

These "lower waters" are sprung loose when the springs of the "great abyss" (Heb. תהום רבה) are split. The verb here is *baqa* (Heb. בקע) which is alternatively translated "to split, cleave, break open, or divide." Not coincidentally this verb is used at some point in the OT canon to describe every other major water event in Israel's history: it describes Yahweh's manipulation of the waters of creation in Ps 74:15 and Prov 3:20; it illustrates the "dividing" of the Sea of Reeds in Ex 14:16 and 21 and in the retellings in Neh 9:11, Ps 78:13 and Isa 63:12; and refers to the bringing of water from the rock at Meribah in Ps 78:15; Isa 35:6 and 48:21. Additionally, בקע is used elsewhere to refer to Yahweh bringing water from a rock for Samson in Judg 15:19; Yahweh's creation of the rivers in Job 28:10 and Hab 3:9 (although the latter has overtones of creation imagery); and, interestingly, to refer to the "cleaving" of the Mount of Olives on "the Day of the Lord" in Zech 14:4. This verse does not refer specifically to any water flowing as a result of this splitting of the mountain, but Zech 14:8 does talk about water flowing out from Jerusalem on "that day."[35] Although the source of this water is not specified, the use of this water image in close proximity to the verb בקע is probably not coincidental and would have likely brought to mind the previous uses of the word in the major events of Israel's history. The water imagery of the creation, appropriated as a framework for understanding later water events in the history of Israel, is given a cosmic eschatological application by the prophet.[36]

Some scholars have connected the concept of "splitting" or "cleaving" the water with the Babylonian creation story *Enuma Elish*, in which Marduk creates the heavens above and the earth below by splitting in two the corpse of Tiamat.[37] However, not all uses of the word בקע refer to the splitting or dividing of waters. Some indicate the carving, breaking or "cleaving" of rock or earth to bring forth springs or rivers. So this would not seem to be a universal association. Also, as Hamilton notes, in the *Enuma Elish* the body of Tiamat is split as an act of ordering or control, whereas in Gen 7:11

---

35. Also note the Exodus imagery in Zech 14:5–7, which supports this connection.

36. This connection will be particularly important as a background to Jesus' speech in John 7:37–39.

37. Hamilton, *Genesis*, 292.

the action is the opposite; the "splitting" of the springs of the deep allows for chaos to once again take over the created order.³⁸ בקע is never used to describe creation or the incident at Meribah within the narrative accounts of these events, which indicates that at some point in later development Hebrew authors started to make a connection between these episodes and the actions of Yahweh in the Flood and at the Sea of Reeds. The common element is Yahweh's control of the waters, be it his ability to restrain the seething waters of chaos, his parallel power to release said waters in a catastrophic flood, or the capacity for tapping these waters to provide protection and sustenance for his people.³⁹

However, the waters do not merely "flood" the earth (as in some English translations): they are said to "triumph" or "prevail" (7:18–20, 24; Heb. גבר). Although this word most frequently refers to something or someone being "strong," "great," or "mighty,"⁴⁰ גבר is occasionally used in a military context to refer to succeeding in a battle.⁴¹ Therefore, the translation "triumph" here for the activity of the waves is not inappropriate. The waters have won; they have conquered the foe (the earth); they are victorious. But it is not the waters that deserve the credit, rather Yahweh, the one who set the waters loose on the unsuspecting (and, once again, passive) foe.

Yahweh's role in this drama is finally cemented in 8:1–3 where we are told that God "made a wind blow over the earth, and the waters subsided; the fountains of the deep and the windows of the heavens were closed, the rain from the heavens was restrained, and the waters gradually receded from the earth." There is an undeniable affinity here with Gen 1:2 where the spirit (or wind) of Yahweh "swept" over the waters of the subjugated תהום at creation. It also foreshadows Yahweh's upcoming activity at the Sea of Reeds, driving back the sea with "a strong east wind" which turns the sea into "dry land" (Ex 14:21; cf. also the poetic expression of this action in Ex 15:8, 10).⁴² In essence, this constitutes a second creation; Yahweh has wiped

---

38. Ibid., 293.

39. There is yet another, more subtle, affinity between this passage and the creation narrative of Gen 1. Wenham points out that the phrase "on the earth" occurs together with "waters" six times in 7:17–24, "produc[ing] a strong resonance with Gen 1" [*Genesis*, 16], but a search of these terms reveals that they do not appear together in any intervening passage. This, again, shows the desire of the author to forge a close connection between the events of creation and the events of the Flood.

40. Gen 49:26; 2 Sam 1:23; Job 15:25; 21:7; 36:9; Ps 65:3; 103:11; 117:2; Jer 9:3

41. Ex 17:11; Is 42:13; Lam 1:16.

42. Also note that the language in 8:3: "the waters receded" (Heb. שוב) is the same

out the old and is beginning anew with Noah and his family as the only humans, as Adam and Eve inhabited his first creation. Just as he brought forth solid land out of the midst of the in Gen 1:9–10, in Gen 8:1 he again pushes back the waters to allow space for life.

In conclusion, the language and imagery of the Gen 1 creation narrative constitutes the primary interpretive lens through which the events of the flood are remembered and interpreted. It is impossible to borrow this construct without also making a connection between the characteristics of the Deity who was wholly responsible for both events. Two of the most formative narratives of the Hebrew nation deeply reflect—indeed, completely demand—the notion of Yahweh as the sole and absolute master of the waters.

WATER AND YAHWEH'S IDENTITY IN THE CROSSING OF THE SEA OF REEDS: EXODUS 14:1—15:21

The next water incident in Israelite history, the Crossing of the Sea of Reeds, has independent significance apart from the Creation story, but the authors have chosen to use language and imagery from Creation to give a cosmic and eternal importance to Yahweh's salvation of his people in the exodus. Indeed, as we shall see, Yahweh is only able to do what he does at the Sea of Reeds **because** of what he has done at Creation.

The central image in Israelite history and identity is the incident at the Sea of Reeds, which in its various retellings is sometimes fused with mythic elements involving the creation of the world and God's defeat of the sea dragon (see below). This event, then, becomes the lens through which other salvific acts of Yahweh are expressed and interpreted. While focus is most often given in the exodus narrative to its climax at the Sea of Reeds it must be noted that water, and Yahweh's control of it, is a recurring theme throughout the entire story of Moses. Beginning with his birth and hasty concealment in a basket on the Nile (Ex. 2:1–10), Moses himself is closely connected with water from his earliest days. Indeed, the Scripture tells us

---

word used to describe the "returning" of the Sea of Reeds to its normal position, which drowns the Egyptians, in Exodus 14:26–28; 15:19. Although שוב is a very common word in the OT meaning "to return"—appearing over 950 times—in light of the other evidence of connection to OT water events, its use in this pericope and the Sea of Reeds passage is more than just coincidental.

that the name "Moses," given him by the Egyptian woman who raises him, means "because I drew him out of the water" (Ex 2:10).[43]

After fleeing the wrath of Pharaoh in Egypt, Moses finds himself among the Midianites where he rescues his future wife and her sisters and their flocks at a well (Ex 2:15ff.). When Moses, following the call of the Lord, returns to Egypt to confront Pharaoh, Yahweh emphasizes his message with a series of plagues. In one he turns the Nile into blood (Ex 7:15ff.) effectively bringing on a drought for the people of the land, who frantically look elsewhere for potable water (Ex 7:24). In another Yahweh brings on a plague of frogs, which is depicted as coming from the Nile and other water sources (Ex 8:6ff.). So, long before the incident at the Sea of Reeds, we are introduced to the fact that Yahweh, as well as his servant Moses, is completely capable of manipulating the waters of the earth to bring about his purposes. This serves as a foreshadowing of what Yahweh will do at the Sea of Reeds; anyone who has been paying attention should not be surprised at how the story turns out—it has been adumbrated by all the previous interactions between Yahweh (or Moses) and water up to this point.

But, of course, the climax of the exodus narrative comes at the Sea of Reeds. Here Yahweh demonstrates his complete control of the waters when he manipulates them in such a way as to allow the Israelites to pass on dry land without harm and then drowns the pursuing Egyptians. We have two "accounts" of this event. Exodus 14 contains the prose narrative of the crossing which is immediately followed in Exodus 15:1–21 by the "Song of the Sea," a (most-likely older) poetic expression of the same event.[44] The

---

43. It appears that the name *Mosheh* is from an Egyptian word meaning "to beget a child," and may be connected to the Egyptian deity Thut-mose, but in the text of Exodus it has been given a Hebrew etymology, *mashah*, "he who draws out," (cf. Propp, *Exodus*, 152–53) because he will one day "draw his people out" at the sea. The Reed Sea incident is also prefigured in the "rushes" (Heb. סוּף—Ex. 2:3) amongst which the baby Moses is hidden—they are parallel to the *Yam Suph* ("Sea of Reeds"—Heb. יָם סוּף —Ex 15:4) from which Moses will "draw out" his people.

44. Voluminous material has been written on the dating of the Song of the Sea, so a complete treatment is not possible here. In short, popular scholarly opinion from the early twentieth century that held the poem to be of rather late date, post-exilic or even intertestamental [for examples cf. Bender, *ZAW*, 46–48; Haupt, *AJSL* 20, 150–58], has been challenged by more recent scholars suggesting a much earlier date. Cross (*Caananite Myth*, 121–25) suggests a 10th century BCE date for the actual written version of an older oral work, which could date as early as the 11th or 12th century BCE. Others argue that the poem, while retaining a core of ancient historical recollection (especially in vv. 1–12), was reworked and expanded through many centuries and reflects influence from a variety of other sources (including Second Isaiah) and historical events such as

prose narrative says: "Then Moses stretched out his hand over the sea. The Lord drove the sea back by a strong east wind all night, and turned the sea into dry land; and the waters were divided. The Israelites went into the sea on dry ground, the waters forming a wall for them on their right and on their left" (14:21–22; cf. v. 29). The Egyptians pursued, at which Moses stretched out his hand over the sea, the water returned and "the Lord tossed the Egyptians into the sea. The waters returned and covered the chariots and the chariot drivers, the entire army of Pharaoh that had followed them into the sea; not one of them remained" (14:27–28).

This pivotal narrative involving Yahweh's control of the waters on behalf of his people naturally borrows imagery and language from the previous narratives relating God's command of the waters: the Priestly creation narrative (Gen 1) and the story of the Flood (Gen 6–9). We see this most clearly in the use of the word תמהת ("ancient deeps") in Exodus 15:5, as a pivotal part of the poetic retelling of the event:

> The floods (תמהת) covered them;
> they went down into the depths like a stone. (15:5)

This contrasts with the use of the words ים and מים uniformly to describe the Sea of Reeds in the narrative account of chapter 14.[45] The use of this language in the poetic account suggests that Yahweh does more in this event than simply sweep away the waters of the Sea of Reeds. Something much more basic, more miraculous, and ultimately more powerful happens here: Yahweh calls the primordial waters of the very deep itself to his aid—the same waters that he "defeated" in Genesis 1, and therefore controls; the same waters that he unleashed in the great Flood. Durham perhaps summarizes it best: "The implication, at the very least, is that the visible waters in their everyday flow were thrust aside to make way for the temporary release of the devastating rebellion-waters from their subterranean prison."[46] This image confirms that what happens at the Sea of Reeds is not a fluke or accident. This salvation is purposefully brought about by Yahweh alone because he, and he only, is the one who can call the primordial depths

---

the conquest, the building of Solomon's temple, etc. Cf. Hyatt, *Exodus*, 163. The question is probably best answered by a theory which includes the possibility of very early source material that was reworked through several centuries of Israelite worship into the form we have now, which may indeed be post-exilic in date. Cf. Durham, *Exodus*, 203.

45. Cf. 14:9, 16, 21–23, 26–29.
46. Durham, *Exodus*, 207.

of chaos to do his bidding. This understanding of the event is reinforced by verse 8:

> At the blast of your nostrils the waters (מים) piled up,
> the floods (נזלים) stood up in a heap;
> the deeps (תהמת) congealed in the heart of the sea (15:8) (ים)

Note here that the participial נזלים has at its root a meaning of "flow, trickle, run or stream," emphasizing the nature of the water as moving, usually in a downward direction, as in rain or flowing streams.[47] Therefore, its use to refer to waters of the sea is unexpected.[48] The progression here from "waters" and "floods" of the Sea of Reeds to "the deeps" of the primordial ocean also supports the idea that there are two levels of water being referred to here—earthly and subterranean. This is more than just Yahweh controlling the currents of one particular sea. All the water in the universe—the very foundation of the world itself—is doing Yahweh's bidding in this miracle.

Note once again in both narratives that the waters, even those of the primordial deep, are always under Yahweh's control; there is no sign of rebellion or restlessness. Indeed, one can argue that everything in the narrative of Exodus 14 is carefully orchestrated and controlled by Yahweh: he chooses the perfect location of the Israelite's encampment (by the sea, vv. 1–2) in order to lure Pharaoh to pursuing them (v. 3); he "hardens" Pharaoh's heart against the Israelites (v. 8) which results in the Egyptian pursuit; he carefully instructs Moses in what to do to bring the miracle about (v. 16); he creates a barrier between the Israelites and the Egyptians using the pillar of cloud, creating both darkness for the Egyptians and light for the Israelites (vv. 19–20); he drives back the waters of the sea all night long with a wind (v. 21); he creates confusion and chaos among the Egyptian army so that they become stuck on the floor of the sea, unable to cross (vv. 23–25)[49]; and finally he brings the waters back into their place to drown the terrified Egyptians (vv. 26–28).

---

47. Durham, *Exodus*, 206; Propp, *Exodus*, 521–22.

48. Propp sees this use as part of a greater scheme of "elevation and depression, rising and falling" throughout the story in both language and theme (Propp, *Exodus*, 510, 521, 542).

49. The interpretation of the verb סור here is a notorious crux. It can mean "bound" (as in, the wheels became locked up, either because of the thick mud or through mechanical failure), "removed" (the wheels fell off, perhaps?) or even "diverted" (did Yahweh confuse the drivers so that they lost control of the chariots?). The most likely answer, given the

Each of these steps is carefully supervised by Yahweh to accomplish his purpose, which is stated three times in the story: to gain glory for himself (vv. 4, 17–18). And in this he is successful, as is testified to in vv. 30–31. Everything and everyone in this story is firmly under Yahweh's command, including even the hearts and minds of Pharaoh and the other Egyptians. They may feel they are acting of their own accord, but the story makes it clear that Yahweh manipulates them at every turn—a fact which some of the Egyptians eventually come to realize, to their dismay (v. 25b: "Let us flee from the Israelites, for the Lord is fighting for them against Egypt.")

The power of Yahweh is also emphasized in the story by the constant reminder that the Israelites themselves are to do nothing to bring about their rescue. Indeed they are incapable of doing so. Moses makes it clear that Yahweh and Yahweh alone will bring about their salvation:

> "Do not be afraid, stand firm, and see the deliverance that the Lord will accomplish for you today; for the Egyptians whom you see today you shall never see again. The Lord will fight for you, and you have only to keep still" (14:13–14).

The Israelites have seen the pursuing Egyptians and fear their fate. Moses now commands them to focus their sight instead on Yahweh's imminent salvation. This contrast is skillfully made by the statement that the Egyptians whom they see, and who are the cause of their fear, will soon been seen no more forever, "an ominous anticipation of the medium of the victory to come." Furthermore, as Durham points out: "Seeing, then not seeing; not seeing, then seeing are to be . . . the extent of their [Israel's] activity. Yahweh is going to do their fighting. In addition to watching, they have only to keep quiet."[50] More was on the line at the Sea of Reeds than just the fate of Yahweh's people, as important as that was: Yahweh's very reputation was at stake.

After all, in the eyes of the world he had abandoned these people; they had been captive slaves in a foreign land for centuries. Was this God actually capable of saving his people? Did he have the power and authority to command the elements of the universe (in this case, water) to bring about his purposes? Would he be defeated by the Egyptian armies which pursued

---

conditions that are described in the narrative, seems to be that the wheels became stuck in the mud, although the idea of Yahweh throwing the drivers into a confusion would be consistent with his actions earlier in the story (cf. 14:24). For a full discussion cf. Propp, *Exodus*, 500; Cassuto, *Exodus*, 169–70.

50. Durham, *Exodus*, 192.

and forever after be a laughing stalk to generations of Pharaohs and Egyptians? Clearly Yahweh had to do more than simply ensure the welfare of his people by conquering their enemies. Indeed, if defeat of the pursuing Egyptians had been the only issue, it could surely have been accomplished by other means well before the people had made it all the way to the Sea of Reeds.

There is clearly more intended in this story than just proving that Yahweh is capable of saving his people. The more subtle, but clear, message is that Yahweh is God. He alone controls the primordial waters, which were held back at creation by his command and are now unleashed by him on behalf of his people. He has complete power over the waters, and can manipulate both those of the deep and the surface waters ("currents"), just as he can manipulate the minds and motives of Pharaoh and his men. By his control of the water, Yahweh reveals himself to be the only God, a force to be reckoned with. There is no one like him (cf. 15:11). Not only can he blow the surface waters around with a mere breath from his nostrils, he can actually call to his aid the crushing force of the waters of the very deep itself

WATER AND YAHWEH'S IDENTITY AT MERIBAH/MASSAH: EXODUS 17:1-7; NUMBERS 20:1-13

In Exodus 17 and Numbers 20 we are given two differing accounts of the experience of the Israelites at Meribah, also called Massah. Here the Israelites' complaint that there was no water is answered by God who instructs Moses to bring forth water from a rock. At the core of this story, especially as it is told in the Exodus version, is the very identity and nature of Yahweh himself. Is Yahweh able to keep his promise and sustain his people in the wilderness against all odds? Or have they been led there by a madman and left to die?

This story is part of a larger motif in the wilderness accounts where the people of Israel question Yahweh's abilities to protect them and complain to Moses about the adverse conditions. Moses then presents the situation to Yahweh, who solves the problem, proving himself as the one true God in the process. Yahweh's identity is central to each of these narratives, not just to the incident at Meribah. In Exodus 15:22-27 we read the story of the Israelites, immediately after the Reed Sea incident, complaining or "grumbling" because they have gone three days in the desert without water and when they do finally come to a spring, called Marah, the water is found to

Water and Yahweh's Identity in the Old Testament Tradition

be non-potable. Moses takes the problem to Yahweh who tells him to throw a particular piece of wood into the water and it will become drinkable. This Moses does, after which Yahweh makes a declaration to the people: "If you will listen carefully to the voice of the Lord your God, and do what is right in his sight, and give heed to his commandments and keep all his statutes, I will not bring upon you any of the diseases that I brought upon the Egyptians; for I am the Lord who heals you" (v. 26).

The important part of this pronouncement for our purposes is the last clause: "I am the Lord, who heals you." It is noteworthy that immediately after a miracle involving Yahweh's ability to control the waters of the earth, he proclaims his unique identity, as the one who heals Israel. This miracle was not about simply providing drinkable water for the Israelites, although that was the people's main focus. Instead, it was about the fundamental nature of Yahweh as one who can nurture and heal his people.

We see an even stronger example of this connection of Yahweh's identity with a "grumbling" narrative in Exodus 16:1–18. Here the people complain to Moses and Aaron that they have no food. They are desirous of returning to Egypt where they at least had plenty to eat (vv. 2–3). Yahweh informs Moses of what he will do to remedy the situation: he will provide bread from heaven for them and they are to follow very specific instructions about how to collect it (vv. 4–5). Thus, Yahweh turns this gift into a test of the people's faith (v. 4)—will they trust him enough to only collect enough for the day ahead? What started as a test of Yahweh by the people turns into a test of the people by Yahweh. Significantly, in relaying God's instructions to the people Moses emphasizes that the Lord's actions will confirm his identity: "In the evening you shall know that it was the Lord who brought you out of Egypt, and in the morning you shall see the glory of the Lord. . . . You shall know that it was the Lord when he gives you meat to eat in the evening and all the bread you want in the morning. . . ." (vv. 6–8). And later in the story Yahweh himself tells Moses that through the eating of the meat and bread "you shall know that I am the Lord your God" (v. 12). God's actions here will prove that he is who he says he is.

This all leads us up to the passage we are most concerned with in this work: the production of water from the rock at Meribah. We can see that the story fits the general pattern already established of the people doubting Moses, and Yahweh by extension (Ex 17:2–3; Num 20:2–5), Moses (and Aaron) taking the people's complaint to Yahweh (Ex 17:4; Num 20:6), and Yahweh providing a solution (Ex 17:5–6a; Num 20:7–8). Moses then does as Yahweh commands (Ex 17:6b; Num 20:9–11) and water rushes forth from the rock (Ex 17:6b; Num 20:11). Like the other desert passages which relate to the "grumblings" of the people, the issue of Yahweh's identity factors in to the event, although in a far subtler way. The Numbers account portrays Yahweh as revealing something of his identity through this action. In the conclusion to the story in v. 13 the narrator says: "These are the waters of Meribah, where the people of Israel quarreled with the Lord, and by which he showed his holiness." Yet, the Exodus account contains no direct reference to Yahweh revealing himself, or to the people knowing Yahweh's identity.

However, that is not to say that the question of God's identity is not present in the Exodus narrative; it is very much an issue that hovers in the background of the story. This is patent in the etymology of the name of the place where the event occurred. The name Meribah (מריבה), which appears in both the Exodus and Numbers accounts, means "place of strife or contention," deriving from the root ריב meaning "to strive or quarrel." This name, therefore, emphasizes the "quarrelling" or "grumbling" aspect of the event. The people are portrayed as fighting against Yahweh and his appointed leaders. The word Massah (מסה) means "test, temptation or trial." This name only appears in the Exodus account (v. 7) but is paired together with "Meribah" indicating that the quarrelling and contention implied by the name מריבה resulted in a testing (מסה).

The very idea of "testing" someone naturally involves the notion of integrity: is someone who he says he is, or is he capable of delivering something that he promised; is he trustworthy? Yahweh claims to be the only God, the God of Abraham, Isaac and Jacob, but can he prove it? Of course, the ultimate irony in the Meribah account, along with the other wilderness testings, is that Yahweh has already proven himself in a hugely miraculous manner at the Sea of Reeds. And yet for the people it isn't enough. Every new difficulty brings about new doubt as to Yahweh's integrity of character.[51] Can he sustain them? Or should they return to Egypt and her gods? This is the dilemma that is paramount in the wilderness stories of Exodus and Numbers. God's very identity as the creator and ruler of the universe is at stake. And their complaints against Moses' leadership are clearly revealed by him for what they are—distrust of Yahweh. An attack on Moses was an

---

51. As Durham states, in discussing the question asked by the people, "Is Yahweh present with us or not?" (Ex 17:7): "The only unbelievable aspect of the narrative is that the Israelites could possibly ask such a question at such a time, and on the basis of so flimsy a provocation." (*Exodus*, 231).

attack on the Lord himself; the test of one was the test of the other (cf. Ex 17:2, 7; Num 20:13)

In her commentary, Carol Meyers contends that the questioning of God's presence by the people at Meribah is directly related to the lack of water. The people apparently believe that if God was with them, they would not be in need of water, because he is the one who provides water. Since there is none, perhaps Yahweh has left them.[52] This reading understands the people as specifically identifying Yahweh with his previous control over the waters in both their folklore and in their own recent experience. The flow of water from the rock was not just a provision that ensured Israel's livelihood, but was an affirmation of Yahweh's presence among them. In much mythology of the ANE water was envisioned as flowing from a deity's dwelling place, usually from the underside of a holy mountain where the god or gods resided.[53] Therefore, the flowing of the water from the rock at Meribah was also a tacit proclamation by Yahweh of his presence in another sense: he was not only with his people but intended to dwell among them, as will indeed will become a tangible reality very shortly in the narrative as the people arrive at Mt. Sinai, the place where the Lord will reveal himself to Moses.

In this context, then, Yahweh's ability to provide water from a completely dry place is notable. Through this action Yahweh is not simply demonstrating his ability to provide, but tapping into his already established sovereignty and control of the waters of the universe and the earth. Indeed, Propp suggests that this action was seen as a necessary part of the Creation activity that Yahweh had already begun: "Creation is incomplete until Yahweh shows his power not only to make the wet dry [as in Creation] but to make the dry wet, i.e., to sustain life."[54]

In terms of degree this miracle isn't necessarily any more indicative of Yahweh's abilities than his previous actions in parting the Sea of Reeds, providing potable water at Marah, or providing bread and quail for the people to eat. However, from the standpoint of later poetic and prophetic interpretation, the Meribah incident seems to have held a special place in the nation's collective memory. The imagery of water flowing from barren places to bring life is picked up on and repeated over and over again in various forms and contexts for the rest of Israelite history and is commandeered

---

52. Meyers, *Exodus*, 134.
53. Ross, *Recalling*, 91.
54. Propp, *Exodus*, 610.

by early Christian authors as well; the bread (manna) and quail provided in the wilderness appear far less often in later poetic interpretations (cf. Ps 78:24–25; 105:40).[55] This suggests the deep importance of the image of their God as the sole and absolute ruler of the waters of the universe. As seen in the earlier passages of Creation, Flood and Exodus, Yahweh was only able to direct the waters of the cosmos and the world because he was had created them; his control over the waters, therefore, implied both his role as sole Creator and his absolute sovereignty over all the universe. These concepts will be fleshed out in more detail in the poetic and prophetic reinterpretations of the events which we will examine next.

YAHWEH'S IDENTITY AS MASTER OF THE WATERS: POETIC AND PROPHETIC INTERPRETATIONS OF ISRAEL'S WATER EVENTS

The Hebrew Scriptures are packed with allusions to Yahweh's manipulation of the תהום, either at the beginning of time or in the Sea of Reeds incident and his provision of life-giving waters in the desert, as at Meribah. These references are found in a variety of genres from various time periods of Jewish history. In many places these acts on Yahweh's part qualify him to be God. These actions are therefore an integral part of who he is in the eyes of the ancient Hebrew authors. Here we will examine a few of the more prominent examples of this type of reference to uncover the role that Yahweh's control of the waters played in the formation of his identity in ancient Israel.

Job 38:4–38 and Isaiah 40:12–31

Job 38:4–38 begins the climactic section (chs. 38–41) of the Book of Job where Yahweh finally answers Job's plaintive questions about the justice of his fate. The rationale that God gives is simple, if not necessarily heartening to Job: I am God and I know what I'm doing. He then elaborates on his answer quite poetically by listing the great deeds that qualify him to be the one who controls Job's life. Chapter 38 describes in lyric terms Yahweh's

---

55. However, both the water from the rock and the manna will become major symbols in the Gospel of John: the manna in Jesus' discourse in chapter 6 and the water in his speech in chapter 7. For linguistic and narrative connections between Exodus 17:1–7 and John chapter 6, see Janzen, *Exodus*, 120–21.

Water and Yahweh's Identity in the Old Testament Tradition

creation of the universe and particularly focuses on his manipulation of the waters of creation and his subsequent authority over them. Chapter 39 describes Yahweh's power over the animals within his creation. Chapter 40 begins with Yahweh's challenge to Job to sit in judgment over the people of the earth and dole out punishment. The section concludes with a long passage that uses Yahweh's control of the sea monsters behemoth (40:15–24) and leviathan (41:1–34) as proof, once again, of his right to be King.

In this section Yahweh first presents his credentials as Creator and then as Ruler. As Creator, Yahweh established the earth firmly on its foundations (38:4–7), made boundaries for the sea (38:8–11), and created the light (38:12–15). As Creator, he has knowledge of and rules over the recesses of the universe: the deep (38:16–18); the distant horizons, where light and darkness reside (38:19–21); and the heights, also known as the storehouse of snow and hail (38:22–24). As Ruler, Yahweh judiciously manages all the elements in the heavens (38:25–38) and all creatures on earth (38:39—39:30). His argument is clear: whoever knows or controls the extremities of the world is truly master of the created order. And it is this status that gives Yahweh the right and power to call himself Lord of the universe.

One of the main themes in this passage is identity: the identity of Yahweh as God over against Job. The whole point of Yahweh's argument is that his identity as creator of the universe gives him the right and authority to operate in the universe as he sees fit. The implication is that Yahweh, in his infinite wisdom, knows what he is doing and his creatures (including Job) should trust him, even when there seems to be no good reason to do so. What is significant for our study is the role that water takes in this self-identification of Yahweh as ruler of the universe.

Many OT texts affirm that Yahweh is the master of the sea.[56] However, the imagery used in Job 38:8–11 is unique in the Hebrew Scriptures:[57]

---

56. Job 9:8; 26:12; 41:31; Ps 18:15; 33:7; 65:7; 66:6; 74:13; 77:19; 78:13, 53; 89:9; 93:3–4; 104: 6–9; 107:29; 114:3–5; Prov 8:29; Isa 43:16; 51:10, 15; Jer 5:22; Amos 5:8; 9:6; Nah 1:4; Hab 3:8, 15.

57. Pope, *Job*, 293 mentions a possible parallel in a Ugaritic text [BH (75 I 18–19)] where swaddling bands are referred to in the birth of the bovine monsters called Eaters and Devourers, but that is one of the few parallels to be found in ANE literature. The use of the birth metaphor is common in ancient mythology to express the origin of something—cf. Ps 90:2 which speaks of the "birth" of the mountains when the earth was formed.

> Who shut in the sea with doors
> when it burst out from the womb?—
> when I made the clouds its garment,
> and thick darkness its swaddling band,
> and prescribed bounds for it,
> and set bars and doors,
> and said, "Thus far shall you come, and no farther,
> and here shall your proud waves be stopped"?

In a deliberate contrast to the mythical concept of a threatening and chaotic תהום, the sea here is portrayed as a helpless infant completely dependent on Yahweh, who brought it out of the womb when its gestation was complete. Since he brought it into existence, Yahweh never had to subdue it in primordial combat as the gods Marduk or Baal had to do. It has always been subservient to him. In fact, Yahweh took care of the sea as gently as one would care for a newborn infant. He clothed it with clouds and swaddled it with dark mist. He set boundaries for the infant, as any parent would do, so he could not harm himself or others, with the implication that the baby obeys and does not try to cross the line. This metaphor is quite striking, perhaps even shocking, within the context of ancient Near Eastern mythology. As Normal Habel says: "The image is deliberately absurd: this violent chaos monster is but an infant, born from a womb, wrapped in baby clothes, placed in a playpen, and told to stay in its place."[58] Having brought forth the sea and having harnessed it, Yahweh commands it and it does his bidding. The message is clearly that there are no hostile cosmic forces beyond Yahweh's control.

There are obvious parallels between Yahweh's monologue in Job 38–41 and Yahweh's trial speeches in Second Isaiah,[59] where similar challenge questions are posed.[60] Indeed, in one of these speeches (Isa 40:12–31) we find a metaphor of God's control over the waters of creation that is comparable to the imagery in Job 38:

> Who has measured the waters in the hollow of his hand
> and marked off the heavens with a span,
> enclosed the dust of the earth in a measure,

---

58. Habel, *Job: A Commentary*, 538. A similar reduction of a figure of chaos to a non-threatening entity can be found in Psalm 104:26 where the Leviathan is portrayed as "an aquatic pet with which Yahweh sports" (Habel, *Job*, 569). This passage will be discussed below. Cf. also the discussion of this passage in Watson, *Chaos Uncreated*, 274–78.

59. Isa 40:12–31; 41:1–5, 21–29; 43:8–15; 44:6ff; 45:20–25.

60. For detailed discussion cf. Kubina, *Gottesreden*, 131–42; and Rowold, *Theology*.

and weighed the mountains in scales
and the hills in a balance? (40:12)

This verse, especially within the context of the larger passage, is probably not intended so much to say something about Yahweh's control of the cosmic waters as it is to express that God is infinitely greater than the created world. However, it is not insignificant that in the long litany of God's supreme characteristics his greatness in comparison to the waters of creation is given first place. It is indicative of the importance of this image to the ancient Hebrews.

In both these passages the rhetorical questions do not solicit information, but challenge the party to whom they are directed. The answer is intended to focus on God as the only possible power who could perform the action described in the question. The answer to the question, "Who shut up the Sea behind doors?" is not "Who knows?" or "I did not," but "You alone did," just as the answer to the challenge question, "Who measured the waters?" (Isa 40:12) or "Who created these?" (Isa 40:26) is "Yahweh alone. No other deity was involved." As Westermann says, "In the trial speeches of Second Isaiah Yahweh and the gods of the nations confront each other in a legal process, the purpose of which is to decide who is truly God."[61]

The structure of both Job 38 and Isaiah 40:12–31 then, is designed to emphasize the total inadequacy of humans or any other forces in the universe when compared to the Lord. The cumulative effect of the many rhetorical questions which are posed is that Yahweh and Yahweh alone, certainly not with any human agency, or the help of any other creature, created and controls the universe, from the largest activity to the smallest detail. In these recitals, Yahweh's control over the waters of the universe since the beginning of time plays a major role. The fact that he "tamed" these waters at creation is what gives him the power and authority to control them on the earth today. He can call down the waters from the heavens to bring refreshing and life-giving rain (Job 38:26–27, 37)—but he can just as easily call forth the waters of heaven and the springs of the deep to bring on a catastrophic flood (38:34). He has even created the systems by which waters on the earth are controlled and ordered (38:25). Through these both animals and humans receive their very life.

---

61. Westermann, *Isaiah*, 15.

Psalm 104

In this passage the Psalmist marvels in wonder at the greatness of the God he worships. He uses the picture of a divine theophany to convey a sense of the power of Yahweh, who the elemental forces of nature serve as mere minions. Yahweh majestically manifests himself from his celestial tent or palace. He appears royally clad in radiant light (v. 2), travelling on a cloud and wind (v. 3), and attended by the winds and flames of fire (v. 4). He comes down to create the earth and imposes his order, thus demonstrating his dominance over all parts of the universe. The Psalmist cannot resist exclaiming in wonder at the abundant evidence of Yahweh's activity and planning. He is the sole creator, and also the sole sustainer (vv. 24, 27).

Once again in this passage Yahweh's control over the waters of creation is prominently featured. The first reference is found in v. 3 where we are told that Yahweh "set the beams of [his] chambers on the waters." This comes in the midst of a passage describing his creative activity at the beginning of time and is probably a reference to the restriction of the primordial waters above the earth which occurred when God created the "expanse" or "firmament" to separate the waters above from the waters below (Gen 1:6–8). However, the attention soon turns from the mythological sea to the everyday waters of the earth:

> You cover it [the earth] with the deep as with a garment;
>   the waters stood above the mountains.
> At your rebuke they flee;
>   at the sound of your thunder they take to flight.
> They rose up to the mountains, ran down to the valleys
>   to the place that you appointed for them.
> You set a boundary that they may not pass,
>   so that they might not again cover the earth.
>
> You make springs gush forth in the valleys;
>   they flow between the hills,
> giving drink to every wild animal;
>   the wild asses quench their thirst.
> By the streams the birds of the air have their habitation;
>   they sing among the branches.
> From your lofty abode you water the mountains;
>   the earth is satisfied with the fruit of your work.
>
> You cause the grass to grow for the cattle,

    and plants for people to use,
to bring forth food from the earth,
    and wine to gladden the human heart,
oil to make the face shine,
    and bread to strengthen the human heart.
The trees of the Lord are watered abundantly,
    the cedars of Lebanon that he planted. (Ps 104:6–16)

Here we see that Yahweh's mastery over the waters of creation and his continual provision of water on the earth today are closely related. It is because Yahweh as Creator controlled the seas *then* that he can make the waters of the earth do his bidding *now*. Indeed, there is a direct equation between those waters that God "rebuked" at creation (v. 7) and the waters that flow on the earth today (vv. 8–10). Yahweh not only tames the waters, and keeps them in their place by setting boundaries (mentioned again here in v. 9), but he then proceeds to use the subdued waters to serve his good purposes of sustaining life on the earth (vv. 8–16).[62] This is perhaps the ultimate irony: the waters that represent chaos and death are now used by Yahweh to bring forth and sustain life, order and peace. Those springs then provide sustenance for the whole of Yahweh's living creation: beasts of the field (v. 11); birds (v. 12); the earth itself (v. 13); grass and plants (v. 14); trees (specifically the Cedars of Lebanon—v. 16); and finally, humankind's food—wine, oil and bread (v. 15).[63] This provides yet another subtle hint at the uniqueness of Yahweh among the gods of the nations: he not only conquers the rebellious sea (although notice that in v. 7 there is no indication of combat—the sea "flees" when it sees Yahweh coming; there was no contest) but he manages to find a way to turn this mythological enemy into his servant—fulfilling his purpose and doing his bidding.

Another metaphor that expresses the same idea is found a bit later on in the psalm:

    O Lord, how manifold are your works!
    In wisdom you have made them all;

---

62. Cf. Propp, *Exodus*, 608, who notes that a "two-stage Creation" is a typical feature of ANE cosmogony myths. The first stage involves the Creator establishing "the basic physical and hierarchical distinctions in the Cosmos," which is a one-time event, and the second depicts the Creator as producing the conditions for life—particularly irrigating the earth to support plants, animals and humanity. This second stage is never complete but "must be renewed daily."

63. Referring to the actual crops needed to make these items: grapes, olives and grain, which, naturally, require water in order to grow

> the earth is full of your creatures.
> Yonder is the sea, great and wide,
>   creeping things innumerable are there,
>   living things both small and great.
> There go the ships,
>   and Leviathan that you formed to sport in it.
> These all look to you
>   to give them their food in due season (vv. 24–27)

Here the fearsome sea monster "Leviathan" is not portrayed as a terrifying personification of watery chaos which must be subdued by Yahweh, as is found in other texts of the ancient Near East as well as the Hebrew Scriptures.[64] Instead, he is reduced to simply another peaceful sea creature, playing in the waters, dependent on the Lord to care for him. Leviathan has become simply God's toy[65] or pet[66]; just as the cosmic waters of chaos in Job 38:8–9 become a mere helpless baby in the presence of the great Yahweh, so has Leviathan in this passage become completely domesticated.

So, as in the Job passages discussed above, the Hebrew writers use Yahweh's sovereignty over the waters of the universe as a key plank in their argument that he alone was the king and ruler of all things.

Proverbs 3:19–20 and 8:22–29

In the prologue of the Book of Proverbs (chapters 1–9), the theme of creation appears twice, in 3:19–20 and 8:22–31. These two passages are similar enough in subject, imagery, and background that they are often discussed together. They both refer to the Lord creating the foundations of the earth, although in different language. Prov. 3:19 (NIV) describes Yahweh as "laying the earth's foundations" while 8:29 (NIV) says that he "marked out the foundations of the earth." The verb in each case is different, carrying divergent connotations, but the message is essentially the same: Yahweh is the ultimate founder of the universe.

However, the purpose of these passages is not so much to demonstrate that Yahweh is the Creator—that is taken for granted—but rather to lend

---

64. Ps 74:14; 89:10; Job 3:8; 26:12; 41:1; Isa 27:1; 51:9–10; on the topic of *Chaoskampf* and the sea monster in the OT cf. Day, *Conflict*.

65. Schaefer, *Psalms*, 258.

66. Allen, *Psalms*, 34.

authority and antiquity to the figure of Wisdom.⁶⁷ The author in each case argues for why Wisdom is so desirable for humans to attain. The answer: because it is not something new or fleeting—it was the first of God's creations and was a witness and companion to Yahweh in his creative work.⁶⁸ Indeed, Wisdom appears to have been actually instrumental in those acts in some way.⁶⁹ Therefore, she has an unparalleled relationship to God, and a unique perspective, which can only benefit those who acquire her. As Waltke explains it: "If the Lord with wisdom as his tool accomplished the wonders of the various phases of creation—setting the earth on its foundations by splitting the primeval waters and setting the heavens in their appointed place and watering the earth with dew from its clouds—think what his revealed wisdom will do in the lives of those who find it."⁷⁰

Both passages borrow imagery and expressions from the creation myths of the ancient Near East and from other passages in the Hebrew Scriptures. First we have a reference in 3:20a to Yahweh breaking open the deeps. This phrase calls up imagery from both creation and from the Flood and Reed Sea events. "The deeps" here is תמהת, the plural form of the word used in Genesis 1:2 for the waters of the deep. The word for "break" is בקע which, as we saw above, is used in Gen 7:11 to refer to Yahweh's "splitting" or "breaking open" the fountains of the deep to cause the Flood, and in Exodus 14:16, 21 and Neh 9:11 to describe what Yahweh does to the waters of the Sea of Reeds.⁷¹

The mention of "dew" falling from the clouds in 3:20b might initially seem unrelated to Yahweh's control over either the תהום or the Sea of Reeds. Indeed the image of the swirling, untamed waters of the abyss juxtaposed

---

67. Scott, *Proverbs/Ecclesiastes*, 71–72; Waltke, *Proverbs*, 69.

68. For discussion of the long-standing debate over the meanings of אמון—alternatively translated "artisan, master craftsman" or "child, nursling or ward"—and סחק—which can mean either "to rejoice" or "to play, jest" in 8:30 see Clifford, *Proverbs*, 96–97; Murphy, *Proverbs*, 48; Scott, *Proverbs/Ecclesiastes*, 72; Scott, "Wisdom," 213–23; Waltke, *Proverbs*, 417–22 contains one of the best summaries of the major viewpoints on the issue.

69. Wisdom's exact role in creation is unclear, but the preposition translated "by" in 3:19 is taken as instrumental by nearly all translators and commentators, meaning the Lord created the earth somehow "through" wisdom as an instrument. But how this was accomplished is less clear. For discussion see Murphy, *Proverbs*, 22. The image of Wisdom's instrumental role in creation has clearly influenced New Testament thought where the concept of Wisdom is applied to Jesus Christ (cf. John 1:3; Col 1:15–16).

70. Waltke, *Proverbs*, 261.

71. It also appears in Pss 74:15 and 78:13 in relation to the Sea of Reeds event.

next to succulent and life-giving drops of water from above does seem odd, although they also appear together in Deut 33:13 which may serve as a guide for understanding their relationship here. In Deut 33:13 we read: "May the LORD bless his land with the precious dew from heaven above and with the deep waters that lie below" (NIV).

This verse makes clear that the relationship between the two is their shared role in providing water for the earth. The ancients believed the waters of the earth were fed by springs that drew water up from the deep abyss below the earth. This water, along with the waters which fell from above (rain, dew) was the primary means of sustaining life. Ironically, these were also the same means used to destroy life in the Flood, described as a "splitting" (בקע) of these fountains and causing them to burst open, which together with a deluge of rain from the heavens covered the entire earth with water (Gen 7:11; 8:2).

This "dew" probably describes the bringing of moisture from the Mediterranean Sea via the west wind to the land of Canaan during the otherwise dry months. This was a vital meteorological phenomenon for the ancient Hebrews: "In Canaan's almost rainless summer the land was dependent on this moisture for life, and so dew was more impressive to Orientals than to Westerners who, having a more abundant amount of rainfall, have less dependence on dew."[72] The point seems to be that Yahweh, far from simply creating the earth and then letting it fend for itself, actually continues to provide life-giving water to sustain his "good" creation.[73] The connection between this life-giving water and the waters of the תהום or "deep" in Psalm 104 (discussed above) has a different emphasis, but it is clear from both passages that Yahweh is considered to be the master over all waters, whether metaphorical, primeval, cosmological or actual.

The second passage, 8:22–31, also presents wisdom in connection with the Lord as Creator and Sustainer of the world, but this time instead of being his instrument through which creation came to be, Wisdom is personified as the Lord's companion throughout his creating process. To prove that she was with Yahweh from the beginning, Wisdom describes the events she witnessed. She also talks about her origin. In verses 24–26 she proclaims that she was "brought forth" before the oceans or springs, mountains or hills or even the earth were created. Waltke notes that the "life-threatening oceans" and the "life-giving springs" of v. 24 may be intended as a merism

---

72. Waltke, *Proverbs*, 262.
73. Ibid., 261–62.

to indicate the completeness of the emptiness that existed before Yahweh began creating.[74] Murphy suggests that in v. 24 "deeps" and "fountains" are parallel, indicating that the primeval waters, when split yielded these fountains to provide water for the earth.[75] While it is clear that this connection was sometimes made in Hebrew thought, as evinced in Ps 104:7ff. and possibly hinted at in Prov 3:20, the relationship is not portrayed definitively here. If this is the author's intention, it is not made clear, although it is certainly possible that this link hovers in the background of this verse.

This passage also makes reference twice to Yahweh's restriction of the sea so that the earth can be safe from its dangers, in v. 27b and 28b. The latter in particular reads like a reprise of Job 38:11 where Yahweh says to the seas: "Thus far shall you come, and no farther, and here shall your proud waves be stopped." Once again we are reminded that the ancient Hebrews did not believe Yahweh had destroyed the chaotic sea, or made it disappear, but had performed what, to them, seemed a greater feat: forcing chaos to operate within strict limits. This concept fits well within the Wisdom tradition where order and structure were a major theme. As these passages demonstrate Yahweh's ability to control chaos was considered an important part of his divine wisdom, which is extolled in these passages: "God's masterful handling of the waters displays his wisdom in a special way. Wisdom is after all the capacity to *act wisely*, which God has done by mastering the primordial waters and delicately tapping them to make the earth fertile."[76]

CHAPTER SUMMARY AND CONCLUSIONS

The goal of this necessarily brief review has been to demonstrate that Yahweh's identity as the master of the waters of the universe was a very basic concept in Jewish consciousness. From his taming of the sea at creation and his flooding of the earth in the time of Noah, to his manipulation of the Sea of Reeds and his provision of water for the Israelites in the desert, some of the events most basic to Israel's story all hinge on Yahweh's ability to control the waters of the earth. In the ancient Jewish mindset, then, Yahweh's control of the waters became an integral part of who he was—his identity and reputation as the one true God in a world full of gods—were, at least partly, founded on this ability. The breadth of the location of these

---

74. Ibid., 413.
75. Murphy, *Proverbs*, 52.
76. Clifford. *Proverbs*, 55.

references, throughout every section of Hebrew scriptures, is testament to the firm and fundamental place of this concept in the ancient Hebrew mind: Yahweh's nature as God was bound up with his ability to control the waters. Yahweh would not be who he was without this capacity.

God's mastery of the waters of creation is more than just a fantastical image out of an Israelite fairy tale; it is a vital part of the theology and mindset of the Old Testament authors. Much theological development was founded on the idea that Yahweh had created the world and controlled everything in it. The image of Yahweh commanding the ultimate symbol of chaos—the primordial sea—to obey him and follow his direction was one of the most powerful visual illustrations of this most basic theological concept. That this image had significant influence on Hebrew thought and doctrine is evident from the dozens of times it recurs throughout later Hebrew writings, and through its interplay with other symbols, images and ideas. Yahweh's control of the waters—both cosmic and earthly—was a fundamental part of his identity to the ancient Israelite people.

In the next few chapters we shall move towards our goal of demonstrating how the author of the Gospel of John uses water imagery to help integrate the person of Jesus into the identity of God by utilizing a similar technique and connecting Jesus' identity as the Son of God with his control over water.

CHAPTER 3

Setting Up the Motif
Water and Identity in John 1 & 3

INTRODUCTION

Now that we have briefly reviewed the relationship of Yahweh's identity in OT writing, history and thought to his ability to control the waters, we will turn our attention to Jesus' relationship with water in the Gospel of John. We propose that the author of the Gospel uses Jesus' connection to water as a way to integrate the person of Jesus into the divine identity of Yahweh. In the OT Yahweh is distinguished from all other beings by his ability to control the waters of the universe and the earth. Jesus in the Gospel of John is also portrayed as frequently interacting with water, either literal or figurative. It is reasonable, therefore, to ask if Jesus in the Gospel of John also has his deity partially signified by this relationship with water. To answer this question we will spend the next four chapters examining Jesus' connection with water and water imagery in each of the relevant water passages.

We will begin in this chapter with the first water passage of the Gospel, Jesus' baptism by John (1:19–51), as well as a later section which revisits the topic of baptism, expounding on the relative merits of the baptism administered by Jesus to that offered by John (3:22–36). Since both passages deal with the common theme of baptism and, therefore, share somewhat similar metaphoric and historical backgrounds, we will deal with them together in this chapter and discuss the Jewish backgrounds in a unified section.

"THAT HE MIGHT BE REVEALED TO ISRAEL": THE BAPTISM OF JESUS (JOHN 1:19-51)

The first water passage in the Gospel is the account usually referred to as Jesus' baptism, although in reality the text never states that Jesus was baptized. John sees Jesus coming toward him and declares him to be "the Lamb of God who takes away the sin of the world" (v. 29) and "he of whom I said, 'After me comes a man who ranks ahead of me because he was before me'" (v. 30). John then goes on to recount a previous revelatory experience in which Jesus' true identity was confirmed by the descent of the Spirit in the form of a dove (vv. 32–33).

We are not told that this revelatory event specifically took place in the context of Jesus' baptismal experience, as it did in the Synoptics.[1] Despite this, however, it is not unreasonable to speak of a connection between Jesus' water baptism and the revelation of his identity. The author here reinterprets what he expects to be a familiar story to most of his audience, and therefore assumes they can supply the context themselves.[2] Furthermore, John's description of the revelatory experience is given within the *narrative context* of John's baptismal ministry, as the verse immediately preceding references the purpose of baptism in John's ministry, and the entire scene is set on the shore of the Jordan where John was baptizing (v. 28). Therefore we may properly say that the revelation of the identity of Jesus appears within the context of water baptism, even if the connection is never explicitly made.

In this section we will see that water, specifically water baptism, plays an important role in the initial revelation of Jesus' identity in the Gospel. We shall begin by looking at the issue of identity in the passage, and then move on to the interplay of water and Jesus' identity.

---

1. Cf. Matt 3:16; Mark 1:9–11 where the dove descends just as Jesus is coming up out of the baptismal waters; cf. Luke 3:21–22 where we are specifically told the Holy Spirit descended *after* Jesus had been baptized, but it is clear that it was still within the context of the baptismal event.

2. Bertrand, *Le baptême*, 17; Ferguson, *Baptism*, 103; Keener, *Gospel*, 42; there has been a long debate about whether the author of John knew or used material from the Synoptics or whether he relied wholly on a separate tradition. For a succinct history of the discussion cf. Beasley-Murray, *John*, xxxv–xxxvii.

Water, Identity and Revelation in John 1:19–34

Questions of identity are paramount in this first water passage in the Gospel of John and, indeed, in all of chapter 1.³ The narrative can be divided neatly into three sections based on the identity being discussed in each: the first (vv. 19–28) focuses on the identity of John the Baptist, and the second (vv. 29–34) on the identity of Jesus, and the third (vv. 35–51) on the identity of Nathanael, as a representative of all the disciples coming to Jesus and of Israel itself. However, the sections, while structurally separated,⁴ are not thematically distinct: the coming "one" who is revealed in the second section (v. 34), is introduced in the first (vv. 26–27). John never discusses his identity or ministry except in relation to the identity and ministry of the coming "one." Likewise, the climax to the story—the revelation of Jesus as the "Son of God; the King of Israel" by Nathanael in v. 49—only comes about as a result of Jesus' prescient identification of Nathanael.

The passage begins immediately dealing with the identity of John the Baptist when priests and Levites from Jerusalem are sent to inquire about who he is (v. 19). It is typical of the author's concern for issues of identity that he does not begin with a description of the appearance and lifestyle of John, as Matthew and Mark both do (Matt 3:4; Mark 1:6). Nor does the Gospel take the time to situate him in his historical context, as Luke does (3:1–2) before launching into the narrative of his ministry. For the Fourth Evangelist John's relative time and place are of little consequence; John and his ministry serve no other purpose in the narrative than the revelation of the Christ (1:31).⁵ The Johannine Baptist is not a full character in his own right and is allowed to have no personality or identity except as they relate to the identity of Jesus. Everything he does and everything he is centers on the coming Christ.

This becomes clear in his responses to the authorities sent to question him. The first sentence out of John's mouth in the entire Gospel is focused on describing himself in relationship to the coming Messiah. When the authorities ask, "Who are you?" (1:19) John responds not with who he *is*, but rather with who he is *not*: "I am not the Messiah" (1:20). As Westcott points

---

3. Croatto suggests nearly thirty references to issues of identity in John 1—Croatto, "La epifania," 33.

4. The two narrative sections take place on two separate days (cf. v. 29 which begins with τῇ ἐπαύριον).

5. Brown says: "the evangelist is not interested in John the Baptist as a baptizer or as a prophet, but only in his being a herald of Jesus . . ." (*Gospel*, 1.45); Jones, *Symbol*, 41.

out "the answer is addressed rather to the spirit than to the form of the question,"[6] for John clearly knew the authorities were not enquiring about his name; they were concerned with whether he was claiming to be the coming Messiah, or perhaps one of the Messiah's traditional forerunners, Elijah[7] or the prophet like Moses[8] (1:21). John denies all of these identities and instead quotes the words of Isa 40:3 (1:23).[9]

But the authorities are not satisfied with this answer; in particular, they wonder why John is engaging in an eschatological activity like baptism if he is not one of the expected eschatological forerunners (1:25).[10] John describes the significance of his baptismal ministry as secondary to the ministry of "the one coming after [him]" (1:27), the one who stands among them whom they do not know (1:26). This is the first direct mention of this "one" coming after John and, it is perhaps significant that the very first thing we learn about this person is that he is "not known" to the authorities and, by extension perhaps, to the watching crowds. John gives little actual information about this mysterious "one," for he himself does not yet know him (cf. vv. 31, 33), but declares this "one" is so great that John is not worthy to even do the work of a slave on his behalf (v. 27).

The Synoptic accounts of John the Baptist's words all refer to the "one who is coming after me who is mightier than I." John, instead, replaces this phrase with "the one among you whom you do not know" (v. 26), indicating a concern for the identity of this coming "one" that is more pronounced than in the Synoptic accounts. Brown sees in these verses a possible reference to the popular contemporary theory of the "Hidden Messiah": the idea that the Messiah would be concealed among humanity and unknown until the proper time for his revelation.[11] This differs from the "normal" form of

---

6. Westcott, *Gospel*, 18.

7. Cf. Mal 4:5 (Heb 3:23).

8. Cf. Deut. 18:15.

9. It is perhaps telling that the issue of John's identity is never questioned in Matthew or Mark. In both Matthew 3:3 and Mark 1:2–3 the words of Isaiah 40 are cited by the narrator in reference to John, not in response to any query. The question of identity does come into play in the Lucan passage, when we are told that the people listening to John preach were "filled with expectation" and "questioning in the hearts" whether John might be the Messiah (3:15). However, this is still a far cry from the point-blank questioning the Baptist gets from the Jewish authorities in John chapter 1. Luke focuses on John's apocalyptic (3:7–9, 17) and ethical (3:10–14) message much more than on the issue of his identity.

10. Brown, *Gospel*, 1:51.

11. Brown, *Gospel*, 1:52–53. This belief may also lie behind the "Messianic secret"

expectation in which the Messiah would be known because he would make his appearance at Bethlehem (John 4:42; Matt 2:5). Instead, the Gospel of John demonstrates what Brown calls "an apocalyptic strain" of messianic expectation, where the Messiah's presence on earth would be hidden until suddenly he would be shown to his people when Elijah returned to earth and anointed him. He believes John 1:26, 31, and 33 reflect this "apocalyptic" strain of Messianic understanding.[12]

The revelation of this unknown "one" will not come until later, but is foreshadowed in the answer John gives to his inquisitors in 1:20. The ἐγώ here is emphatic[13]: "*I* am not the Messiah," implying that while John is not the Messiah, he knows of one who is, or at least has confidence that such a one is nigh. Indeed, the emphatic ἐγώ is used repeatedly in this passage (vv. 23, 26, 27, 30, 31, 33, 34) by John the Baptist, to highlight the contrast between himself, who is *not* the Messiah, who is *not* first in precedence or eminence, who does *not* baptize with the Holy Spirit, etc., and the coming "one" who will be and do all of these things.[14] In this way the Messiah plays a critical role in 1:19–28 even though he is not identified and introduced by the Baptist until v. 29; he is the silent figure that lies just behind all of the Baptist's remarks. Westcott sums it up nicely saying, "The relation of the Baptist to Christ is suggested everywhere" in this passage.[15]

The section beginning in v. 29 focuses more on the identity of Jesus as this coming "one," but, as might be expected from the previous passage, the issue of John's identity does not disappear just yet as it is only with the revelation of the identity of Jesus that John's true identity can be fully appreciated. In v. 29 we get the first direct identification of Jesus by John. In this case he declares Jesus to be "the Lamb of God who takes away the sin of the world!"[16] and then immediately clarifies that this is the man of

---

idea in Mark. For a detailed discussion of earlier Jewish works which reflect this idea cf. Mowinckel, *Cometh*, 304–8. There may also be an hint of this idea in John 4:27; it also will be seen in the narrative of chapter 7.

12. This apocalyptic messianic understanding is succinctly expressed in Justin's *Dialogue with Trypho*, 8.4 and 49.1.

13. So Barrett, *Gospel*, 143; also Beasley-Murray, *John*, 23; John's declaration "I am not" deliberately contrasts to Jesus' later "I Am" statements and, therefore, continues the theme of John's inferiority to Jesus in this passage.

14. Barrett, *Gospel*, 144; Keener, *Gospel*, 1.434; Westcott, *Gospel*, 18; *contra* Brown, *Gospel*, 1.43.

15. Westcott, *Gospel*, 18.

16. For discussion of the background and meaning of this title cf. Brown, *Gospel*,

whom he spoke earlier in v. 27 who was coming after him. He finishes his proclamation with the rather curious statement: "I myself did not know him; but I came baptizing with water for this reason, that he might be revealed to Israel" (v. 31). This is followed by John's "testimony" about the Spirit having descended on Jesus in a previous revelatory experience which verified Jesus' identity as "the one," because John had been told "He on whom you see the Spirit descend and remain is the one who baptizes with the Holy Spirit" (v. 33).[17] The passage concludes with John's testimony verifying the event and proclaiming that Jesus is the Son of God (v. 34).[18]

John's role in the narrative is now nearly complete. He again points out Jesus as "the Lamb of God" in v. 35, at which two of John's disciples immediately begin following Jesus (v. 37) and, after spending some time with him (v. 39), go out and begin gathering others to follow Jesus (vv. 41–45). The two accounts of disciples bringing their relatives and friends to Jesus (vv. 40–42 and vv. 43–48) are parallel in structure. In both sections we are given information about the disciple who recruits (Andrew, v. 40; Philip, v. 44), then, in both cases the recruiting disciple finds (εὑρίσκει both times) his recruitee (Simon Peter, v. 41; Nathanael, v. 45) and testifies to him about Jesus (vv. 41, 45). Andrew refers to Jesus as "the Messiah" (v. 41) while Philip calls him "him about whom Moses in the law and also the prophets wrote" (v. 45). In both cases when the recruitee meets Jesus he "reveals" something about the character of the new disciple. In v. 42 Jesus reveals Peter's true nature by changing his name from Simon to Cephas or Peter. In v. 47 Jesus calls Nathanael, whom he has not even met yet, "an Israelite in whom there is no deceit."

In this last scenario in particular we see, once again, the connection of identity to the revelation of the Christ. In this case, there is a dual

---

1.58–63; Keener, *Gospel*, 1:452–56.

17. For a discussion of the differences between narrative time and story time ("anachronies") in this passage, cf. Culpepper, *Anatomy*, 54–57.

18. The alternative reading "the Chosen One of God" is also a possibility here. Both readings are well-attested and good arguments can be made for either. For this reason scholars have long been divided over which phrase is original. In light of the connection between Spirit baptism and the revelation of Jesus as the Son of God that we will discuss below, we choose to read "Son of God" here, while not denying that the alternate reading is also plausible. For discussion of the textual evidence cf. Metzger, *Textual*, 200. For commentators supporting the "Son of God" reading cf. Bultmann, *Gospel*, 92–93; Dodd, *Interpretation*, 228; Keener, *Commentary*, 1.463–65. For those preferring "the Chosen One of God" cf. Barrett, *Gospel*, 149; Brown, *Gospel*, 1.47; Carson, *Gospel*, 152; and Schnackenburg, *Gospel*, 1:305–6.

revelation. Jesus reveals the nature of Nathanael, who, as a direct result (cf. v. 48), reveals the true identity of Jesus: "You are the Son of God! You are the King of Israel!" (v. 49).[19] Just as the first half of this passage (vv. 19–34) built up to the climactic reveal of Jesus as "the Son of God" (v. 34), this second passage also concludes with the revelation of Jesus' identity as "the Son of God" (v. 49). The difference is that while John the Baptist himself testified to Jesus as the Son of God in the first instance, in this second occurrence it is a disciple, more significantly, a person associated directly with the nation of Israel, who proclaims Jesus' true nature. This is the pinnacle of the entire chapter 1 narrative. John the Baptist has fulfilled his purpose by pointing out the Messiah and Son of God to his future disciples; it is now time for the disciples to discover Jesus' true identity for themselves and proclaim it to the world. The fact that the disciple who does this is referred to by Jesus as "an Israelite in whom there is no deceit" (v. 47), and is also compared to Jacob—"Israel" himself—in 1:51, is a hopeful anticipation of the recognition of Jesus' identity as the Son of God by all of Israel and the fulfillment of the Baptist's commission to reveal him to Israel.

The Baptist's statement in v. 31 is not the only evidence of a relationship between water baptism and the revelation of Jesus Christ in this passage. The connection is also apparent in the structure of John's proclamations. Every time John mentions his baptism with water it is always immediately preceded or followed by a statement about the mystery of Jesus' identity. In 1:26 he says, "I baptize with water. Among you stands one whom you do not know . . ."; then later in 1:31, "I myself did not know him; but I came baptizing with water for this reason, that he might be revealed to Israel." Finally, in 1:33 John states, "I myself did not know him, but the one who sent me to baptize with water said to me . . ."

Taken together the first two instances, 1:26 and 31, are structured chiastically:

    A   I *baptize with water*

           B   Among you stands one whom you *do not know*

           B'   I myself *did not know* him

    A'   I came *baptizing with water* for this reason

---

19. In the Fourth Gospel the titles "the Son of God" and "the Messiah" (or "King of Israel") are equivalent as is seen by their occasional pairing (1:49; 11:27). This is consistent with contemporaneous messianic thought that identified the Messiah as God's son (based in part on 2 Sam 7:14. Cf. 4 Ezra 7:28–29; 13:32, 37, 52; 14:9; 4QFlor 1:10–12.)

Cullmann rightly recognizes that the connection here is not between "I baptize with water" and "He will baptize with the Holy Spirit," as is found in the Synoptics, but rather between water baptism ("I baptize with water") and the revelation of identity ("Among you stands one whom you do not know").[20] This structural formation underscores the fact that John's water baptism is inexorably linked to revelation of the identity of the unknown coming "one." Most scholars and commentators on this passage recognize this relationship and that the Fourth Evangelist is using the character of John the Baptist and his ministry in a very different way from the Synoptics: as a witness to the person of Jesus and nothing more. However, few have questioned why the act involved in this revelation, water baptism, is significant. What is it about baptism with water that makes it the appropriate vehicle for the revelation of Jesus? The significant element, it would seem, is *water*. John pointedly and repeatedly describes his as a baptism with water (vv. 26, 31, 33) to distinguish it from the spirit-baptism that the Messiah will administer (vv. 33); additionally, the location of John's ministry is specifically pointed out as near the Jordan River (v. 28). So it would seem that the water is important in some way. But how?

A natural answer to this might be that water baptism is used as some sort of rite of purification, cleansing or initiation; such rituals were certainly common enough in the first century.[21] Jewish practice included lustrations for purification and removal of ritual taboos, as well as proselyte baptism.[22] The cult of Enki in Babylon, the Osiris myth in Egypt, Mandaean rituals, and the Orphic tablets, among others, all attribute purifying properties to water and some associate baptism with immortality.[23] Others considered water baptism a necessary preparation for sacred tasks, prayer, worship, marriage, and death.[24] While these images may surface in the mind of the reader, John limits the purpose of his baptism exclusively to enabling him to reveal Jesus to Israel. In fact, the verb βαπίζω never has a direct object in these verses. Neither the narrator nor John makes reference to the baptism of John as a precursor of Christian baptism, to a declaration of baptism for repentance, or to any other impact on those baptized.

20. Cullmann, *Worship*, 60ff.

21. Beasley-Murray, *Baptism*; Ferguson, *Baptism*; Flemington, *Baptism*; Schnackenburg, *Baptism*; Wagner, *Pauline Baptism*.

22. Lindars, *Gospel*, 106; Schnackenburg, *Gospel*, 1.293.

23. Meslin, "Baptism," 59–63.

24. Drijvers, "Ablutions," 9–13.

While such silence does not refute or eliminate any of those possibilities, it does give them a secondary status at best. In addition we have already seen that the author goes out of his way to separate water baptism from its normal connection with cleansing or purification, which is evident in the Synoptic accounts. John never implies that his water baptism is efficacious in any way for those who experience it.[25] Indeed, we are never told that anyone (including Jesus) is actually baptized in this passage. In the Synoptics we are told that crowds of people came to John to be baptized (Matt 3:5–6; Mark 1:5; Luke 3:7, 10, 15, 21), but here there are no other characters around while John is baptizing, other than the Jewish authorities who are sent to question him. While John's baptismal ministry implies that there must have been people coming to him to be baptized, in the Johannine account these crowds fade into the narrative background, underscoring the fact that for the Fourth Evangelist any other effect of John's baptism is secondary to the primary goal of revealing the Christ.

"THE ONE WHO COMES FROM HEAVEN IS ABOVE ALL": JOHN'S BAPTISM (JOHN 3:22–36)

Water, Identity and Revelation in John 3:22–36

At this point of the Gospel the author reintroduces the character of John the Baptist. In direct contrast to the Synoptic witness, 3:22–23 portrays the ministries of John the Baptist and Jesus overlapping, at least for a short time. In the Synoptics John appears to be imprisoned—and, at some unspecified point, executed—very early in Jesus' ministry, which would have made this overlap impossible. The Gospel of John does not recount the narrative of John's arrest or death; its only mention is in an aside in 3:24 which appears to have been placed there precisely so that those familiar with the Synoptic timeline of events will not be confused.[26]

This disconnect has given rise to the theory that the narrative at 3:22–36 has been "displaced" from its original historical context around the time of Jesus' baptism by John, recounted in 1:19–51, and inserted in a later point in Jesus' ministry, recorded at the end of chapter three.[27] This

---

25. Hodges, "Water and Spirit."
26. Keener, 1.577.
27. Some scholars see only vv. 31–36 as being out of place including Schnackenburg 1.380–96.

movement both allows for Jesus and John to have concurrent ministries for a time, and also necessitates the parenthetical comment about John having not yet been put in prison in 3:24. Proponents of displacement theories point to several pieces of evidence that support this conclusion.[28] However, it is possible that these consonances may be explained without resorting to a theory of historical displacement. We will not take up this argument here, but make note of it because it is testament to the strong connection that is evident between these two passages and justifies treating them in juxtaposition to each other.

John 3:22–23 tell us that Jesus and John the Baptist went out to the Judean countryside, each with his disciples, and baptized. They apparently were located in the same general area, but carrying out separate baptismal ministries. A dispute about baptism broke out between John's disciples and another Jew (or group of Jews).[29] The nature of the disagreement is not entirely clear, but it appears that the crux of this debate, at least as it is framed by John, came down to the question of who was superior, John the Baptist or Jesus. People would naturally prefer the baptism of the one who was greater. While from an earthly point of view John came first—which in ANE modes of thought would indicate his supremacy—John himself upturns this traditional thinking when he admits that the one coming after him is actually greater than himself because he came "before" him (1:30), not in an earthly temporal sense, but in a spiritual and cosmic one.

One of the specific marks of this superior one is his ability to impart the Spirit through his baptism (1:33), whereas John's baptism only serves to help reveal him. As we shall argue in connection with chapter 4:4–42 and 9:1–41, it is the identity of this coming one, that is, his role as the one sent by the Father, that gives his water baptism, which on the surface appears no different than John's, its significance and efficacy. So, in a sense, it is the *identity* of the giver that makes Jesus' baptism special and, by extension, its water; the water by itself has no particular potency.

In response to his disciples' concern that more people were flocking to Jesus' baptism than that of John (v. 26), John indicates that things are happening as they should. Jesus should be winning over more and more of the people because John himself is merely the "lesser" or "inferior" who is

---

28. For a summary see Keener, *Gospel*, 1.575ff.

29. Depending on which textual reading you accept. We prefer the singular here as the *lectio difficilior*, although we do not support those who interpret this "Jew" as a circumlocution for Jesus himself.

being supplanted by the "better" or "superior" (a theme already introduced in the Wedding at Cana passage in chapter 2—see discussion below) in the coming of Jesus Christ. John's use of wedding imagery here only strengthens the theory that he (or the author) is thinking about the miracle at Cana when he makes this statement. Just as at that wedding where Jesus turned water into wine, the friend of the bridegroom (the "best man" in Western parlance) is considered inferior in importance to the bridegroom himself, so is John "lesser" than Jesus. The day of the prophets is over and the era of Yahweh's direct salvation has begun.

John then proceeds to expound on this relationship of water baptism to the identity of the giver: "The one who comes from above is above all; the one who is of the earth belongs to the earth and speaks about earthly things. The one who comes from heaven is above all" (3:31). John, as "the one who is of the earth" is only able to pass on what he has been given by God. The gift of the Holy Spirit is the unique possession of "the one who comes from heaven," for "he gives the Spirit without measure" (v. 34). The "he" in this last statement could be understood as either "God" or "Jesus," but we prefer to read it as referring to God.

Firstly, God is mentioned in the phrase immediately preceding and therefore would seem to be the proper antecedent of the pronoun. Secondly, throughout the Gospel Jesus is portrayed as receiving everything he has from the Father, and appealing to the Father. Jesus says that he does nothing on his own but only speaks what his Father taught him (8:28). Therefore, it is most likely that he (and John) would both view God as the ultimate giver of the Spirit, even if it was mediated through Jesus' baptism.[30] The fact that the gift which can only come from the Father is now distributed by Jesus, then, is a profound statement of his identity.

The connection between the Spirit and water has already been a major point in the discussion Jesus has with Nicodemus earlier in chapter 3 (vv. 1–21). In 3:5 Jesus tells Nicodemus: "no one can enter the kingdom of God without being born of water and Spirit." Much has been written through the centuries on the meaning of this somewhat cryptic phrase. We do not have room to review them all here.[31] For our purposes the important un-

---

30. This understanding of the relationship between God, Jesus, the Spirit, and the water that Jesus provides will become very important in our interpretation of John 7:37–39, below.

31. A review of the major positions on the relationship of water and spirit here may be found in Beasley-Murray, *John*, 48–49; Brown, *Gospel*, 1.137–44; Keener, *Gospel*, 1.546–52; also Beasley-Murray, "Baptism"; Fowler, "Born," 159; Hodges, "Water and

derstanding is that water alone is not enough for spiritual cleansing (be that in baptism or any other ritual lustration); the spirit must be in it. And that spirit can come only through God or, by Johannine extension, Jesus. Therefore, John's baptism, while once useful, is no longer efficacious. And since the self-admitted purpose of his baptism—the revelation of this "one from above" (cf. 1:31)—has been completed, both John's baptism and, by extension, John himself, no longer have relevance.

Jones makes much of the statement in 3:23 which relates that John was baptizing at Aenon near Salim "because there was plenty of water." Since John is portrayed as ministering at a location where water was plentiful, while the place of Jesus' baptizing is not disclosed, Jones takes this to mean that Jesus could naturally provide from himself that which John had to rely on from nature. This is yet another indication that John's baptism and ministry were becoming obsolete. Jones reads the "water" here metaphorically while the text seems to be speaking literally (i.e., one would not attempt public baptisms at a place where water wasn't available). While this is perhaps pushing too far to wring meaning out of a water image, Jones does strike the right note of understanding when he concludes from this passage: "Apart from Jesus water loses value and lacks meaning."[32]

And this is precisely the point. John is still capable of performing a baptism by water; indeed, he has abundant water with which to do so. Yet people are no longer flocking to him because the water in itself is not the point. The water must be administered along with the spirit (3:5), and only Jesus can dispense that through his baptism. As Koester says, "What made Jesus unique was not that he and his followers used water for a rite of washing but that God's Spirit worked through him."[33] This ability to impart the spirit with his baptism was, as we've seen, the result of his special relationship with the Father—his identity as the Son of God.

Therefore, in this passage we see the author of the Gospel weaving together the themes of water (baptism) and identity in such a way that Jesus is revealed as "the one who comes from above" who has a singular relationship with the Father. The water itself is not necessarily special; John baptizing with similar water does not have the same effect. The baptism, and

---

Spirit," 206–20; McCabe, "Born of Water," 85–107; Pamment, "John 3:5," 190; Sandnes, "Whence and Whither," 153–73; Söding, "Wiedergeburt," 168–219; Spriggs, "Meaning," 149–50; Witherington, "Waters of Birth," 155–60.

32. Jones, *Symbol*, 85.

33. Koester, *Symbolism*, 184–5.

Setting Up the Motif

the water by extension, receives its potency from the nature of the person administering it. Therefore, the special relationship of Jesus and the Father is both the basis of and reflected by Jesus' baptismal ministry.

Water and Revelation of Identity in Previous Jewish Literature

In the baptism passage in 1:19–51 we demonstrated that an association exists not between water and purification or cleansing, as is found in the Synoptics, but between water and the revelation of identity. This seems to be the Fourth Evangelist's unique take on the purpose of John's baptism. Likewise in 3:22–36 we have seen that the quality of Jesus' water baptism marks him as having a unique relationship to the Father. How and why exactly the ideas of water baptism and revelation of identity came to be related is unclear; but there is precedent for their connection in Jewish literature. We will here review some of the more prominent examples as a step toward understanding how water and revelation of identity are related in Jewish thought.

A very strong correlation between water and "illumination" of identity can be detected in several places in non-canonical Jewish writings. For example, SibOr 1.336–341:

> But when a certain voice will come through the desert land
> bringing tidings to mortals, and will cry out to all
> to make the paths straight and cast away
> evils from the heart, and that every human person
> **be illumined by waters, so that, being born from above**
> they may no longer in any respect at all transgress justice (emphasis added)

This passage has clear connections to Jesus' baptism narrative in the Fourth Gospel. As this text is roughly contemporaneous with the writing of the Gospel there is no way to know the exact relationship of the two. It is possible that the ideas and language of the Sibylline Oracles passage are dependent on John, or the two may have simply arisen from the same tradition around the same time.[34] Whatever its origin, the similarity to the lan-

---

34. Although the Sibylline Oracles are difficult to date accurately the Christian sections of Books 1 & 2 were probably completed no later than 150 CE, and possibly quite a bit earlier. Books 4 & 5 also probably date to the late first-century/early-second century CE (although Book 4 contains some material which likely dates back to the 3rd cent. BCE). Books 6, 7, and 8 are impossible to date more accurately than 300 CE, when they

guage and thought of the Gospel here is quite striking. The description of John the Baptist using the words of Isaiah 40:3 ("a certain voice through the desert land," "cry[ing] out to all to make the paths straight") is clearly related to both the Johannine and Synoptic versions of Jesus' baptism.[35] However, the latter part of the passage contains some distinctively Johannine ideas, especially the γεννηθέντες ἄνωθεν ("being born from above" or "again"), which is also found in John 3:3 where the double-meaning creates confusion for Nicodemus.

Likewise, it is quite possible that the phrase "illumined by waters" (καὶ ὕδασι φωτίζεσθαι) has a parallel to Jesus' being "revealed" by water in John 1. The meanings of the Greek words for "illumine" (φωτίζω) and "reveal" (φανερόω) overlap and both have a dual-level of significance. They can each be understood within a sensory context, meaning "to cause to become visible," in the sense of making a person or thing physically visible which is invisible. Or, they can be used with the cognitive sense "to cause to become known," wherein knowledge or understanding of some sort is made available where it had previously been unavailable. φωτίζω by its nature is a more concrete image which implies the literal shining of light onto something hidden in the darkness or, in a more metaphorical sense, the making understood of something not previously comprehended. Nevertheless, the words have very similar meanings, and may at times be interchangeable.

Indeed, these concepts do stand in parallel to one another in chapter 1 of John. In vv. 7–9 of the prologue John the Baptist is said to have come as a "witness" to the "light" that has come into the world in the form of Jesus "so that all might believe through him" (NRSV). The Baptist describes the purpose of his ministry as the revelation of the one who was coming after him who ranked ahead of him (v. 30). It seems clear that for the author of the Gospel these two functions, witnessing/testifying and revealing were synonymous.

What exactly is revealed to us about the nature of Jesus in the Sibylline Oracles passage is not clear, but the writer seems to find the connection between "illumination" and the waters of baptism quite natural. Indeed,

---

were quoted by Lactantius, but it is not implausible that they pre-date him by a century or more. Only Book 3, which is Jewish and probably originated during the post-Maccabean or early Roman era (163–45 BCE), can lay serious claim to definitely pre-dating the Gospel of John. For detailed discussion of dating issues see the introduction to each book in Charlesworth, *Pseudepigrapha*.

35. Matt 3:1–3; Mark 1:2–3; Luke 3:4.

the association of water in general and "illumination" appears in two other Sibylline passages as well:

> All will come to the tribunal of God the king.
> A *river of fire and brimstone will flow from heaven.*
> There will then be a sign for all men, a most clear seal:
> the wood among the faithful, the desired horn,
> the life of pious men, but the scandal of the world,
> *illuminating the elect with waters in twelve streams.* (SibOr 8.242–247, emphasis added)

> Mindful therefore of this resolution, he will come to creation
> bearing a corresponding copy to the holy virgin,
> *illuminating by water,* at the same time through the hands of elders
> (SibOr 8.269–271, emphasis added)

The Greek words here for "illuminating by water" are the same as in SibOr 1.336–341. While these passages from Book 8 are undoubtedly later than the passage in Book 1,[36] and may in some way be dependent upon it, they still serve to show the ongoing importance and use of the metaphorical connection between water and "illumination" in one early Christian tradition.

Is there any evidence of this connection between "revelation" or "illumination" and water baptism in the Jewish or Christian tradition prior to John? As we saw in chapter 2 water plays a large role in the self-revelation of God in the history and writings of the Jewish people. But there are also hints of events in which the true character of people is determined on the basis of a water experience. Referring to the Exodus event the Psalmist in 66:8–12 says that the Israelite people were "tried as silver is tried" and passed through "fire and through water," meaning the wilderness and Reed Sea experience.[37] The use of the terms "fire and water" here to describe the Israelites' trial foreshadows a combination of water and fire used to distinguish the righteous from the unrighteous which flourishes in intertestamental literature.[38]

---

36. See note 34 above.

37. Dahood, *Psalms*, 122–23; Kraus, *Psalms* 60–150, 37–38

38. Ps. 81:7 refers to the people of Israel being "tested" at Meribah where Yahweh produced water from the rock, another interesting connection between water and the revelation of character as the result of testing.

For example, 1 Enoch 22:9–10 describes a "spring of water with light upon it"[39] which is used to distinguish sinners from the righteous. Because this is clearly a metaphor intended to describe an otherworldly phenomenon, we cannot determine precisely how the light and water are related, but the connection is clear even in the Greek manuscripts, one of which refers to "this bright spring of water."[40] It is an easy metaphorical step from light and water to heat and water, as seen later in 1 Enoch 67:11–13 where the visionary describes the use of fountains of hot water as the tool of punishment for evil angels.

Vision of Ezra 23–33 puts a slightly different spin on the metaphor by describing a large cauldron of boiling sulphur and bitumen "roiling just like the waves of the sea." Into this concoction the "just" enter and pass over the fiery waves without harm "just like those who walk over dew or cold water." But the "sinners" come and "the angels of hell" submerge them in "the fiery stream." Here it is clear that the burning water serves two purposes: first to distinguish the "just" from the "unjust" and, secondly, as the actual vehicle of punishment for the unjust, who are submerged into its fiery depths while the just escape unharmed.

The combination of water and heat to illuminate or reveal a person's character and then mete out punishment based on that determination reaches its fullest metaphorical form in the image of the river of fire, which is widespread in both Jewish and Christian apocalyptic visions.[41] In Second Temple visionary literature the river of fire is frequently found as a feature of the heavenly realms.[42] Rivers of water and/or rivers of fire are commonly used as a tool of punishment or destruction in eschatological visions of the final annihilation of the world.[43] But much more frequent are descriptions of a sort of ordeal or test of righteousness that takes place in the river of fire.

In Testament of Isaac 5:21–24 we clearly see the purpose of the river of fire to be the discernment of character. Here the visionary sees many weeping souls immersed in the river of fire. These are the ones who have been declared wicked for the narrator tells us that "that river had wisdom

---

39. Reference to a "fountain of light" is also found in 2Bar 54:13; all translations of the pseudepigrapha are taken from Charlesworth. See note 34 for bibliographic information.

40. Cf. Charlesworth, *Pseudepigrapha*, 1:25n22t.

41. Cf. Rev. 20:14–15 where the image takes the form of a "lake of fire."

42. Cf. 1En 14:19; 17:5; 71:2,6; 2En 10:2; 3En 18:19, 33:4, 37:1–2; 42:7; 47:1–2; TIsaac 5:21–26.

43. SibOr 2:196–205, 3:461–62, 7:118–122; LAE 49:3, 50:2

in its fire: It would not harm the righteous, but only the sinners by burning them." The language implies that their characters were not known prior to their entering the river—it appears to be the river of fire itself that evaluates their spiritual states.

Another example is found in Sibylline Oracles 2.283-88; 296-97. Here we have a description of "sorcerers and sorceresses" who have evoked the "anger of the heavenly imperishable God" and are punished "by whips of flame" on a pillar "around which an undying fiery river flows in a circle." After enduring this punishment they will be "press[ed] hard all around" by a "fiery wheel from the great river." While this passage does not specifically indicate that the ordeal itself was what determined each person's righteousness or lack thereof, it is implied in the following section: "But as for the others, as many as were concerned with justice and noble deeds, and piety and most righteous thoughts, angels will lift them through the blazing river and bring them to light and to life without care" (2.313-16).

This picture is somewhat different from the Testament of Isaac passage. In this case the distinction between the righteous and the wicked has been made before the ordeal begins. However, the righteous are allowed to pass through the "blazing fire" without harm and are taken away to their eternal reward, which suggests that the river may have played a role in the testing process. This underlying concept is more succinctly presented in Sibylline Oracles 2.252-255: "And then all will pass through the blazing river and the unquenchable flame. All the righteous will be saved, but the impious will then be destroyed for all ages."

From these few examples we can see that the connection between a water experience (often mixed with fire) and the elucidation and evaluation of one's true character or nature was well-established in Jewish thought by the writing of the Gospel of John. As such it is a tradition that could stand in the background of the Fourth Gospel, which was written by a person or group well-steeped in Jewish literature and tradition.

One might argue that John's narrative of Jesus' baptism contains no allusion to fire, which would seem necessary for the "river of fire" passages to serve as a possible background. While it is possible that "river" here is only intended to describe the form or movement of the fire (i.e., it is a type of fire that moves in some way similar to the way water moves in a river—perhaps envisioning something like hot lava?), it is also possible, perhaps even likely, that some type of juxtaposition of actual water and fire is intended in the image. Either way, the use of the word "river" as a descriptor of the fire's form at the very least calls up the association of water with the fire; therefore, it is not inappropriate to see these "river of fire" passages as part of a larger and ongoing association throughout Jewish writings between water and fire.[44]

Secondly, it should be noted that fire is associated with Jesus' baptism in some of the parallel traditions. The Synoptics maintain a connection between fire and the baptism that Jesus will administer: In both Matthew and Luke John the Baptist describes Jesus as the one who will "baptize you with [or in] the Holy Spirit and fire" (Matt 3:11; Lk 3:16). Note here that the preposition traditionally translated "with" can also be "in" which is more consonant with the action of believers being plunged "into" water during baptism, and also with the image of sinners being submerged into the a fiery river as the test of their righteousness.

Likewise, there is evidence of the connection between baptism and fire in some early Christian interpretations like this one in Sibylline Oracles 6:

> I speak from my heart of the great famous son of the Immortal,
> to whom the Most High, his begetter, gave a throne to possess
> before he was born, since he was raised up the second time
> according to the flesh, *when he had washed in the streams of the river Jordan, which moves with gleaming foot, sweeping the waves.*
> *He will escape the fire and be the first to see delightful God*
> coming in the spirit on the white wings of a dove.
> A pure flower will bloom, fountains will burst forth" (SibOr 6.1–8, emphasis added)

Here Jesus is described as "escap[ing] the fire" as a result of his baptism in the river. What exactly is meant here is unclear, but it is similar in concept to SibOr 2:252–255 where the righteous are spared from the punishment of the river of fire and taken away "to light and life without care." This could be a reference to the revelation of Jesus' righteousness as a result of his baptism.

Finally, the water/fire/revelation connection is seen in yet another passage from the Sibylline Oracles:

> You shall pour a libation of *water on pure fire*, crying out as follows:

---

44. For water-fire connections not related to the river of fire imagery cf. Ex 12:9; 32:20; Lev 1:9, 13; 8:21; Num 31:22; 1 Kgs 18:38; Ps 66:12; Prov 30:16; Is 43:2; Joel 1:20; 4Ezra 7:6–8; 8:8; SibOr 7:118–122; 1 En 17:4; 2En 29:1–2 [J]; LAE 49:3 [V]; 50:2; ApAbr 17:1.

> 'As the father begot you, the Word, so I have dispatched a bird,
> a word which is swift reporter of words, sprinkling
> with holy waters your baptism, through which you were *revealed out of fire*. (SibOr 7.81–84, emphasis added)

The emphasis on "the word" in this passage suggests dependence on the Gospel of John or at least familiarity with the tradition behind the Gospel, as does the idea of being "revealed" (φανερόω—the word nearly uniformly used in John for "revealed") in some way through the waters of baptism and fire. This passage connects these concepts more closely than any of the others we have examined and indicates that at least one Christian tradition after the Gospel of John found significance in the connection, whatever its origin, between Jesus' water baptism, revelation of identity and fire.

It is not surprising that the author of the Fourth Gospel would pick up on these connections when it came to the baptism of Jesus. The main concern of the Evangelist was the presenting of Jesus as the Christ, the son of God (cf. 20:31). As such, the "revelation" of his identity unfolds gradually throughout the book. This theme is introduced and established in the very first narrative of the Gospel when Jesus experiences a "testing" through his baptism so that his nature as the Son of God can be revealed to all. His identity is affirmed and attested by the descent of the Spirit (v. 33) and by the witness of John the Baptist himself (v. 34).

Water and Spirit in Previous Jewish Literature

As we have demonstrated, the "spirit" is closely associated with the idea of baptism in both the narrative of Jesus' baptism (1:32–34) and in John's explanation of why Jesus' baptism is superior to his (3:34). When examining the background of the connection of water (or water baptism) and spirit in earlier Jewish literature, the most immediate passage that comes to mind is found in Isaiah 44:3:

> For I will pour water on the thirsty land,
>   and streams on the dry ground;
> I will pour my spirit upon your descendants,
>   and my blessing on your offspring.

Here water and spirit are directly equated via poetic parallelism. This is the only explicit connection of water and spirit in the OT. However, the use of the water-related verb "pour" to describe the activity of the spirit is more common:

> Then afterwards
> I will pour out my spirit on all flesh;
> your sons and your daughters shall prophesy,
>   your old men shall dream dreams,
>   and your young men shall see visions.
> Even on the male and female slaves,
>   in those days, I will pour out my spirit (Joel 2:28–29)

> I will never again hide my face from them, when I pour out my spirit upon the house of Israel, says the Lord God. (Ez 39:29)

A similar connection is found in Zechariah 12:10. Two different words are rendered "pour" in these verses. The first, שפך (as in Ezek 39:29; Joel 2:28–29; Zech 12:10), is interesting from a Johannine standpoint since it is most often used in conjunction with the pouring out of blood.[45] The co-mingling of blood and water will become significant later on in the Gospel, of course (19:34), and has already been somewhat foreshadowed by the turning of water into wine (a blood-like substance) at the Wedding in Cana (2:1–11), as we will demonstrate below. However, שפך is also used in relation to water in Ex 4:9;[46] 1 Sam 7:6; and Amos 5:8; 9:6. The second word, יצק, is used in the Isa 44 passage and also refers to pouring of water in 1 Kgs 18:33; 2 Kgs 3:11; and Ezek 24:3. So these words, while not exclusively related to the pouring of water[47] are used this way more than once in the Scriptures and therefore can be understood to be related to water imagery. The development of the direct connection of water and spirit in Jewish-Christian thought does not come to full fruition until the Gospel of John, but the seeds of the connection can certainly be found in Old Testament thought.

---

45. A non-comprehensive list of verses which use this word to refer to the pouring out or "shedding" of blood includes: Gen 9:6; 37:22; Exod 29:12; Lev 4:7ff.; 17:4, 13; 1 Sam 25:31; 1 Kgs 18:28; 2 Kgs 24:4; 1 Chr 28:3; Ps 79:10; 106:38; Prov 1:16; 6:17; Isa 59:7; Jer 7:6; 22:3, 17; Lam 4:13; Ezek 16:38; 22:3ff.; Joel 3:19; Zeph 1:17.

46. See discussion of the relationship of this verse to John 2:1–11 below.

47. יצק in particular is often used to refer to the pouring out of oil (cf. Gen 28:18; 35:14; Exod 29:7; Lev 2:1ff; 14:15, 26; Num 5:15; 1 Sam 10:1; 2 Kgs 4:4–5; 9:3,6); שפך especially seems to be used to refer to the "pouring out" of God's wrath, anger or contempt (cf. Job 12:21; Ps 79:6;107:40; Is 42:25; Jer 6:11; 10:25; Lam 2:4; 4:11; Ezek 9:8; 14:19; 20:8, 13ff; 21:31; 22:22, 31; 30:15; 36:18; Hab 5:10; Zeph 3:8).

A link that is perhaps less direct in some ways, but probably very powerful in the Jewish collective consciousness is that of the "spirit" (or "wind" or "breath") of Yahweh that is said to "sweep" (NRSV) or "hover" (NIV) over the surface of the waters of creation (the great תהום discussed in more detail in chapter 2 above). As we noted in our section on Genesis 1 the verb used here is מרחפת which carries the connotation of "hovering like a bird." This vision of Yahweh's spirit as a bird is made concrete in the story of Jesus' baptism (John 1:29; cf. Matt 1:16; Mark 1:10; Lk 3:22) perhaps illustrating how vibrant this equation was in the Jewish mindset of the first century.

In John 1:32–34, the Baptist makes clear that the descent of the spirit, in the form of a dove, was the confirming sign of Jesus' identity as "the one who will baptize with the Holy Spirit." The dove descending and "remaining" (Gk. μένω) on Jesus (vv. 32–33) is evocative of the spirit of Yahweh "hovering" over the waters of creation in Gen 1:2. In that passage, the connotation is one of possession and control. Yahweh, as ultimate master of the waters of the universe, in some sense "owns" the תהום over which he carefully watches from his aeolian perch. It is clear that this visual image was intended by the Gospel's author.

In Matthew, Mark and Luke the spirit is said to descend as a dove upon Jesus' baptism, but in each case the true mark of Jesus' unique identity is offered by the heavenly voice which proclaims Jesus as God's son (Matt 3:17; Mark 1:11; Luke 3:22). In the Johannine account no such voice is heard; the dove which descends is the primary marker of Jesus as "the one who will baptize with the Holy Spirit." It is typical of the Fourth Gospel's concern for "witnessing" that it is John the Baptist who proclaims Jesus' identity as the Son of God as a result of seeing the dove descend in the Johannine account (1:34). However, this verse makes it clear that the proclamation was predicated on seeing the spirit descend. This was the sign of Jesus' identity; John simply testified to the validity of the experience.

It certainly seems that the spirit descending on a man as he rises up out of the waters of baptism would be an appropriate sign to mark the one who will administer the spirit through his own baptism. However, by reusing the imagery from Gen 1:2, the author seems to be hinting at even greater things here—a connection that is not yet made explicit, between this man Jesus and the identity of Yahweh as depicted in the first creation narrative.

CHAPTER SUMMARY AND CONCLUSIONS

In mainstream Christian tradition baptism has come to be associated most often with purification or the forgiving of sins, an idea reflected in the Synoptic tradition. However, as we have seen, water in general, and baptism in specific, was viewed as more than just a vehicle for cleansing in Second Temple Jewish and early Christian thought. The narratives of Jesus being baptized by John and subsequently baptizing others, therefore, establishes several themes and features that will be seen throughout the rest of the Gospel, particularly the prominent use of water imagery as a special component in the revelation of identity. Indeed, we suggest that John's description of his baptism as being for the purposes of revelation may provide the key to understanding the purpose of the water symbol throughout the rest of the Gospel. From this point on the concept of the revelation of Jesus' identity will often be tied up with water imagery or water events.[48]

The narratives of Jesus' baptism revolve around the revelation of Jesus' true identity. In chapter 1, the author lays out clearly the role of water in relation to Jesus's identity: its purpose is revelation. Identity is a prominent theme in the chapter 1 narrative, where the identities of Jesus, John the Baptist and the disciples (represented by Nathanel) are questioned and defined. Water, specifically water baptism in this case, is the agent of this revelation of identity. John the Baptist admits as much in 1:31 when he declares that the purpose of his baptism is the revelation of "the one coming after [him]" (1:27) who will 'baptize with the Holy Spirit" (1:33); a few verses later this epiphany is recounted as having occurred within a baptismal context (1:32–33). This connection would not have been foreign to the Jewish mindset given the prevalence of instances of water serving as revelation and illumination in both intertestamental and canonical literature. Nowhere in this passage is water said to have any other effect on those baptized. Therefore, water is intimately linked to the revelation of Jesus' identity as the Christ from the very first narrative of the Gospel. This, then, is the key to understanding the purpose of water (both literal and figurative) throughout the rest of the Gospel and will serve as our interpretive lens: water is intended to reveal something about Christ.

---

48. Indeed, of the nine uses of the word φανερόω ("to reveal") in the Gospel, 7 of them appear in the context of a water-related passage (1:31; 2:11; 3:21; 7:4; 9:3; 21:1 [2x]; 21:14). 17:6 is the only exception. φανερόω is the word nearly uniformly used to talk about revelation in the Gospel. ἀποκαλύπτω only appears one time in the Gospel (12:38) within the context of an OT quote.

Setting Up the Motif

In the next baptismal passage (3:22–36) we start to see something of the content of that revelation: Jesus is the one who administers the spirit with his baptism, something foreshadowed in the earlier baptismal narrative by the descent of the spirit as a dove (1:33–34). It is this characteristic alone which distinguishes Jesus' baptism from John's. Both are using water from the same area, yet John's baptism is not capable of providing what Jesus' can. Just as John's baptism is inferior to that of Jesus, the one who imparts the spirit, so also is John himself merely a minor player compared to the role that Jesus is playing in the world. As seen in previous Jewish writings, the connection of Yahweh's spirit to water is subtle, but still observable: the spirit was often described in water-related terms, and God's spirit at creation is closely connected to the waters of the primordial תהום. This connection is at least partly behind the tradition of Yahweh's spirit descending as a dove on Jesus as part of the identification of him as God's son.

The baptism passages of John 1 and 3 provide us with a foundation for our further examination of the relationship between Jesus' identity and water in the Gospel. The first narrative made the explicit connection between revelation of identity and the waters of baptism; the second introduced the important connection between Jesus' relationship with the Father and the quality of the water he is able to offer. This latter point in particular will become a major motif in the imagery and storyline of the rest of the Gospel.

CHAPTER 4

Weddings and Waterpots
Water and Identity in John 2 & 4

"HIS DISCIPLES BELIEVED IN HIM": THE WEDDING AT CANA (JOHN 2:1–11)

Water, Identity and Revelation in John 2:1–11

The first Johannine narrative which portrays Jesus as actually interacting with water is found in John 2:1–11, the Wedding at Cana. In this passage Jesus takes water which is set aside for the ritual lustrations of the Jews and turns it into wine, sparing the wedding hosts public humiliation. However, there is clearly more going on here than Jesus simply coming to the aid of some friends. The last verse of this pericope (v. 11) tells us that this first "sign" of Jesus "revealed his glory" and that as a result "his disciples believed in him." The question for our purposes is how was Jesus' "glory" revealed in this event and what role did water play in that revelation?

This passage is notoriously challenging to any interpreter. John 2:1–11 is one of the miracles performed by Jesus in John which is not followed by an interpretive discourse (cf. 4:46–54; 6:16–21 for other examples), making interpretation that much more challenging.[1] As John Ashton rightly, if dramatically, describes it: "Tramping the foothills of biblical scholarship, the exegete is often tempted to stray from the beaten track, and nowhere more

---

1. Little, *Echoes*, 13.

so than in the course of investigating the marriage-feast of Cana, where one can easily find oneself waist-high in bracken. The episode is crammed with teasing little problems."[2] Many of these "teasing little problems" we will have, for the sake of space, to ignore: issues like why Jesus' mother was present at the wedding, what the relationship was between Jesus' family and the family holding the wedding, how Jesus and his disciples came to be invited, the question of Mary's role in the festivities, and how the hosts managed to run out of wine are just a few examples. Instead, we will focus on two particular issues in the early part of the passage which seem to hold the interpretive key to understanding why Jesus performed the miracle, what the miracle was supposed to mean, and what role water played in this "revelation" of Jesus.

These issues are found in Jesus' conversation with his mother at the beginning of the narrative. In v. 3 Mary comes to Jesus and reports the lack of wine for the festivities. This would have been a serious situation in first-century Palestine; freely-flowing wine was considered essential to a wedding celebration as a sign of the joy of the new couple and the generosity of the host. To fail to provide enough wine at such an event would open the host family to social stigma and public ridicule. It was even possible for guests to sue the family of the groom for not fulfilling its obligation of hospitality.[3]

It is here that we face a difficulty of interpretation. Mary never directly asks Jesus to take action in the situation, yet Jesus' response to her makes it seem as if she *has* requested something of him. "What concern is that to you and me?" (v. 4)—more literally rendered "what to you and to me?"—is a Semitism found frequently in the OT to indicate a desire to distance oneself from involvement in an activity or issue.[4] In the use of this phrase "there is always some refusal of an inopportune involvement, and a divergence between the views of the two persons concerned."[5] The reason for this distancing by Jesus is given in his next statement: "My hour has not yet come."

---

2. Ashton, *Understanding*, 266.

3. Derrett, "Water," 84–85, 89; for the best treatment on the subject of wedding customs and law in first-century Palestine see Derrett, *Law*.

4. A nuance which is well-captured in the NIV translation: "Why do you involve me?"

5. Brown, *Gospel*, 1.99.

This interaction is often interpreted as Mary requesting Jesus to take some sort of action, and Jesus refusing such action because it would result in a public manifestation of his identity that he is not yet ready for. However, what happens next in the story seems to contradict this understanding: Jesus promptly fulfills Mary's request and solves the problem she has informed him of. Which leads to the obvious question: why would Jesus refuse such a request just to take said action only a few moments later? This seems to lie at the crux of the issue. If Jesus' response to his mother is not a complete refusal to act (since we see that he does act, and rather swiftly), then this exchange must have another significance.

There have been many attempts to make sense of this conversation over the centuries. A common interpretation is that Jesus was indicating by his response that he would not be dictated to in terms of the timeline of his ministry, or that no one other than his Father would determine when he should reveal himself. A related argument is that he is trying to distance himself from his mother's authority—to make clear to her that he no longer takes commands from her, but only from his heavenly Father. When he does act, it is clearly of his own volition, or that of the Father, and not compelled by any earthly person, no matter how closely related. There could certainly be an element of this understanding running in the background of the exchange. It fits the pattern of other situations in the Gospel where Jesus intentionally rebuffs a request or delays an action in order to show that he works on God's timetable, and for his glory only, and not at the behest of any human (cf. 7:1–13; 11:11–15). However, as we shall see, what is really at stake in this event is not *when* Jesus' "true" identity will be revealed, but rather *how much* of his identity will be revealed and to whom.

One of the best holistic expositions of this passage was presented by Karl T. Cooper in a 1979 article.[6] He also believes that the crux of the passage turns on Mary's conversation with Jesus. However, Cooper contends that Jesus' reference to his "hour" alludes not to "the proper time for me to act" but rather to "the time of my glorification—my death and resurrection." There are several pieces of evidence to support this reading. Firstly, this is the common way the term "my hour" seems to be used by both the Evangelist and Jesus in the Gospel (7:30, 8:20; 12:27; see also 13:1 and 17:1 for similar sentiment). John 2:4 is the first occurrence of the phrase "my hour" in the Gospel and as such, "seems to point to an important time in

---

6. Cooper, "Best Wine," 364–80.

his life but its meaning remains mysterious for the reader."[7] However, the narrator later recounts, in 7:30 and 8:20 that the Jewish officials did not arrest Jesus because "his hour had not yet come." Here "hour" clearly refers to a divinely determined time in which Jesus will be glorified in a very specific way. The implication is that any human efforts to "rush" Jesus' hour—to make it come sooner than ordained—will be futile.

The closest Synoptic parallel to this usage is in Mark 14:35 when Jesus, in Gethsemane, prays that "if possible the hour might pass from him" (cf. also Mark 14:41). Outside of this occurrence, the word ὥρα in the Synoptics is generally used to refer to a specific point in time; Matthew and Luke never use the term to refer to Jesus' coming death and glorification.[8] So this seems to be largely a Johannine conception, perhaps borrowed or adapted from the same or a related source that underlies the Marcan Gethsemane narrative. Reading "my hour" here as meaning "the fulfillment of my purpose on earth" instead of "the hour to reveal myself as a miracle-worker" is more consistent with the usage of this term by the Fourth Evangelist.[9]

Secondly, the events of the story itself seem to mitigate against understanding "my hour" as referring to the revelation of Jesus' identity through the performance of a miracle. The very fact that Jesus immediately provides the needed wine makes it obvious that was not denying Mary's request for action. Some would argue that Jesus is not refusing the request but the spirit in which it is made: Jesus rejects his mother's presumption in trying to control the time and manner of his revelation to the people, or the initiation of his Father's salvific plan which will culminate in his death.[10] However, Cooper takes issue with this understanding, contending that Mary nowhere indicates or hints that she is requesting Jesus to do something. Rather, what Mary has in fact done is to bring to Jesus the simple report, "There is no more wine." We need see here no more than a straightforward desire to share her perplexity and concern with Jesus. If she had any idea that he would do something about it, or could do so, it does not appear in the text. She merely laid the situation before Jesus, as something entirely beyond the scope of human resources. A glance at several parallels among the Johan-

---

7. Mlakuzhyil, *Christocentric*, 163.

8. Although the apocalyptic passage in Matthew 24 does use "hour" several times in reference to the end of time (cf. vv. 36, 42, 44, 50).

9. For a comprehensive discussion of the meaning of Jesus' "hour" in the Fourth Gospel cf. Mlakuzhyil, *Christocentric*, 162–66.

10. Keener, *Gospel*, 1.506.

nine sign narratives will show the consistency of this pattern: Jn 5:5–7; 6:5, 9; 9:2; 11:3, 21, 32. In no case does the miracle come into the context of a prior expectation. It is the nature of the sign to burst the bounds of all probability, and to come as a surprise of divine grace.[11]

The signs Jesus performs reveal his glory to only a small audience often in a private setting (2:11; 11:40; 17:4). However, the events of the coming "hour"—his death and resurrection—will manifest his glory to everyone in a very public way (12:23; 12:27–33; 17:1). So, Jesus' reply to Mary is an attempt to warn her that, although he will perform a "sign" in this situation, she should not expect a full public manifestation of his glory. The time for that has not yet come.[12] The reason for the delay of the full public manifestation is, in Cooper's view, the fact that such a revelation would "short-circuit the whole Messianic program, either by an abortive worldly kingship thrust upon Jesus (6:15) or by his seizure and premature execution (5:16, 18; 7:13, 19, 25, 32, 44; 8:20, 59; 10:31, 39; 11:53)."[13]

Following this interpretation of Cooper we can explain why it is only the disciples who are said to believe in Jesus as a result of this miracle. The "sign" was never intended to be for everyone, but only for a select few for whom belief in Jesus at that time was crucial. Note that no one else in the narrative is said to believe in Jesus after this event, neither the servants who presumably witnessed the transformation, or even Jesus' mother, who also must have been aware that he had provided the wine by supernatural means.[14] And although the disciples are, interestingly, never said to be privy

---

11. Cooper, *Best Wine*, 368; cf. also Schnackenburg, *Gospel*, 1.327.

12. Cooper, *Best Wine*, 370–71.

13. Ibid., 371. He contends that this is the same reasoning behind Jesus refusing his brothers' request in 7:3–9: "His refusal to go up to the feast is actually only a refusal to go up to the feast in the way they suggest — a refusal to show his glory publicly — because 'my time has not yet come' (7:6, 9; cf. 7:10)." He also compares these refusals to the commands Jesus gives to people in the Synoptics to not reveal his identity: "The purpose is identical — to forestall a premature unleashing of Jewish opposition and a consequent miscarriage of the Messianic plan."

14. Cooper makes a elaborate argument that Jesus' statement to Mary "what to you and to me" was intended to get Mary to examine the nature of their relationship, because that relationship is about to change since "the purpose of the sign that Jesus has in mind is deeper faith based on a deeper apprehension of who Jesus is." Mary has to transition from seeing Jesus as her Son, to seeing Jesus as her Lord and Savior—which Cooper believes happens by the end of this passage (*Best Wine*, 369–70). However, this interpretation seems speculative at best based on the evidence in the passage, particularly the fact that Mary is nowhere said to "believe" here or anywhere else in the Gospel.

to the details of the transformation, one must assume that they were somehow informed since their subsequent belief would otherwise have no cause.

The most significant and perplexing question for our purposes is born out of verse 11, in which we are told that as a result of Jesus turning water into wine he somehow displayed his glory to his disciples. The connection between these two events is left somewhat obscure. Specifically we are told that as a result of this miracle ἐφανέηρωσεν τὴν δόξαν αυτου and consequently ἐπίστευσαν εἰς αυτον οἱ μαθηταὶ αυτου. So the disciples' belief in Jesus was a direct result of this "revelation" of his "glory." However, the author does not make clear what it was about this miracle in specific that caused his disciples to "believe."

The simple performance of a miracle itself would most likely not have had messianic implications for the disciples. Miracle workers abounded in first century Palestine. But while these men were usually considered to have been sent by God or empowered by God to do their deeds, there was not necessarily a connection to the Messiah or a Son of Man figure. So while the performance of a miracle might lead the disciples to understand that their teacher was no ordinary man, by itself it wouldn't be enough to make them conclude that he was the Messiah. In fact, we are told in chapter 1 that at least three of the disciples already believed in Jesus as the Messiah prior to this event (1:35–41; 43–51). Therefore, it seems that, the disciples' belief in 2:11 involves more than simply a recognition of Jesus as Messiah. This suggests that the event they witness in 2:1–11 brings the disciples to a deeper and more developed level of faith. As Schnackenburg observes: "At the miracle of Cana, as at the other 'signs' and 'works,' it is his [Jesus'] origin from God and his union with the Father that must be believed and recognized."[15] Indeed, Neyrey argues that "glory" is the word used by the Evangelist to describe the manifestation of the relationship between Jesus and God.[16]

This sign, as recounted in the present narrative, is intended for the specific purpose of showing how the disciples first came to deeper belief in Jesus' true identity. It appears that they do not fully comprehend Jesus' relationship to the Father at this point, since later passages in the Gospel indicate that this was a gradual process. However, it is clear that they have apprehended *something* about Jesus that they did not know before the miracle. Jesus' conversation with Mary at the beginning of the account reveals

---

15. Schnackenburg, *Gospel,* 1.337–38; he points to 1:51 as support for this reading.
16. Neyrey, *Gospel,* 25.

to us that this "sign" was not meant for everyone, and was not intended to fully disclose everything about his purpose and mission on earth, but was solely to bring his disciples to some new and deeper level of appreciation of himself and his mission. But to know exactly what this was that the disciples were supposed to understand about Jesus, we must examine more closely the "sign" itself and, in particular, the elements involved therein—water and wine.

As we investigate the relationship of Jesus' identity and water in this passage it is worth noting that the author of this narrative gives the reader astonishingly little detail about how the miracle takes place. The narrative is carefully crafted to highlight only the facets of the story vital to the author's purpose. Likewise, the significance of the miracle—how the audience is to interpret it—is never directly spelled out by the narrator. The audience is left to pick up on narrative clues, both overt and subtle, to make sense of the happenings at Cana.[17] There clearly are such clues in the story, and we shall attempt to follow them to an understanding of the role of the water in this narrative.

In interpreting the meaning of the elements of the miracle, the lion's share of the attention has been given to the wine, and indeed this is the dominant symbol. However, the significance of the water is too often marginalized or overlooked altogether. Jesus did not create the wine *ex nihilo*; the fact that he uses *water* to make the wine is significant. And indeed, the author does place emphasis on particulars concerning the water (and the water jars) in the narrative. The calling of attention to the purpose of the water pots (for Jewish ritual purification—v. 6) seems unnecessary unless they are intended to have some sort of symbolic value and to transfer that value to the elements held within—the water and later the wine.

Attention in the narrative is also directed toward the actions of the servants in filling the jars with water, and then drawing out the liquid and taking it to the head waiter for tasting. This emphasis suggests that the miracle of transformation took place at some point during these actions although the narrative never specifies at what point the water became wine. Likewise, we are not told of the servants' reaction when they drew wine out of a pot which previously held water, only that of the disciples after they hear the words of the head waiter. The entire narrative is structured to

---

17. As Little (*Echoes*, 13) points out, the lack of direct explanation of the miracle's significance is probably an intentional action by the author. Since his text is multi-layered in meaning he may not want "to shackle readers to one interpretation" as "excessive explanation can kill stories as well as jokes."

emphasize the actions taken by the servants with the water, and the reaction of the disciples when they witnessed the miracle. Therefore, the water and wine themselves seem to be the significant ingredients in the disciples' belief.

What significance could these elements have carried for the disciples? We suggest that the answer to this question may be found in past associations in Jewish thought and Scripture which we will examine in the following section.

Water, Signs and Yahweh's Identity in Previous Jewish Literature

When looking for OT parallels to this miracle, one of the first that comes to mind is found in the Exodus events. In Exodus 4:9 Moses is told to pour out water from the Nile onto the ground and it will turn into blood. This is the third of the "signs" Yahweh gives him to perform before Pharaoh. It is particularly cogent as a parallel to John 2:1–11, not only because of the obvious similarities of water/wine and water/blood, but also because of the description of these miraculous actions as "signs." In Exodus 4:8 Yahweh says, "If they do not believe you or pay attention to the first miraculous sign, they may believe the second" referring to the "signs" of the staff turning into a serpent (vv. 2–4) and the leprous hand (vv. 6–7). Verse 9 also refers to these two wonders as "signs." The Hebrew for "sign" (אות) is rendered σημειον in the LXX, the same word used in John 2:11 for Jesus' "sign," and elsewhere throughout the Gospel (cf. 2:18, 23; 4:48, 54; 6:30; 7:31; 9:16; 10:41; 11:47; 12:18, 37; 20:30).

Some authors have found a parallel between the mention of the first two "signs" in Exodus 4 and the enumeration of two "signs" by Jesus in John 2:11 and 4:54. While this is not impossible, and may be a good explanation for why only the first two of Jesus' signs in John are numbered, it is not necessary to force this connection: the Jewish mind would almost certainly have related Jesus' actions to those of Moses by the mere mention of the word "sign" in the context of water turning into a blood-red substance, especially in light of 1:17 in which the greatness of the "Word" over Moses' "Law" has already been set out. If the author does intend the first two enumerated signs to be an echo of those two signs in Exodus 4:8–9, it would only be to underscore the echo already present.

There also is the related passage in Exodus 7:14–24 where Moses and Aaron turn the Nile to blood. Although this miracle is not referred to as a "sign" anywhere in the narrative, there is one possible hint of a connection to John 2:1–11. Exodus 7:19 describes the breadth of the plague of blood: "Blood will be everywhere in Egypt, even in the wooden buckets and stone jars." The LXX uses λίθνιος here to describe the stone pots, as does the author of John in 2:6 in introducing the stone pots that held the water for ritual purification at the wedding. Although the Hebrew of Exodus 7:19 leaves the word for "vessel" implied, using אבן for "in stone," parallel with the עץ in the same verse meaning "in wood," in both cases the reference is clearly to vessels made of these materials. The disciples, who were surely at least moderately knowledgeable about Jewish history and Scripture, could hardly miss the fact that Jesus was recreating one of Moses' great signs, albeit in a smaller scale.

But is there greater meaning here? One might argue that the turning of 20 to 30 gallons of water into wine, while certainly impressive in its context, can't begin to compare with the feat of turning the water of the Nile River to blood. Other miracles of Jesus found later in the Gospel are clearly superior to miracles performed by Old Testament figures—the Feeding of the Five Thousand, for instance, which is a recreation of Elisha's miracle in which he feeds 100 people with 20 loaves of bread (2 Kgs 4:42–44). Jesus, by comparison, feeds five thousand (and probably more) with only 5 loaves and 2 fish. However, the miracle he performs at Cana does not seem to be on an exaggeratedly larger scale than Moses turning the Nile to blood. So what other significance can there be?

We propose that the significance of the miracle of Cana in terms of the revelation of Jesus' identity can be found in Exodus 4:5. Here Yahweh tells Moses that the signs he is giving him to perform before Pharaoh serve a specific revelatory purpose: "'This,' said the LORD, 'is so that they may believe that the LORD, the God of their fathers—the God of Abraham, the God of Isaac and the God of Jacob—has appeared to you.'" In other words, by performing the actions given by Yahweh Moses will prove himself to be not just a mere shepherd, but one to whom God has revealed himself. Thus, Moses' authority comes directly from Yahweh, not from any man, and Pharaoh will ignore his message at his peril.

In John 2:1–11, we see Jesus fulfilling Yahweh's words in Exodus 4:5. Just as the miracle performed by Moses was intended as a sign of Yahweh's special relationship to him, Jesus' "sign" at Cana was intended to point to his unique affiliation with the Father. But in this case, instead of representing the one to whom Yahweh has revealed himself, Jesus demonstrates that he himself *is* this revelation of God. The same God who appeared to Moses is now standing in their midst revealing himself to his disciples. This point is underscored by the fact that Jesus does not complete the necessary actions himself, but rather gives instructions that are followed by the household servants, just as Yahweh performed his miraculous sign through the agency of his servant Moses.

It is with this reading in mind that the statement by the head steward upon tasting the wine that Jesus transformed takes on a new level of meaning: "Everyone serves the good wine first, and then the inferior wine after the guests have become drunk. But you have kept the good wine until now" (2:10). In an instance of Johannine irony, the author shows the steward unconsciously commenting on the relationship of Jesus to Moses. In Jewish thought and history generally older or prior things are better.[18] Moses was considered the greatest of the prophets and the giver of the law—the most important figure in Jewish history. And yet, now that Jesus has come, God himself incarnate, even Moses' greatness fades in comparison, as good wine outshines poor wine. So, instead of the "good wine" being reserved to Israel's past, the steward declares to the audience that in Jesus the "good wine" is here now, even at this late hour, making all before it seem cheap in comparison.

So in a subtle way the audience and, apparently, the disciples, come to see that although what Jesus does with the water and wine is a much smaller accomplishment than turning the Nile to blood, it is, in theological terms, something much, much grander than even Moses was able to accomplish. The changing of water into wine was impressive; the real miracle is that Yahweh has now appeared to them in the flesh, in the form of his Son, a feat that even Moses and all the prophets of Israel together would be not have been able to accomplish.

This interpretation is consistent with the common understanding of the water pots (and the water in them) representing the old Jewish law and customs, and the wine representing the new age that Jesus will usher in with his death and resurrection, and is already in some sense inaugurating. Therefore, Exodus 4:2–9 and 7:15–25 constitute one background which helps explain the revelatory significance of Jesus' act at Cana. Jesus deliberately performs a sign that is intended only for a small group around him, not for the whole world, since that would hasten the arrival of his Messianic hour. The purpose is to clearly demonstrate to that small audience that he is

---

18. Neyrey, *Gospel*, 68.

more than a miracle-worker, more than a prophet, even greater than Moses himself—he is the appearance of Yahweh himself in their midst. This understanding is inherent both in the actions he takes at the wedding and in the elements involved in that action—the water and the wine. The themes of identity, revelation of Yahweh's presence and identity, and water are, therefore, strongly intertwined in the narrative of the first miracle of Jesus' ministry in the Gospel of John.

"HE CANNOT BE THE CHRIST, CAN HE?": THE SAMARITAN WOMAN AT THE WELL (JOHN 4:4–42)

Water, Identity and Revelation in John 4:4–42

When Jesus meets a woman of Samaria at a well on his journey from Judea back to Galilee, their conversation quite naturally involves heavy water imagery. Not coincidentally it also dwells on the question of identity, much as we saw in 3:22–36. As a result of this interaction the character or nature of each is revealed: Jesus reveals himself as the Christ (v. 26), and also exposes the woman's scandalous lifestyle (vv. 16–18).[19] In this section we will discuss the role of water imagery in the revelation of these identities.

It has long been noted that this scene shares many characteristics with the OT stories of a man finding a wife at a well, such as in the narratives of Isaac (Gen 24:10–61), Jacob (Gen 29:1–30) and Moses (Ex 2:15–22).[20] Robert Alter has referred to this form as a "repeated biblical type-scene" and lists five elements that are usually found: First, a future bridegroom or his surrogate travels to a foreign land and, secondly, encounters a girl or a group of girls at a well. Thirdly, one of these characters draws water from the well. Fourthly, the girl or the group goes home to tell about the encounter with the stranger. Finally, a betrothal is arranged and concluded, usually following an invitation to a meal.[21] With the exception of the last element (Jesus and the woman are never betrothed) all of the other elements are

---

19. Spencer points out that the issue of "'who knows what about whom' colors the entire scene"; cf. "Understand,"15–47. Reprinted as chapter 4 in Spencer, *Dancing Girls*, 76–106.

20. Bonneau, "Woman," 1252–59; Carmichael, "Marriage," 332–46; Eslinger, "Wooing," 165–82; Glasson, *Moses*, 57; Neyrey, "Jacob Traditions," 419–37.

21. Alter, *Biblical Narrative*, 51–52.

present in John 4:4–42, even if the drawing of water from the well (element #3) occurs metaphorically rather than literally.

Other areas of similarity include: Jesus' invitation to stay with the Samaritan people in their city, just as the OT patriarchs (or their agents) were welcomed by the family of the girls met at the well (cf. Gen 24:24ff; 29:13ff; Exodus 2:20–21); his request for a drink of water (cf. Gen 24:17); and his refusal to eat until his mission was accomplished (Gen 24:33; cf. John 4:31–34). Two details of place and time also would remind the readers of earlier OT passages: Jesus sits on the edge of the well, just as Moses does (Exodus 2:15); and Jesus meets the woman at noon ("the sixth hour"—4:6) around the same time of day that Jacob meets Rachel (Gen 29:7). These passages also have a number of words in common (γυνή, πηγή, ἀντλέω, ὕδωρ, ὑδρία, μένω) although this is mostly due to the overlap in topic and unlikely to be the result of intentional borrowing.[22]

Despite these similarities, however, John elaborates much more significantly and specifically on the meaning of the water in the well at the center of this scene than any previous story of its kind in Scripture. The discussion of water begins in v. 7 when Jesus asks the woman for a drink. The woman is taken aback because Jews will not normally even speak to Samaritans, much less drink from the same vessel (cf. 4:9b). Jesus responds to her by saying, "If you knew the gift of God, and who it is that is saying to you, 'Give me a drink,' you would have asked him, and he would have given you living water" (v. 10). Noting that he has no bucket with which to draw the water, the woman enquires about Jesus' identity: "Are you greater than our ancestor Jacob?" (v. 12). Instead of answering her question directly, Jesus demonstrates his knowledge of the woman's background and living situation (vv. 16–18), which then leads her to identify him as a prophet (v. 19) and begin to ask questions that a prophet of Yahweh should be able to answer. The conversation concludes with the woman admitting she is anticipating the coming of the Messiah (v. 25) and Jesus finally disclosing that he is that Messiah (v. 26). For our purposes it is significant that the discussion of "living water" leads directly into the conversation about the woman's living situation and her Samaritan religious beliefs (vv.19–24), which then leads to her belief in Jesus' true identity (vv. 25–26). In this passage water once again serves as the means for the elucidation of the true nature or character of Jesus, although this time the water is metaphorical instead of literal.

---

22. Bonneau, *Woman*, 1252.

The connection of water and identity in this passage begins with the woman's response to Jesus' request for water: "How is it that you, a Jew, ask a drink of me, a woman of Samaria?" (v. 9). This translation is a fairly literal rendition of the Greek, Πῶς σὺ Ἰουδαῖος ὢν παρ' ἐμοῦ πιεῖν αἰτεῖς οὔσης γυναικὸς Σαμαρείτιδος; The request for a drink in the preceding verse now becomes the thing that brings up the question of identity. It is the drink of water which connects Jesus, a Jew, with the woman, a Samaritan, both verbally and physically. The request for water, a natural one given the context of the meeting, is both the conversation starter and the vehicle for bringing Jesus and the woman into relationship with each other.

But water at the same time represents everything which separates these two characters: he is a pious Jewish male; she is a Samaritan female who, perhaps, has not always lived in a religiously devout way.[23] These two have almost nothing in common. In their society the two would rarely if ever have had opportunity to meet each other, and if they did, they certainly would not be expected to engage in conversation; they definitely would not drink water from the same vessel.[24] The obstacles to communication between these two were numerous and nearly insurmountable.[25] But Jesus, by the simple act of asking for a drink of water, cuts through these accumulated social, religious and cultural conventions to build a relationship with this woman.

After the woman's quizzical question of why he is even associating with her, Jesus responds: "If you knew the gift of God, and who it is that is saying to you, 'Give me a drink,' you would have asked him, and he would have given you living water" (v. 10). This introduces the topic of Jesus' identity. The "living water," the "gift of God," and Jesus' identity all seem to be related. In this verse Jesus implies that knowing the gift itself is not good enough—one also must know the giver because *the identity of the giver impacts the significance of the gift* in some way. Recognizing Jesus' identity is the crucial element in the recognition of the water's importance.[26]

Although Jesus does not elaborate this point, this interpretation is a natural one after the testimony of John the Baptist in chapter 3 discussed

---

23. Malina and Rohrbaugh, *Social-Science*, note that "such awareness of gender and origin was quite typical of social interaction in antiquity" (98).

24. Ibid., 98–99.

25. For detailed discussion of Jesus' conversation with the woman in terms of the different kinds of "gender speak" used by each see Spencer, "Understand," 15–47.

26. O'Day, "Narrative Mode," 667.

above: "The one who comes from above is above all; the one who is from the earth belongs to the earth, and speaks as one from the earth. The one who comes from heaven is above all" (v. 31) and "for the one whom God has sent speaks the words of God, for God gives the Spirit without measure" (v. 34). Jesus applies these principles in his conversation with the woman of Samaria. Earthly water comes from the one who is from the earth and represents earthly things and earthly concerns; but the water that comes from him will be different because he is different—he is the one "from above" (cf. 3:3) and so his water is also "from above."

Only God can give the spirit; therefore, when Jesus offers the woman living water, a common symbol for the coming of the spirit, he makes a profound statement about who he is. The woman didn't ask him for literal water because Jews and Samaritans do not share things in common. However, Jesus is more interested in why she does not ask him for spiritual "water" and concludes that it is because she does not know who he is. If she had, she would have asked and he would have given it to her (v. 10). The implication, then, is that if she knew that he was special, she would also have known that the water he gave was special. She doesn't recognize the unique qualities of the water because she does not recognize the unique person of Jesus as the Son of God. Therefore, the properties of this spiritual "water" result from its association with Jesus and, by extension, the Father. It has no particular significance on its own.

This is consistent with the Johannine theme of the inferiority of everyone and everything to Jesus and those things associated with him that has been prevalent thus far in the Gospel. John the Baptist is inferior to Jesus, and only serves as a pointer to him. Both the water of Jewish purification and the earlier wine at the Wedding of Cana is inferior to the "last wine" which Jesus created. The temple at Jerusalem is inferior to Christ's body, because while the temple will be destroyed never to be rebuilt, Jesus' body will be destroyed, but will rise up again (2:19–21). Physical birth (the birth "of water") is far inferior to the spiritual birth (from the spirit and from "above"—3:3–6) that Jesus offers. Finally, the best man is subordinate to the bridegroom at a wedding, just as the one who is from the earth is inferior to the one "from above." Jesus' conversation with the woman in chapter 4 is the next plank in John's elaborate argument for the superiority of Jesus.

As Jesus predicted in v. 10, the woman only understands him on a physical level, for she responds to his remark with: "Sir, you have no bucket and the well is deep. Where do you get that living water?" (v. 11). The woman clearly demonstrates that she neither recognizes Jesus nor catches the double meaning of "living water" (ὕδωρ ζῶν). Understanding this play on words is crucial to recognizing Jesus' identity, and the woman does neither. Instead, she is fixated on the physical difficulties presented by his statement—namely, how Jesus is going to be able to reach to the bottom of a very deep well to extract water since he has no vessel with which to do so. She then seemingly switches subjects abruptly asking, "Are you greater than our ancestor Jacob, who gave us the well, and with his sons and flocks drank from it?" (v. 11).

When the woman finally does think to investigate Jesus' identity with this question, it seems to have been prompted by a combination of amazement and confusion that this Jew would count himself to have special powers by which he could draw water from a well without a bucket. Neyrey has suggested that this question reflects the woman's knowledge of an ancient Palestinian tradition in which water sprang up from a well at Jacob's command.[27] This seems plausible as Jacob's relationship to the area has already been mentioned in v. 3 and the well is referred to as "Jacob's well" in v. 6.[28] It also would make clear the connection between the woman's two statements in verses 11 and 12. If he does not have a bucket, how would he expect to draw the water? The woman must assume that he thinks he can get the water through supernatural means, which leads to her curiosity about his identity.

---

27. Neyrey, "Jacob Traditions," 421–25; the majority of the evidence is from extra-canonical sources, many of which are dated later than the Gospel. But Neyrey argues convincingly that this is an ancient tradition which was preserved in much later documents. Num. 21:16–18 may be related to an early version of the tradition (cf. *Tg. Yer. I* Num 21:17–18). However, the tradition would not necessarily have to be ancient for the woman of Samaria and the author of the Gospel to be familiar with it. The fact that it exists in documents that ante-date the Gospel of John could just as well support the possibility of it being well-known in 1st century Palestine.

28. There is no mention in the OT of Jacob owning a well. The first references come from Christian pilgrim sources in the 4th century (cf. Brown, *Gospel*, 1.169). There is indeed a place known today as "Jacob's well" at the foot of Mt. Gerizim whose location makes it a plausible candidate for the well mentioned in Jn 4, but there is no way to be certain. Jacob's connection with Shechem, and the plot of land he purchased, is mentioned in Gen 33:18–19 and Josh 24:32. Although nearly all sources read "Sychar" as the name of the town in 4:5, many scholars identify Shechem as the more likely location, although this is by no means unanimous. It is possible that the Greek for Shechem (*Sychem*) was corrupted into *Sychar*, which accounts for the reading as it stands today. For discussion see Brown, *Gospel*, 1.169; Keener, *Gospel*, 1.590.

Jesus does not directly answer the question about Jacob, but instead returns to the issues of water and identity: "Everyone who drinks of this water will be thirsty again, but those who drink of the water that I will give them will never be thirsty. The water that I will give will become in them a spring of water gushing up to eternal life" (vv. 13–14). It is significant that here the spiritual or "living" water is qualified and described by its relationship to the person of Christ: "those who drink of the water *that I will give them* will never be thirsty. The water *that I give* will become in them a spring of living water. . . ." This is in contrast to the water of the well ("this water"), which will leave people perpetually thirsty. The distinction between the two is the fact that the "living" water originates from Jesus himself. This relationship is what gives the water both its significance and its efficacy.

The woman responds, enthusiastically one assumes: "Sir, give me this water, so that I may never be thirsty or have to keep coming here to draw water" (v. 15). The woman now *thinks* she understands Jesus' identity; she at least comprehends that this source of perpetual water will come from him. However, it is clear she is still thinking in earthly terms, which means she still does not know who Jesus truly is. At this point she believes him only to be someone who may be able to provide her with an everlasting source of fresh water which will save her the dreary daily task of hauling water from the well to her house. She has not yet got the point that Jesus is speaking metaphorically. But she should not be expected to be able to do this yet, as she has not yet fully grasped Jesus' identity. It is only when she does this that she can understand what the water he is offering her represents.[29]

In verses 16–18 Jesus turns the conversation from tentative questioning about who he is to a discussion of the woman's identity. This may not seem to modern eyes like a conversation about identity, but in a patriarchal society where a woman was largely identified by her husband and/or his standing in the community, the question of whether she was married and to whom was significant.[30] Jesus asking her to call her husband could imply

---

29. In his survey of medieval and early Reformation commentaries on John 4 Farmer notes that commentators from both periods see the woman as wrestling with issues of identity. However, the medieval commentators generally portray her as coming to understand Jesus' identity while those of the Reformation focus on the woman coming to terms with her own identity as a sinner. Cf. Farmer, "Changing Images," 365–75.

30. According to Malina marriage in the 1st century Jewish context resulted "in the embedding of the female in the honor of her husband." Cf. Malina, *New Testament World*, 143.

that he wants to meet him in order to know more about her. It likewise could be an instance of Jesus observing the niceties of proper social interaction; he really should not be talking to a woman alone, especially not a married woman. Her husband should be present before their conversation progresses any further. Either of these could be legitimate reasons, on one level, that Jesus wants her to call her husband. However, since this conversation has operated on two different levels throughout, it seems that Jesus probably had another more "spiritual" intention as well: that of revealing a bit more of his identity to the woman by revealing his knowledge of her.

By subtly implying that he knows all about her marital situation, despite the fact that they met only moments before, Jesus reveals his omniscience. This brings the woman one step further down the path to understanding who Jesus is when she identifies him as a prophet (v. 19). She reinforces this understanding of him by quizzing him on a major point of contention between the Jews and Samaritans—the proper place for worship. Something in Jesus' speech to her about worship (vv. 21–24) causes her to bring up the topic of the coming Messiah (the *taheb* in Samaritan belief) who will "proclaim all things to us" (v. 25). Jesus then, finally, directly identifies himself as this coming Messiah in v. 26.

The revelation of Jesus' identity in this passage is gradual. The woman goes from knowing him as only a generic "Jew" (v. 9) to a mysterious man who can do miraculous things, such as supply her with endless water (v. 15), to a prophet who can tell her things about her life no normal stranger would know (v. 19), to finally recognizing that he is more than a prophet, but rather the coming Messiah himself (v. 26). Actually, even at this point the woman may still not be completely convinced, although she has caught a glimpse of who Jesus might be. Significantly when she goes back to her village and tells everyone what has happened she does not confidently proclaim that she has found the Messiah, but instead asks, "He cannot be the Messiah, can he?" (4:29)[31] in what was probably a mixture of awe and confusion.

What is the role of the water imagery in all this? In the early part of the Gospel water imagery is closely linked with the identity of Jesus, as only the "one who is from above" is capable of providing the living water that is associated with the spirit. If Jesus has not come from God, then the water

31. The μήτι in 4:29 makes it clear that the question is expected to be answered in the negative. The NRSV ("He cannot be the Messiah, can he?") or NASB ("This is not the Christ, is it?") are thus to be preferred over the NIV's less precise "Could this be the Christ?"

he provides would be no more potent than that in Jacob's well; but the fact that he does come from God *is what makes his water unique*. For one to recognize the water as special, one must also acknowledge the unique identity of the giver. Conversely, if one knows who the giver is, then one must assume that what he gives is more than just ordinary water. Therefore, the nature of the water and the identity of the giver are intimately intertwined. Just as Jacob's well was set apart as special because of its association with one of Israel's great forefathers (cf. vv. 6, 12), so also is the water Jesus gives distinct from all around it by virtue of its relationship to his person.

The leaving behind of the water jar in v. 28 has been interpreted in various ways. This detail could have been included simply to show the woman's excitement and haste to get back to her village and spread the word about the man she had met. But it might have more symbolic significance: since she has now found the spiritual "living water" she has no need for the physical water or, by extension, for a jar to carry it in. Of course, John, the literary master that he is, could have intended both interpretations at once. It also could be an indication of her permanent change of mind about the identity of Jesus. Since his identity and the nature of water are so linked in this passage, the leaving of the jar could also represent the leaving behind of the previous misunderstandings of Jesus' identity as a Jewish rabbi, a miracle worker, and a prophet. Now that she has grasped his true identity, she has left behind the lesser conceptions of who he is. Now that she has acknowledged his true identity, she also recognizes the potency of the spiritual "water" that he offers.

She originally thinks he is just an ordinary man, which is why she interprets things on a literal, earthly level. It is only through understanding his divine origins that she comes to understand his other statements as referring to a spiritual, rather than an earthly, reality. So recognizing Jesus as the coming Messiah, sent from God, is crucial in this entire narrative. The woman doesn't learn about the spiritual aspects of the "living water" and then from that deduce that Jesus must be from God; it is the other way around. By recognizing his unique character the woman can then understand, in a flash of intuition, that the "water" he offers refers to more than just an earthly substance to quench thirst. This is what causes the immediate abandonment of the water jar and her flight back to town.

Wells, Springs, Living Water and Yahweh's Identity in Previous Jewish Literature

The OT texts that have the most consonance with the water imagery of this passage, and which would most likely have quickly come to the mind of those familiar with Scripture, are found in Jeremiah. In Jeremiah chapter 2 Yahweh laments, through the prophet, that Israel has rejected and abandoned him despite all his care for them. Part of that grief is expressed in rather striking water imagery:

> My people have committed two sins:
> They have forsaken me,
> the spring of living water,
> and have dug their own cisterns,
> broken cisterns that cannot hold water. (Jer 2:13)

A similar sentiment is expressed, in consonant language, in Jeremiah 17:13:

> O LORD, the hope of Israel,
> all who forsake you will be put to shame.
> Those who turn away from you will be written in the dust
> because they have forsaken the LORD,
> the spring of living water.[32]

The word translated as "spring" in both cases is מקור which may also be translated as "fountain." The LXX renders this as πηγή the same word used for "spring" in John 4. It appears frequently in conjunction with the image of water, naturally, and often with the concept of "living" or "running" water. The "living water" in both instances is the Hebrew מים חיים. This phrase is found relatively few times in the OT. It appears most frequently in Leviticus to describe the type of water to be used in the process of ritual or sacrificial purity (Lev. 14:5–6; 50–52; 15:13; 19:17; also Num 19:17). Proper purification required water that was "running" or "living" as opposed to stagnant water from a jar.

While these instances are not of primary importance in understanding the imagery of John 4, given the context and content of Jesus' discussion with the Samaritan woman, it is possible that the idea of ritual purity hovers in the background of the narrative. After all, the Samaritan woman would have been considered perpetually ritually impure by Jewish standards and

---

32. Cp. 1En 96:6.

Jesus' touching her or anything she had touched would render him impure as well.[33] Furthermore, their debate about the proper place of worship brings to mind all the differences that stand between the two nations, not just which Temple they worship at. The most profound of these differences was the illegitimacy, in the Jewish mind, of the Samaritan people and their religion. Jesus' offer of "living water," to the woman, then, might suggest that through belief in him she can become "ritually pure."[34] This is not to say that Jesus is calling her to become a Jew. Indeed, the point he makes in their discussion is that "true worshippers" need not adhere to the ritualistic standards of either religion, but instead will stand before Yahweh directly "in spirit and in truth" alone (4:23). So in one sense his offer of water to her may represent the ritual purity necessary to stand before Yahweh, and at the same time signify the power to transcend human religious distinctions.

However, the more significant connections are found in the other three instances of מים חיים ("living water") in the OT. The first appearance of the phrase in the OT comes in Genesis 26:19 in reference to Isaac's digging of wells to search for fresh water: "Isaac's servants dug in the valley and discovered a well of springing [or living] water." Even though it is mentioned as a well, the מים חיים presumably refers to a natural spring over which a well was eventually built. Still, this is the first instance in the OT where the image of a well and that of "living water" are found together, and although the story involves Isaac rather than Jacob, it still might have come to the mind of the original audience of John 4.

The second place that מים חיים is found outside of Leviticus is in Song of Solomon. In 4:12 the singer describes his lover as "a garden enclosed, a spring shut up, a fountain sealed and later calls her "a well of living waters" (4:15). The "spring," "fountain," and "well" are clearly euphemisms for her sexuality; the fact that the spring and fountain are "shut" and "sealed" either refers to the woman's virginity, or to her fidelity to her husband. Water-related imagery is used elsewhere in the OT in reference to sexual behavior. Prov. 5:15–18 employs such imagery to warn against adultery:

> Drink water from your own cistern,
>   running water from your own well.
> Should your springs overflow in the streets,
>   your streams of water in the public squares?

---

33. Malina and Rohrbaugh, *Social-Science*, 98–99.
34. Derrett, "Purity," 291–98.

> Let them be yours alone,
>> never to be shared with strangers.
> May your fountain be blessed,
>> and may you rejoice in the wife of your youth.

Similar sentiments expressed with related imagery can be found in Prov. 9:17 and 23:27.

These verses throw an interesting light on the interpretation of the Jeremiah passages above. It is quite plausible that there is a double *entendre* intended when Yahweh accuses his people of "forsaking the fountain of living water" and digging "cisterns" instead (Jer 2:13). In Jeremiah 2 Yahweh uses the language of adultery and prostitution to describe Israel's turning away from him toward false gods. The marriage context is set up in v. 1 when Yahweh recalls "how as a bride you loved me." But since that time Israel has felt the need to "drink water" from the rivers of other lands, particularly Egypt and Assyria (v. 18). They have acted the part of a prostitute (vv. 20, 33) and chased after other gods like a donkey in heat chases after a mate (v. 24). In striking contrast to a woman's chastity being like a well-tended garden blossoming with abundant fruits and spices (Song of Sol 4:12–15), Yahweh calls Israel a "corrupt and wild vine" (v. 21). So the metaphor of Israel digging cisterns for themselves instead of drinking from the spring of living water does not just represent Israel turning its back on Yahweh, but has overtones of sexual infidelity.

At first glance this would seem to have little in common with the use of "living water" in John 4. However, it may be very significant if one sees sexual innuendo hovering just beneath the surface of Jesus' conversation with the woman of Samaria. While scholars have long talked about the dual level of meaning in this conversation, e.g. the physical level and the spiritual level, which causes the woman to misunderstand Jesus, Brant suggests that there really are three levels of meaning in play here: a "supratext" which carries the spiritual meaning of "living water," the "text" which refers to physical things like running water, wells, etc., and the "subtext" in which the water imagery brings up issues of sexuality and fertility.[35] The context and setting of the meeting certainly prepare the reader to expect a betrothal story similar to those in the OT, as discussed above. The perceptive audience, who was familiar with Jewish tradition and Scripture, might naturally assume that Jesus, a single male, meeting a (presumably) single female near

---

35. Brant, "Husband Hunting," 213.

a well and asking her for water would be a set up for the two to become married.

The issue of whether Jesus and the woman were actually intentionally engaging in double *entendre* is a debated question.[36] One assumes that Jesus would not have knowingly led the woman to believe he was interested in a sexual relationship with her. However, it is possible that the woman interpreted the events in this way, which may partly explain the reason she is so slow to understand Jesus' true meaning. Even if she was not well-versed in the traditions of a man finding his wife at a well, or the symbolism of wells and springs for sexual relations, she still may have assumed that Jesus was interested in her on a physical, rather than spiritual level. After all, he was acting outside the boundaries of normally accepted social behavior by even talking to her; it would be easy to assume that he had a less than honorable goal in mind.

Following this interpretation of the woman's thought processes, Keener suggests that her less-than-truthful answer to Jesus concerning her marital status may actually be her coy way of intimating that she is open to a sexual encounter: "A denial that one was married may not have always been flirtatious, but it constituted an essential prerequisite for any further steps toward even a casual sexual union."[37] Keener also suggests that Jesus' statement about her marital history may not be only intended to show his omniscience on a spiritual level, but on the physical level it could be his attempt at "clarifying the direction of the discussion."[38] Jesus realizes that the woman has misunderstood him, or, rather, continues to interpret everything he says and does on a very physical, human level, rather than a spiritual one. To make it plain to her that he has no sexual designs on her, he brings up the subject of her husband(s). Even if this understanding of the sexual *entendres* under the surface of the conversation does not do justice to the actual situation, an interpreter could be forgiven for making these kinds of assumptions about the text given the context, the background and the language and imagery used.

It is also possible that the original audience would have understood this as one of the levels of meaning of the narrative. They certainly are led to

---

36. Haenchen, *Gospel*, 221.

37. Keener, *Gospel*, 1.606.

38. Ibid., 1.605. Conversely, Brant sees the woman as the one who is "resisting the relationship" by pointing out that he and she are not the traditional couple in a standard betrothal scene. Cf. Brant, "Husband Hunting," 213

expect such a type of story by the setting, type-scene, imagery and language used in the conversation. Although it is difficult to pin down the precise reason for the woman's marital history, the legal and traditional material marshalled by Keener[39] makes it difficult to imagine a scenario in which the woman comes off looking good, although apologists of the feminist camp have tried valiantly.[40] It is true that her character has often been undeservedly maligned by critics throughout the centuries who assume that her multiple marriages were the result of some type of promiscuity when, in reality, there might be other viable explanations for her five marriages. However, it is hard to find a morally justifiable reason for her to be living with a man she is not married to, whether he is someone else's husband or not. This fact at the very least makes her character seem morally suspect, even if she is not the great whore that some commentators have sought to make her. Therefore, we cannot rule out the reading of the water imagery in this passage as possible sexual innuendo, even if it plays out as only a subtext of the narrative.

Perhaps most significant for our purposes is the fact that in Jeremiah 2:13 Yahweh compares *himself* to the spring of living water, in contrast to the broken cisterns that the people have created for themselves. This comparison is actually relatively rare in the OT. While fountains, springs and rivers of water are often used as a metaphor for life, wisdom and, by extension, for the Torah itself (especially in later Rabbinic sources) there are relatively few places in ancient Jewish writings where we find Yahweh appropriating this imagery to describe himself. However, there are many places where Yahweh claims to be the source and giver of all waters. For example, in Isaiah 43:19–20 the Lord says:

> See, I am doing a new thing!
> > Now it springs up; do you not perceive it?
> > I am making a way in the desert
> > and streams in the wasteland.
> The wild animals honor me,
> > the jackals and the owls,
> > because I provide water in the desert
> > and streams in the wasteland,
> > to give drink to my people, my chosen.

---

39. Keener, *Gospel*, 1.605–8.
40. Dube, "Post-Colonial," 19; Kim, "Korean," 109–19.

Water, especially life-giving or living water, is specifically and solely the gift of Yahweh in the Old Testament and in Apocryphal and Pseudepigraphical sources as well. Psalm 36:9: "For with you is the fountain of life; in your light we see light." This identifies the "fountain of life" as being "with" the Lord, so it was clearly seen as his possession, and, therefore, he had the ability to give it. There are several passages in the Odes of Solomon which talk about living water as Yahweh's gift, in language tantalizingly similar to that found in John 4. The most cogent example comes from Odes of Solomon 30:1–7:

> Fill for yourselves water from the living spring of the Lord, because it has been opened for you.
> And come all you thirsty and take a drink, and rest beside the spring of the Lord. Because it is pleasing and sparkling and perpetually pleases the self.
> For more refreshing is its water than honey, and the honeycomb of bees is not to be compared with it;
> because it flowed from the lips of the Lord, and it named from the heart of the Lord.
> And it came boundless and invisible, and until it was set in the middle they knew it not. Blessed are they who have drunk from it, and have rested by it.[41]

This "spring" is called "the spring of the Lord" and it comes "from the lips of the Lord" and is "named from the heart of the Lord." Note that its origin is what gives it its superlative qualities: "more refreshing is its water than honey, and the honeycomb of bees is not to be compared with it; *because it flowed from the lips of the Lord.*" So Yahweh is not only the provider of the gift of this "living spring" but also what gives the water its unique properties. In a sense, then, he *is* this spring because without him, it would not be what it is.

This is the key to understanding how the equation of Yahweh with springs of living water works metaphorically; it also applies to Christ and his offer of living water to the woman at the well of Samaria.[42] The water he offers her is special because of its source, just as the water Yahweh offers has qualities that can only come from him. In this way the gift and the giver are inextricably linked. Indeed, in some sense, they are identical. The

---

41. Similar imagery can be found in OdSol 11:6–7, 16c.

42. It will also be cogent as a background for John 7:38–39, which we will discuss in a later chapter.

water Jesus offers is qualitatively different from any other water because it is associated with his person. At the same time Jesus' unique characteristics are revealed through the association of the water with himself. This understanding helps make sense of the first part of John 4:10: "If you knew the gift of God, and who it is that asks you for a drink, you would have asked...." Jesus is saying that if she knew the gift she would know the giver, and vice versa, because the two are inseparable. When Jesus offers the woman the water he is not offering something separate or distinct from himself; he is offering her his very self as the Son of God.

In John chapter 4 the author deliberately plays on a rich heritage of Jewish water imagery related to the nature and person of Yahweh as a means of revealing Jesus' true identity as the Son of God to the woman of Samaria. Although the woman does not catch on right away, the readers/hearers of the story would understand that Jesus' offer of "living water" casts him in the role of the God of the OT offering to provide that which can only be offered by him because it can only originate from him. The revelation of Jesus' true identity is once again inextricably intertwined with the water motif of the Gospel.

CHAPTER SUMMARY AND CONCLUSIONS

In the baptism passages of John 1 and 3 the author sets out the connection between water baptism and the revelation of Jesus as one who is uniquely related to the Father. This relationship manifests itself in 2:1–11 when Jesus and his disciples attend a wedding in Cana. Here Jesus' turning of water into wine was clearly intended to reveal something about himself, specifically his special relationship to Yahweh. We are told that as a direct result of this "sign" he "revealed his glory" and "his disciples believed in him" (2:11). Jesus understood that granting his mother's request to help with the shortage of wine would involve some revelation of his true nature and identity, which is why he seems to resist initially. Jesus warns his mother not to expect a full public revelation of his identity, because his "hour has not yet come" (2:4). The Johannine Jesus recognizes that the fullest revelation of his relationship to Yahweh will only come from his glorification on the cross, an event that still lies in the future. Nevertheless, by changing the water into a blood-red substance, Jesus symbolically repeats Moses' miracle of turning the Nile to blood (Ex 4:9; 7:19–21) introducing into the passage the echo of Yahweh's words to Moses stating that this "sign" was to be done "so that they may believe that the Lord, the God of their ancestors, the God of Abraham, the God of Isaac, and the God of Jacob, has appeared to you" (Ex 4:5). Jesus' miracle at Cana, which required manipulation of earthly waters, was a sign that Jesus was not merely another miracle-worker; he was Yahweh himself come among them in the flesh.

Jesus is only able to do what he does at Cana because of his unique relationship to the Father. The "sign" he performs, therefore, reveals his true purpose: Jesus has come to inaugurate the new age represented by the wine. However, this new age is born out of God's previous revelation to his people, represented by the water, in much the same way that Jesus' "new" identity as divine is born out of, and expressed in terms of, Yahweh's previous dealings with his people.

This leads, then, into chapter 4 and Jesus' discussion with the woman at the well. From the opening exchange where the differences in their social and religious situations are highlighted to Jesus' prescient knowledge about her living arrangements, this passage crackles with tension over identity. And once again, Jesus' identity and the efficacy of the water he provides—this time the metaphorical "living water"—are dependent on one another. This offer of living water does reveal something of Jesus' relationship to the Father, at least to those familiar with the Old Testament references to Yahweh as the "spring of living water." By offering to provide "springs of living water" Jesus boldly unites himself with Yahweh. Conversely, Jesus' identity as one with the Father is what gives the living water its efficacy. If the woman had known Jesus' identity she would have known the quality of the water he offered because the two are defined by each other.

The theme of the revelation of Jesus' identity by water takes a big step, then, in chapter 4. Up to this point water has been literal—specifically the waters of baptism or ritual purification. Now water starts to represent something—the life that is characteristic of the age to come which Jesus is even now ushering in. His ability to offer this life, represented by the water, is the direct result of his unique relationship with Yahweh: the acceptance of one requires the acceptance of the other.

CHAPTER 5

Bethesda and Siloam
Water and Identity in John 5 & 9

INTRODUCTION

The Gospel of John records two healing miracles in which both water and the question of identity figure prominently. The narratives in John 5:1–18 (The Healing at the Pool of Bethesda) and 9:1–41 (The Healing of the Blind Man) demonstrate related concerns and emphases and exhibit a comparable narrative structure. The setting is similar in both stories—pools in Jerusalem—and both unnamed characters are introduced as having long-term disabilities (a thirty-eight year infirmity and blindness from birth). Both healings are followed by discourses and debates with the Jewish authorities. And because both men are healed on the Sabbath, the stories share the similar theological themes of work, sin and the identity of Jesus. Keener, among others, has noted these similarities calling the passage in chapter 5 a "clear antithetical parallel" and "foil" for the miracle in chapter 9.[1] In addition, Culpepper has produced a detailed outline of the similarities between the two narratives.[2] The story in chapter 9 can be seen an expansion

---

1. Keener, *Gospel*, 1.639. Cf. also Bultmann, *Gospel*, 239; Lee, 108–9 (esp. note 4); Staley, "Stumbling," 55–80.

2. Culpepper, *Anatomy*, 139–40.

of the form introduced in chapter 5 to create the most theologically and narratively significant healing story in the Gospel.[3]

These two narratives are also important tent-posts in the structure of the Gospel, as Culpepper[4] and Brown[5] both point out. Some also note that the story in 5:1–18 begins the escalation of the plot against Jesus which eventually leads to his death in the Gospel.[6] It is as a result of his healing of the man at Bethesda that Jesus is first reported in John as coming into conflict with the Jewish authorities. This clash continues and increases throughout the following chapters, culminating after Jesus' final sign, the Raising of Lazarus (11:1–44) when the Sanhedrin meets (11:47) and decides to have Jesus removed (11:53). It has also been suggested that the narratives in chs. 5 and 9 are the first part of a set of bookended structures that begin and end the section of John 5–10. Culpepper notes this major section of the Gospel begins with the healing of a man by a pool (Bethesda; 5:1–18) followed by a discourse in response to the Jews (5:19–47), and then ends with a similar healing by a pool (Siloam; 9:1–7), followed by dialogues and discourses with the Jews (9:8–41; 10:1–38) and concludes with Jesus' withdrawal from Jerusalem.[7] So in a sense these two narratives are seen as supporting on either end the second major division of the Gospel, chapters 5–10. Deeks has also suggested that these two stories are parallel to each other in a giant chiastic layout of the Gospel.[8]

Most importantly for our purposes, the use of water imagery and its relationship to the theme of revelation of identity is similar in both passages, as we will demonstrate. For this reason, we will deal with these two stories together in this chapter. First we will briefly look at the major elements of identity and water in each pericope and then examine the possible OT precedents and echoes that may be seen in these stories. Since the events are similar, particularly on matters of water, revelation and identity, the Jewish background section will cover and apply to both passages.

3. The condensed form of 5:1–18 as compared to other miracles stories in John and the Synoptics has led some scholars to speculate that it was developed at an earlier stage of the composition of the Gospel before the author had perfected the form. However, there are certainly other possible explanations. Cf. Lee, *Symbolic Narratives*, 108; Lindars, *Gospel of John*, 208.

4. Culpepper, *Sample*, 196–97.
5. Brown, *Gospel*, 1.cxliv.
6. Carter, *Storyteller*, 39–41; Jones, *Symbol*, 122; Ridderbos, *Gospel of John*, 181.
7. Culpepper, *Sample*, 196–97.
8. Deeks, "Structure," 107–28.

"IT WAS JESUS WHO HAD MADE HIM WELL": HEALING AT THE POOL OF BETHESDA (JOHN 5:1-47)

Water, Identity, and Revelation in John 5:1-47

The story of the healing of the lame man at Bethesda presents interpreters with several intriguing problems. We shall briefly visit several of these as we examine the roles of water and identity in this passage.

On its surface 5:1-15 appears to be simply another miracle tale: Jesus sees a man who is lame and makes it possible for him to walk. However, the story quickly takes an ominous turn as the man who was healed runs up again Jewish legal authorities who charge him with breaking the Sabbath for carrying his mat as Jesus had told him to do. Suddenly, the story takes on a very different focus, and for the rest of the section the actual healing becomes of secondary importance. The remainder of the chapter centers around the Sabbath violation and a discourse by Jesus on the Father, His work, and the responsibility of the Son in relationship to the Father's work (vv. 16-47).

Immediately the setting is described as a pool near the Sheep Gate[9] where persons with infirmities or illnesses went to seek healing (vv. 2-3a). The situation depicted shares many similarities with ancient Greek healing shrines, particularly ones associated with the gods Asclepius and Serapis.[10] Such sanctuaries, which often included pools or springs of water thought to have therapeutic powers, were found in virtually every major city in the ancient world from at least the 5th century B.C.E.[11] Whether what is represented in this story is actually a Greek healing shrine or a Jewish adaptation of the pattern, substituting Yahweh for the pagan gods, is unclear. The editor who inserted the commentary in vv. 3b-4 credits the powers of the pool to "the Lord," but this could be a later gloss to cover up the pagan connections. There is archaeological evidence that the sanctuary at Bethesda[12] was used as a pagan shrine in the 2nd century CE, but it is unclear whether

---

9. Or perhaps it should read "sheep pool." The proper translation is unclear. Cf. Beasley-Murray, *John*, 69-70; Brown, *Gospel*, 1.206; Metzger, *Textual*, 207-8.

10. Avalos, *Illness*, 37ff; Broer, "Knowledge," 83-90; Davies, *Land*, 302-13; Koester, *Symbolism*, 53.

11. Poirier, "Hatred," 29.

12. That is assuming that the current day St. Anne's is the actual location of the pool described in John 5, which seems plausible given the evidence. Cf. Keener, *Gospel*, 1.636-37.

Bethesda and Siloam

it was pagan at the time of Jesus or originally Jewish and converted to pagan use after the destruction of Jerusalem.[13] Even if John's audience had not experienced these shrines first-hand, they were common enough in the Roman world that they would have been familiar with their operation.[14]

Verse 3b and all of what would be v. 4 consist of a very early textual variant: "and they [those needing healing] waited for the moving of the waters. From time to time an angel of the Lord would come down and stir up the waters. The first one into the pool after each such disturbance would be cured of whatever disease he had." It is generally agreed that this is a later interpolation to explain the situation for those audience members not familiar with the Pool of Bethesda or its purported healing capabilities.[15] However, there is no compelling reason to doubt that this statement accurately reflects an ancient tradition concerning the Pool of Bethesda[16], even if the author of the verse advances a supernatural explanation for the 'stirring' of the waters (an angel) rather than a natural one (an underground spring?). The more important question, to some scholars, is how knowledge of the information in this variation has affected interpretations of this passage through the years. We will return to this issue later in our examination.

The narrator's attention next turns to one particular man at the pool (v. 5). We are not given his name or the exact nature of his affliction. The audience only knows that he has been unable to walk for 38 years. Some read this figure allegorically as the number of years the Israelites wandered in the wilderness.[17] It seems more likely that it has no specific significance outside of underlining the seriousness of the man's condition, although Waetjen is probably correct in reading this number as representative of the kind of heartbreaking longing for rescue that the man at the pool must have felt after waiting for such a long time.[18] How Jesus learned about the man's problem is also not narrated. The NIV renders the γινώσκω in v. 6 as "learned" implying that Jesus somehow discovered the information about the man's condition through normal means, perhaps by enquiring of someone at the pool. However, γινώσκω can also be read as "to know" or "per-

---

13. Koester, *Symbolism*, 53. There are eyewitness reports of the pool still being used for healing as late as the 6th century CE (cf. Poirier, "Hatred," 29).

14. Koester, *Symbolism*, 53.

15. Cf. Brown, *Gospel*, 1.207; Beasley-Murray, *John*, 70; Metzger, *Textual*, 209.

16. So Morris, *Gospel*, 267–68.

17. For just one recent example see Waetjen, *Beloved*, 184.

18. Ibid.

ceive," which is the choice of most other English translations (NRSV, NASB, KJV, ESV, ASV). This seems the more likely intention as Jesus' unnatural knowledge about people is a recurring motif in the Gospel (cf. 1:47–49; 2:24–25; 4:16–19; 11:11; 13:11, 21; 13:38).

The next element of the story is the somewhat puzzling conversation that takes place between Jesus and the man (vv. 6–7). Unlike other miracle stories in the Gospels, Jesus initiates the conversation with the man, not the other way around. There have been differing interpretations of Jesus' question, "Do you want to get well?" (v. 6). In one sense it seems like a ridiculous query. The man has been unable to walk for 38 years—of course he wants to be healed! Why does Jesus even feel it necessary to pose such a question? The suggestions have been many. Some see Jesus as testing the man's faith, or at least his will to regain his health.[19] Others see Jesus as rebuking the man for not really wanting to get well.[20] At least one scholar has proposed that the man might not want to lose his lucrative position as a beggar.[21] However, none of these suggestions seems completely satisfactory.

First of all, as Thomas astutely notes, the understanding that Jesus is testing the man's faith is based on a reading of the text in light of the textual variation in vv. 3–4. If one removes this section from the text, which most scholars agree we should, then there is no hint anywhere of Yahweh working through the waters of the Pool of Bethesda. The means by which the healing occurs is not specified. Therefore, there is no reason to assume that the man's problem is a lack of faith, because there is no evidence that being healed by the pool was a matter of faith.[22] It is not impossible that at least some of the people at the pool did consider Yahweh to work through the waters to effect their healing.[23] This would account for the tradition that is preserved in the textual variant. However, the man in the story never indicates whether he believes this or not, so we have no way of knowing.

The second reason that these interpretations of Jesus' question fail to satisfy is that they do not account for the man's answer; they assume

---

19. Dodd, *Interpretation*, 319–20.

20. This was an especially popular interpretation by commentators in the first half of the 20th century, but has persisted in a small minority of modern scholars. Cf. Barclay, *Gospel*, 1.175; Culpepper, "Sample," 193–208; Dods, *Gospel*, 1.178; Finch, "Interpretation," 195; Morton, "Diagnosis," 424–25.

21. Findlay, *Fourth Gospel*, 271.

22. Thomas, "Stop Sinning," 9.

23. It should be noted we don't know that all the people at the pool were Jewish. There may well have been many ethnicities and religions among those seeking healing.

that Jesus is asking something that has no relation to the answer given. This leads to speculation of poor editing by the author, or a combination of sources.[24] However, this approach is backwards because it is based on the interpreter's *assumption* of what the question means. We should interpret the intent of the question through the lens of the answer the man gives, instead of interpreting the answer from what we assume the question means. With this method we can at least understand what the man *thought* Jesus was asking and perhaps come up with a more reasonable understanding of the conversation.

If Jesus is enquiring about his faith or willpower, the man's answer is indeed nonsensical. Instead, the man seems to understand Jesus' question as an offer to help him to be healed.[25] He has been waiting for a person to come along to help him to the edge of the pool when the water is stirred so he can be made well, and he assumes Jesus is offering to do that. The irony is that Jesus is fully capable of healing without the pool, but the man does not understand this. He only knows of one method of possible healing—the pool—and assumes Jesus is going to help him to it. Under this scenario, then, his answer makes perfect sense—in case Jesus is not familiar with the workings of the pool, the man hurriedly fills him in. Everything the man says is requisite information for anyone intending to assist him—he has to be helped to the edge of the pool when it is stirred, and he has to get there quickly, before anyone else does.[26]

In terms of the narrative, this is the best interpretation of the conversation. Jesus is offering to heal the man, but the man misunderstands him, or only understands him partly. It is a great instance of dramatic irony: Jesus, the one who is able to heal the man entirely on his own and instantly, is standing before him, but the man sees Jesus only as someone who could possibly help him to the pool's edge in time to be healed. It is a classic Johannine case of a character misunderstanding because he thinks in physical rather than spiritual terms. And this is perhaps the most compelling argument in favor of this reading for it positions this passage as part of the larger "misunderstanding" motif that is an important and widely-recognized device of the Fourth Evangelist,[27] although this instance has been

24. Cf. Keener, *Gospel*, 1.635ff.
25. Witkamp, "Use, 24."
26. Thomas, "Stop Sinning," 9; Witkamp, "Use," 24.
27. Thomas, "Stop Sinning," 10; Witkamp, "Use," 24. Other ironic misunderstandings are found in 2:19–21; 3:3–5; 4:10–15, 32–34; 8:21–23; 11:11–13, 23–26.

often overlooked by scholars or obscured by an inadequate interpretation of Jesus' question to the man in v. 7.[28]

Jesus then makes his meaning clear to the man by simply commanding him to take up his mat and walk (v. 8). The man obeys and is healed. The actual means of healing is not disclosed. It appears that the picking up of the mat was integral to the healing process because it required that the man demonstrate faith—the action was not only confirmation of his healing but also the means of his cure; the picking up of the mat is otherwise not essential to the miracle part of the story. Jesus could just as easily have said, "You are healed" and gone on his way. However, the man's actions do become a very important plot point in what is to come.

Up to this point the narrative has been a fairly basic miracle story seemingly designed to demonstrate Jesus' supernatural knowledge of people and his healing abilities. Therefore, readers might feel a bit disoriented when they get to verse 9b: "The day on which this took place was a Sabbath." There has previously been no mention of the Sabbath by the characters or narrator, or any indication that anything remotely negative has happened. The story seems perfectly complete with the statement in v. 9a: "At once the man was cured; he picked up his mat and walked." However, with the addition of this new information in v. 9b, the story takes a serious turn in another direction.[29] Instantly a negative tension is introduced: Jesus has broken Jewish law by healing on the Sabbath, as has the healed man, by carrying his mat.

Interpreters debate what drove the author to hold off this valuable piece of information until after the narration of the miracle. The Synoptic stories of Jesus healing on the Sabbath invariably mention the Sabbath near the beginning of the narrative, before the healing occurs.[30] It's possible to see in v. 9b the mark of clumsy editing of traditional sources: the author used the Sabbath reference as a crude transition from the healing miracle to the Sabbath controversy that follows it, which may not originate in the same context as the healing narrative but has been spliced together with it by the author. However, narrative examinations of the passage have found ways of explaining the author's rationale in terms of intentional narrative

---

28. This passage is not discussed in the major works on misunderstanding in the Fourth Gospel, e.g., Leroy, *Rätsel*; and D.A. Carson, "Understanding."

29. Staley, *Stumbling*, 59.

30. Mark 3:1–6; Luke 6:6–11; 13:10–17; 14:1–6; cf. Matt 12:1–12; Mark 2:23–28; Luek 6:1–5.

creation without resorting to a conclusion based on form, source or redaction critical methods.[31] The author may have intended to surprise the audience with this information, which requires them to view the previous miracle story in a very different light.[32] No longer is it a simple healing narrative; the knowledge that it took place on a Sabbath adds a new layer of subtext that would not have been present on first reading.

The healed man is now caught by the Jewish authorities carrying his mat on the Sabbath, a clear violation of Sabbath law (v. 10). They question him and he explains that the man who healed him had commanded him to take up the mat.[33] When the authorities ask who had healed him (v. 12), the man cannot tell them because he knows nothing of Jesus' identity; Jesus had slipped away before the man could question him (v. 13). Then, without warning, the scene shifts from the man's confrontation with the authorities to Jesus finding him in the temple sometime later (v. 14). This leads us to the two final, and perhaps, most perplexing dilemmas raised by this passage: the riddle of Jesus' final words to the healed man in v. 14, and the man's behavior in v. 15. In v. 14, when Jesus encounters the man again in the temple, he says to him, rather cryptically, "See, you are well again. Stop sinning or something worse may happen to you."

This is a puzzling command since neither sin nor faith has been mentioned anywhere in the narrative thus far. Unlike some other recorded miracles of Jesus, the man does not profess faith in Jesus as a prerequisite to healing (cf. Matt 9:20–22; 15:22–28; Mark 5:25–34; 10:46–52; Luke 8:43–48; 18:35–43), nor does Jesus indicate that his physical cure was accompanied by the forgiveness of sins (cf. Matt 9:2–8; Mark 2:1–12; Luke 5:17–26). From the standpoint of the narrative, it would seem that Jesus' command in v. 14 is somehow related to the man's encounter with the Jewish authorities in the previous verses for it is not until after this event that Jesus feels the need to warn the man about his spiritual fate (e.g., "something worse may happen to you."—v. 14).

In what way could the man have been 'sinning?' He didn't originally give the authorities any information about the identity of his healer that could get Jesus into trouble. But immediately after this conversation, he

31. For a reading of this passage as an example of "unstable irony" and the effects of such a device on the audience, cf. Thatcher, "Sabbath Trick," 53–77.

32. E.g., Asiedu-Peprah, *Sabbath*, 66; Thatcher, "Sabbath Trick," 58–61.

33. Is this another possible indication that the healing itself was dependent upon the man obeying Jesus' command? Otherwise why would the man have risked censure for what he surely knew was a Sabbath violation?

does go back to the authorities to tell them who Jesus is (v. 15). This has been interpreted as an act of rebellion, betrayal, cowardice, or all three.[34] Why would he turn in the man who had done such a great thing for him if he didn't have to?[35] However, we don't have to assume that the man had sinister or self-serving motives. In light of Jesus' discourse about his work on the Sabbath which follows (vv. 17–24), it is possible to view the man's actions in a positive light.

Staley suggests that the man's "sin," which Jesus warns him to stop, is his failure to testify to the identity of Jesus before the Jewish authorities.[36] Jesus is not interested in hiding his identity, as he often is in the Synoptics.[37] In John he is generally very willing for people to know that he is from above, one with the Father, sent by the Father, etc., as the revelation of his identity is a major goal of the Gospel. Therefore, it is possible that Jesus wanted the man to serve as a witness (another major theme in John) to his identity and healing abilities. The man testified to the healing abilities, but by not naming Jesus, did not carry out the other half of the mission. Therefore, Jesus' warning for him to "stop sinning" drives him back to the authorities to tell them who Jesus is.

In revealing this information to the authorities, the man may also have been arguing that Jesus' identity gave him the right to heal on the Sabbath. Because he now knows who Jesus is, he knows something about his relationship to the Father. Jesus is about to begin a discourse on how his relationship to the Father means that he has authority to work on the Sabbath just as the Father does. The man's "testimony" to the authorities may be seen as a prelude into this theme. The man tells the authorities about Jesus' identity not to get him in trouble, but to justify why his healing on the Sabbath was legitimate. Because it was Jesus, it was alright because he has a special relationship to the Father. Staley summarizes it thusly:

> In his final narrated sentence, the healed man may unequivocally be making the case for the charismatic healer's authority over and above Torah authority—this time supplying the name of the healer in the hope that his interrogators will be impressed. Perhaps he is

---

34. Morris, *Gospel*, 271–73.

35. Note that the authorities have apparently stopped questioning him and let him go as in v. 14 he is found on his own at the temple. It doesn't appear that he was in immediate danger or under serious pressure to reveal Jesus' identity; he does it voluntarily.

36. Staley, "Stumbling," 62–64.

37. Matt 8:4; 12:16; 16:20; 17:9; Mark 1:44; 3:12; 7:36; 8:30; 9:9; Luke 5:14; 8:56; 9:21.

BETHESDA AND SILOAM

not a tattle-tale, but a character who serves in his own way, with his own theological argument, as a faithful witness to the sign performed.[38]

This interpretation not only makes sense of the actions of Jesus and the man in vv. 14–15, but also places this passage firmly into the larger themes of witness and revelation of identity that are of paramount importance in the Gospel. This also works as an example of not "replacing" the law, but rather, supplementing it. After all, healing the lame (along with the blind) was a sign of the eschatological age to come as predicted by Israel's prophets (Isa 35:6; Jer 31:8; Mic 4:6–7; Zeph 3:19). Ironically Jesus is both fulfilling and replacing the Jewish understanding of the law at the same time; he proves that as the son of God he has the right, even the duty, to work on the Sabbath as his father is working, regardless of the law. At the same time he subtly shows that he is fulfilling the law (and the prophets) by performing some specific signs related to the eschatological kingdom that had been long expected.

Now that we have looked at some of the major critical issues in the passage, we will turn to an examination of the themes of water and identity and how they interact. One of the most striking things about water in this passage is its relative unimportance to the action of the narrative. Unlike the water in the stories of John's baptizing in chs. 1 and 3, the wedding at Cana in ch. 2, or the conversation with the woman at the well in ch. 4, the water of the pool of Bethesda is never "used" either physically or metaphorically in this passage. In fact, aside from the mention of the pool as the setting for the story in v. 2 and the man's reference to it as a possible agent of healing in v. 7, the waters play no significant role in the narrative, as they will do in Ch. 9. Moreover, the pool is never referenced by Jesus nor connected in any specific way (outside of the scribal interpolation) with Yahweh.[39] Keener perhaps sums it up best by describing the waters of the pool as mere "stage props for the miracle."[40] It is likely for this reason that this passage is very often overlooked or intentionally ignored by critics dealing with the water imagery of the Gospel.

However, given that a large section of the chapter right before this (4:1–42) has also dealt significantly with water as a symbol, it seems that we cannot simply write off the water of the pool as totally incidental or

---

38. Staley, *Stumbling*, 63.
39. Koester, *Symbolism*, 90, 191.
40. Keener, *Gospel*, 1.638.

insignificant. It seems unlikely that an author with the literary skill of the Fourth Evangelist would randomly drop another reference to water into the narrative mix so soon unless the two were supposed to be understood as somehow related. One attempting a narrative or literary examination should at the very least be cautious in assuming that there is no connection without first examining the matter.

Since patristic times, some interpreters have detected a baptismal motif in this passage.[41] John 5:1–15 along with the story of Nicodemus in chapter 3 and the blind man in chapter 9 were the three great Johannine readings used to prepare candidates for baptism in the early church. However, as Brown has pointed out, this was likely not an intended focus of the author as the narrative does not support such an interpretation.[42] Not only does the mention of water seem incidental to the story, but the narrative emphasizes the Sabbath controversy much more than the healing itself. Then there is the simple fact that the lame man never enters the water. In fact, no character interacts with the water in any way. Additionally apart from the textual variation in vv. 3b-4, which credits "an angel of the Lord" with "stirring" the pool, there is no indication in the story that Yahweh or any other spiritual entity is at work through the waters of Bethesda. If the author intended a message about baptism, surely the water would have had a more prominent role and its connection with Yahweh, Christ or the Holy Spirit would have been more blatant.

When pressed to find a connection between Jesus and the water of the Pool in this story, most authors have interpreted Jesus as doing what the water cannot do: he performs the healing that the water cannot perform. However, this is not precisely accurate. Assuming the tradition of the pool's healing powers is reliable (and there is no reason to believe that people did not at least sometimes receive relief from various diseases at Bethesda) then the explanation of his continuing affliction has nothing to do with the water's efficacy. The real hindrance to healing is his inability to get into the water in time. The important point for the present study is not so much that Jesus does what the water could not do, but rather that Jesus accomplishes what the water could do *without the water*. It is a subtle but important distinction.

Interpreting this passage in light of what we learned about "living water" in chapter 4, we suggest that Jesus intentionally ignores the earthly

41 For more information cf. Brown, *Gospel*, 1.211.
42. Ibid.; also Jones, *Symbol*, 135–36.

waters of the pool because they are of no use to him. The one who can provide "living water" from within himself (4:10–14; 7:37–39) is not dependent on any other source.[43] That which he gives (from the father, from above, ch. 3) is efficacious for healing and salvation. So, in essence, he did heal the man using water—the metaphorical "living water" that comes from his person which later will be identified with the Spirit (7:37–39). The water that Jesus offers is effective even for those who cannot avail themselves of it on their own. It is not a matter of the one who can best help himself being healed. In fact, Jesus may have sought out this particular paralytic precisely because he knew that he was unable to help himself to healing. So, God may at times work directly through the pool, as folklore attested, but in this instance he works through his son Jesus Christ, the one whom he sent.

There is a bit of irony here which also often goes unnoticed. As mentioned above the Pool of Bethesda was mostly likely part of a healing shrine in which some sort of deity was considered to be active. If this is true, then the fact that Jesus walked into such a place and boldly healed the man without assistance from the water associated with the deity is both ironic and an important statement about his identity. If Bethesda is associated with the cult of a pagan god, then this statement is even more significant: Jesus is more powerful than the pagan god who can only heal through the waters of the pool when they are stirred. Jesus can heal without an intermediary. Seen this way, then, this passage also becomes part of the greater "replacement" motif of the Gospel.[44] Jesus not only "replaces" the rites and rituals of Judaism, but also proves himself superior to pagan gods and the symbols of their cults.

"THAT GOD'S WORKS MIGHT BE REVEALED IN HIM": HEALING AT THE POOL OF SILOAM (9:1–41)

Water, Identity, and Revelation in 9:1–41

The narrative of Jesus' healing of the man born blind in John 9:1–41 is one of the longest in the Gospel. Much has been written concerning the background and interpretation of this passage.[45] Here we will limit our

---

43. Culpepper, *Anatomy*, 138.
44. E.g., Burge, "Revisiting."
45. For a sample see Beasley-Murray, *Gospel*, 148–62; Brown, *Gospel*, 1.369–82; Jones, *Symbol*, 161–76; Keener, *Gospel*, 1.775–94.

remarks to elements of the narrative that impact the relationship of water and identity. The story has many obvious similarities with the healing of the paralytic in chapter 5. Both scenes play out on a background of pools of water and take place on a Sabbath, in both cases the healed man is confronted by Jewish authorities demanding to know who had healed him, and both stories end with Jesus meeting with the man one-on-one and revealing his identity.

However, there are differences as well. Unlike the story of the paralytic, the story of the blind man is preceded by a theological setup. We are told that Jesus and his disciples pass a man "blind from birth." The narrator imparts this information to the audience, but how the characters learn about the man's affliction we are never told. That the man was blind would be obvious to anyone, but how did they know he had been that way since birth? Was it perhaps another instance of Jesus' omniscience? We don't know, but the disciples are clearly aware of the man's condition because they ask Jesus: "Rabbi, who sinned, this man or his parents, that he was born blind?" (v. 2). Such congenital infirmities, and particularly blindness, were often believed to be the result of sin, either on the part of the person or the parents.[46]

Jesus' response rejects this explanation in favour of an even deeper theological one: "'Neither this man nor his parents sinned,' said Jesus, 'but this happened so that the work of God might be displayed in his life. As long as it is day, we must do the work of him who sent me. Night is coming, when no one can work'" (vv. 3–4). So again we encounter the theme of God's work in the world through Jesus. In chapter 5 Jesus justified his healing on the Sabbath by appealing to his relationship with the Father, who was always working. Now he builds on this theme including the disciples (and, by extension, all of God's servants) in the work of the Lord. Note that v. 4 says, "*we* must do the work of him who sent me" whereas in ch. 5 Jesus only spoke of himself as working for the Father (5:17ff.).

Like the paralytic at Bethesda, this man has not requested Jesus' assistance; Jesus is once again the initiator of the healing. In fact, the author here doesn't even portray Jesus as asking the man whether he wants to be healed or not. He simply performs the act. The blind man doesn't speak in the narrative until v. 11, after the healing and the report of all the neighbors debating the legitimacy of the healing. In verse 6 Jesus "spit on the ground, made some mud with the saliva, and put it on the man's eyes." Saliva was

---

46. Brown, *Gospel*, 1.371; Keener, *Gospel*, 1.777–79.

commonly believed to have healing properties in the ancient world; there are examples in ancient folklore of saliva being combined with other ingredients to form a therapeutic substance.[47] The original audience of the miracle, as well as of the original story, would not have reacted to this with the type of hygienic bias that readers from the western world might today.

Next Jesus, somewhat surprisingly, orders the man to go and wash the mud off in the pool of Siloam. Despite this unusual instruction, the man obeys unquestioningly. Again, as in ch. 5, it appears that the action may have been the actual means of healing.[48] The man expresses his faith in actions rather than words. That it is not yet a fully-formed faith becomes clear as the narrative progresses: shortly after the miracle the formerly blind man referred to his healer as "the man they call Jesus" (v. 11). During his debate with the Pharisees Jesus is first "a prophet" (v. 17) and later "from God" (v. 33). Then, at Jesus' questioning in v. 38 the man finally declares his belief in Jesus as "the Son of Man." However, while his faith may not have been complete at the time of the actual healing, he believed enough in Jesus' words to take the actions that would lead to his healing. This was the first step on the road to truly understanding Jesus' identity.

And surely it is Jesus' identity that is at the core of this story, although the issue is presented in a slightly different way than it was in chapter 5. There, the healed man did not know either Jesus' physical identity (what his name was, where he could be found, etc.) or his "true" identity in terms of his relationship to the Father. However, in chapter 9 the formerly blind man knows Jesus' name (v. 11) and presumably could pick him out of a crowd if necessary. He knows his earthly identity, and by the end of his interrogation by the Pharisees seems to come to some understanding of his spiritual significance. At the very least he believes that Jesus may be a prophet and knows that he must be sent from God because "if this man were not from God he could do nothing" (v. 33). This distinction is echoed by a reverse dichotomy concerning the knowledge of the man's interrogators. In the ch. 5 narrative the authorities apparently do not doubt that the man has been healed, but focus their questions on the identity of his healer. In ch. 9, the authorities at first question whether the man has really been healed. They realize that if he really was healed, a valid case could more easily be made for Jesus' identity.

---

47. Keener, *Gospel*, 1.779–81.
48. Schnackenburg, *Gospel*, 2.242.

One might make a stronger argument for associating this passage with baptismal imagery than the healing in chapter 5. In this story the man does actually cleanse himself in water which is efficacious for healing by its association with Christ. And we find that as a result of the healing through water the man comes to understand who Jesus is and believe in him. Indeed, there is a robust history of this passage being used in baptismal liturgy.[49] Brown points out the connection made by some early Christian writers and church fathers between baptism and "enlightenment." The fact that this connection is at least partly based on the John 9 passage is made clear by the words of Tertullian: "The present work will treat of our sacrament of water which washes away the sins of our original blindness and sets us free unto eternal life."[50] This association between Jesus' opening of the man's eyes and the idea of the washing away of sins is only possible if one considers the waters of Siloam as associated with and empowered by Jesus himself.

Since the Pool of Siloam was instrumental in the healing in this chapter, it is crucial to know more about it when interpreting the story. The Pool of Siloam (Gk. Σιλωάμ; Heb. שלח) is located at the bottom of the eastern hill of Jerusalem.[51] It is fed by the waters of the Gihon spring, which are channeled into the pool by a canal.[52] The Hebrew root שלח means "to send," however, in OT usage it often has a decidedly hydraulic connotation. Watts notes that the verb in *piel* means specifically "to send water." He draws attention to the related Akkadian words *šalhu*, which means "water pipe," and *šilihtu*, meaning "water course."[53] Nehemiah 3:15 contains the related

49. For summary and discussion cf. Brown, *Gospel*, 1.380–82.

50. SC 35:64; Augustine makes a similar connection (*In Jo.* XLIV 1–2; PL 35:1713–14).

51. The location that for years was assumed to be the Pool of Siloam has recently become the center of scholarly attention due to the findings of excavations begun in 2004. These excavations uncovered the remains of a much larger pool to the south of the traditional site which appears to have been a large public *miqveh* and into which the water of the northern pool empties. The relationship of the two pools is a matter of open scholarly debate, but von Wahlde may be correct in seeing the northern pool as an *otzer* for the southern pool, which allowed the non-living (and therefore ritually impure) water of the southern pool to come into contact with flowing ("living") water from the Gihon spring and therefore be considered ritually clean again, a requirement for waters of a *miqveh* or that used in the water festival at the festival of Booths. For description (including photos and diagrams) and discussion, cf. von Wahlde, "Siloam," 155–74.

52. For detailed discussion of the archeological evidence, see Adan, "Fountain," 92–100; Burge, "Revisiting"; Burrows, "Conduit," 226; Elitzur, "Siloam," 17–25; Issar, "Evolution," 130–36; Shaheen, "Tunnel," 107–12; Shanks, "Siloam," 16–23; von Wahlde, "Pool," 155–74.

53. Watts, *Isaiah*, 117.

Hebrew word הַשֶּׁלַח which refers to an aqueduct or conduit for water. So, even though we are told that the name "Siloam" means "sent" (v. 7), there is a sense in which this word was closely related to water imagery and may have conjured up the same in the minds of the original audience and later readers from a Jewish background.

HEALING WATERS AND THE ONE WHO SENDS IN PREVIOUS JEWISH LITERATURE

The first OT passage that might naturally come to mind when reading John 9 is the story of the healing of Naaman by the prophet Elisha in 2 Kings 5. There are a number of cogent parallels. Both men have long-term incurable diseases; both are given instructions that require them to immerse themselves in a body of water; both are cured as a result; and, perhaps most importantly for our study, both stories emphasize the fact that the man was "sent" to the water by the person mediating the healing. It is this last point that seems most significant for our purposes.

Both Elisha and Jesus effect the healing of their respective subjects indirectly, at a distance. Neither is actually present at the moment of the healing. This, of course, has been seen before in the Gospel of John; in 4:43–54 Jesus heals the official's son from afar, simply by giving the command and never actually seeing the boy. Naaman is persuaded to seek out the prophet Elisha by his wife's Israelite slave girl, supported by his master, the king of Aram. When he finally arrives at Elisha's house, the prophet does not meet or speak to him, but instead sends a servant with the message: "Go, wash yourself seven times in the Jordan, and your flesh will be restored and you will be cleansed" (5:10). Elisha doesn't interact with Naaman in any way until *after* the healing is completed.

Similarly, Jesus only has modest interaction with the blind man in John 9. Before sending him to wash in Siloam, Jesus does make mud and put it on the man's eyes. But the narrative makes it clear that the healing is not complete until the man washes in the pool, which happens at a distance from Jesus. In fact, the man never speaks to Jesus at all, neither to ask for healing (it was wholly instigated by Jesus) nor to question Jesus' curious instructions. The character doesn't speak at all in the narrative until after the healing when he answers his skeptical neighbors who don't believe he is the same man who used to beg. He doesn't see, talk to or otherwise interact with Jesus again until v. 36, well after his interrogation by the Pharisees.

A related element found in both stories is the transformation of normally innocuous water sources into places with therapeutic power. Unlike the Pool of Bethesda in John 5, neither the Jordan River nor the Pool of Siloam was necessarily renowned as a center of healing. The fact that Naaman initially refuses to consider immersing himself in the Jordan ("Are not Abana and Pharpar, the rivers of Damascus, better than any of the waters of Israel? Couldn't I wash in them and be cleansed?"—5:12) indicates that the Jordan was not known as a place of healing. If their waters had been proven effective for healing, surely the infirm of Judea would have flocked to them as they did to Bethesda, and Naaman would not have questioned Elisha's instructions. But neither story gives any indication that this is the case, nor is their outside evidence that the people thought of these water sources in this way.

Naaman or the blind man could have washed in these places a thousand times previously and never have been healed because their waters had no particular efficacy on their own; they are only turned into means of healing through the power of the person who "sends" the patient there. Avalos specifically notes this:

> The ritual that Elisha prescribes for Naaman . . . . consists of the repetition of an action a specific number of times. This is not unlike some of the prescriptions of Asclepius. The latter's prescriptions may not always appear to be the most obvious ones to use, but it was the fact that they were prescribed by Asclepius which was their reason for their supposed efficacy. Similarly, Elisha's prescription may not have been the expected one, but it was one that worked because it was the prophet of Yahweh who provided it.[54]

Likewise, while in John 5 we have an instance of water which is efficacious for healing but not needed by Jesus, in John 9 we have water which in and of itself is of no particular importance but gains its significance and abilities completely by its association with the person of Christ. The first story emphasizes the distinction between Jesus and the water while the latter assumes a connection between the two. Moreover, Jesus is only able to impart this power to the waters because of his own identity as the one who was "sent" from Yahweh and who now "sends." In this way the healing of the blind man in John 9 is completely intertwined with the issue of Jesus' identity.

---

54. Avalos, *Illness*, 264.

The final meeting between the healer and the healed is similar in both stories. After his healing, Naaman and his men return to Elisha to give thanks. In the course of this meeting, Naaman declares his new allegiance to the god of Israel (vv. 15–18). In similar fashion, Jesus and the formerly blind man meet up again in Jn 9:35, once again at the initiation of Jesus. They proceed to have a conversation which resonates with the echoes of Naaman's conversation with Elisha. "Do you believe in the Son of Man?" Jesus asks him. The man responds with eagerness: "Who is he, sir? Tell me so that I may believe in him" (vv. 35–36). Although the man has not instigated the meeting, he clearly has a fervent desire to prove his belief in the man whom he had so valiantly defended against the Pharisees. Jesus' revelation of himself as the Son of Man elicits the surely heartfelt response from the man, "Lord, I believe" (v. 38).[55]

The motives for the healing are also analogous. In Jn 9:3 Jesus indicates that the healing he is about to administer is for the purpose of revealing God's work in the man's life. Similarly, in 2 Kings 5:8 Elisha declares that Naaman should come to him for healing because then "he will know that there is a prophet in Israel." Then, immediately after he is healed, Naaman returns to Elisha and announces: "Now I know that there is no God in all the world except in Israel" (5:15) and he vows not to worship any other gods, except as required in his duty to his master (vv. 17–18). In both cases the healings result not only in a physical cure but also (and more importantly to John) in spiritual insight into the identity of the true God, in Naaman's case, and the "true" nature of the person of Jesus in John 9.

Of course, the man in Jn 9 is more faithful than Naaman for he never questions Jesus' order while Naaman is skeptical of Elisha's instructions to the point that his servants have to convince him to follow them. But this is just another example of the way in which the blind man in Jn 9 is designed as a deliberate contrast to those who do not believe in Christ (and, by extension, Yahweh). Also, in both cases, the story of the healing itself is set up almost as an object lesson to the healer's audience. In the case of Elisha, he invites Naaman to come to him for healing at least partly as a rebuke of the doubt of the King of Israel, to whom Naaman's master sent a letter requesting healing (2 Kgs 5:6–8). In John 9, Jesus' healing of the blind man is prompted by a theological question raised by his disciples about the relationship of sin and physical affliction. Jesus makes it clear that the man's

---

55. For discussion of the parallels between Jesus' signs in John and the miracles of Elisha cf. Bostock, "New Elisha," 39–41; Brodie, "Cracking," 39–42; Mayer, "Elijah," 171–73.

blindness, and by extension his subsequent healing, serve the purpose of revealing God's glory. In the first place, this revelation seems to be directed to the disciples themselves, and then later in the story, to the Pharisees. In the latter case it is significant that Jesus makes no mention of the forgiveness of sins, either before or after the healing, as he does in the chapter 5 story. He wants to demonstrate clearly to the disciples that this miracle is about something else entirely: his identity as the one who was "sent" from the Father.

CHAPTER SUMMARY AND CONCLUSIONS

The healings that Jesus effects at two different pools, Bethesda and Siloam, both lead to deep controversy about his identity. In the first narrative Jesus' identity as a miracle-worker is questioned because he healed on a Sabbath, something one from God would presumably not do. Jesus, however, counters with the argument that, indeed, one from God would naturally continue to do God's work on the Sabbath; as the Father never rests from doing good, so also will the one he sent do his work continually. Jesus doesn't use the waters of Bethesda in the actual healing of the man because he has no need to; he is capable of doing the Father's work even without them because he supplies water from within himself. As we saw in John 4, Jesus and the water are one and the same.

Jesus' identity again takes center stage in a very public debate after he heals the blind man through the waters of Siloam. In this case the waters of Siloam have no particular efficacy on their own, but become capable of providing healing because of their association with Jesus: the one who "sent" the blind man there. The similarities to the story of Elisha and Naaman in the Old Testament are intentional: the author of the Gospel casts Jesus in the role of Yahweh "the one who sends" the man to the pool and, therefore, reveals God's work in the man (9:3). The waters of Siloam gain their efficacy from their interaction (in this case, at a distance) with Jesus; the healing produced by this interaction serves as a sign to Jesus' true identity—it is the healing that touches off the identity controversy among the Jewish leaders. But the healing was only possible because of who Jesus was—the one who was "sent" by the Father and therefore had the power to "send," the one who can do nothing on his own but is totally dependent on the Father.

CHAPTER 6

The Water from Jesus' Side
Water and Identity in John 7 & 19

INTRODUCTION

There are two prominent appearances of water in the Fourth Gospel in relation to the identity of Jesus which we will consider together because of their complementary nature. In John 7, during the water ritual of the Feast of Tabernacles, Jesus speaks of "rivers of living water" which will flow out of his belly and out of all those who believe in him. In John 19, as Jesus dies on the cross, we find a literal representation of this metaphor as water and blood flow from Jesus' side after he is pierced with a soldier's lance. Because these two incidents employ such similar imagery, we shall treat them together in this chapter.

"OUT OF HIS BELLY WILL FLOW RIVERS OF LIVING WATER": JESUS AT THE FEAST OF TABERNACLES (JOHN 7:1–39)

Preliminary Discussion

Of the three "core symbols" of the Gospel of John identified by Culpepper (light, water, bread),[1] water is the only one which Jesus does not directly

---

1. Culpepper, *Anatomy*, 189.

connect himself to by means of an "I Am" statement.[2] The closest Jesus comes to saying, "I am the living water" happens in 7:37–38 when he says, "Let anyone who is thirsty come to me, and let the one who believes in me drink." He then goes on to make a declaration about rivers of living water which will flow from either himself or the one who believes in him. Jesus makes this pronouncement against the background of the water libation ritual which was part of the Jewish celebration Sukkoth, the Feast of Tabernacles. Since Jesus deliberately plays off of the imagery of this festival to make his point, it is important for us to understand its major thematic and symbolic elements.

Background of the Water Libation at Feast of Tabernacles

New Testament scholars have long recognized the significance of the context of Jesus' speech in this passage: the culminating water ritual of the Feast of Tabernacles (cf. 7:2). This ritual is not mentioned in the OT, but is detailed in the Mishnah (*m. Sukkoth*). It is generally believed to have evolved as part of the Tabernacles festival in the intertestamental period.[3] It was apparently a well-established practice by the time of the Mishnah, so it is not surprising that it would have been observed during the NT period.[4]

Both Jewish and non-Jewish sources stress that the Feast of Tabernacles was celebrated with special ceremony.[5] It also seems to have been one of the most joyful of the feasts and particularly beloved by the people.[6] The distinguishing feature of this festival was the ritual in which water was drawn from the pool of Siloam and then marched in procession up to the temple. Once there, the priests would pour out the water into one of two pipes at the base of the altar—the other was for wine. Part of the purpose

---

2. Cf. 6:35, 48: "I am the bread of life"; and 8:12; 9:5: "I am the light of the world." Also cf Koester, *Symbolism*, 156.

3. For detailed discussion of the Scriptural and rabbinic evidence for Tabernacles and its evolution from OT to rabbinic times, cf. MacRae, "Meaning," 251–76. Cf. also Malina and Rohrbaugh, *Social-Science*, 140–41.

4. The tradition of illumination associated with this festival was likewise a later addition (cf., MacRae, "Meaning," 273). It is perhaps significant that Jesus associates himself with the two "newest" symbols of the festival.

5. 2 Macc. 10:6–9; Jos. *Ant.* VIII, 100; Plutarch, *Quaestiones Convivales* IV, 6.

6. *M. Sukkah* chs. 4–5; 2 Macc. 10:7; Safrai, "Temple," 865–907 (894–95); For an examination of this festival in the Johannine context as a product of "social memory" cf. Spaulding, *Commemorative*.

of this ritual was to secure rain as the feast took place immediately before the rainy season. Prayer for rain was an important part of the festival, and there is evidence that at least some believed that the water libation at the feast brought on the rains.[7]

We know much about how this water ritual was carried out. On each of the seven mornings of the festival a procession of priests and the people travelled to the Gihon spring, which supplied to waters to the pool of Siloam. There a priest filled a golden pitcher with water, as the people recited Isa 12:3: "With joy you will draw water from the wells of salvation." Then the procession went up to the Temple through the Water Gate. The accompanying crowds carried the symbols of the festival, the *lulab*, a bunch of myrtle and willow twigs tied with palm, and the *ethrog*, a lemon or citron signifying the harvest. They also sang the Hallel psalms (113–118). When they reached the altar in front of the Temple, they proceeded around it waving the *lulabs* and singing Ps 118:25. Then the priest went up the ramp to the altar to pour the water into a silver funnel whence it flowed into the ground. On the seventh day this ritual was repeated 7 times.[8] The water flowing through the pipe into the ground was believed to proceed into an underground spring which flowed into the great "deep" under the earth to which the temple mount gave special access.[9]

The symbolism of the water libation had its roots in the bringing forth of water from the rock in the wilderness (Ex 17:1–7; Num 20:1–13). Since Tabernacles was a festival which remembered the years of wandering in the desert, it makes sense that the water from the rock incident, one of the highlights of the wilderness narratives, would have a special place in the people's collective memory and commemoration at this celebration. But the ritual came to be more than a remembrance of God's past provision; it was also an anticipation of God's coming work expected at the end of the age. Just as the OT prophets had transformed the image of the water from the rock in the wilderness into a signifier of the blessings to come in Yahweh's earthly kingdom,[10] so did the NT Jews allow the water ritual to represent their eschatological expectations. Yet the author of the Gospel plays even more deftly with these hopes. By having Jesus stand up in the midst

---

7. Brown, *Gospel*, 1.326–27; MacRae, "Meaning," 265; Safrai, "Temple," 2.899.
8. Brown, *Gospel*, 1.327.
9. Safrai, "Temple," 882.
10. A particularly frequent metaphor in Isaiah. See Isa 30:25; 32:20; 33:21; 35:6; 41:18; 43:19; 44:3; 66:12; also Ezek 47:1–12; Amos 5:24.

of this water festival and declare himself to be the source of the living water expected in the end times, John is declaring that the hopes of the people represented in the ritual were not relegated to some distant future; rather, they were being fulfilled right in their midst! The eschatological kingdom was not only coming but was already here in the person of Jesus Christ, the source of all blessings.

Water, Identity, and Revelation in John 7:1–39

There are several challenging interpretive issues surrounding this passage, which is evidenced by the large amount of scholarly comment throughout the years. The issues fall into three major categories: 1) the source of the quotation in v. 38; 2) the proper punctuation of vv. 37–38; 3) the source of the water in v. 38. In reality however, as Knapp points out, the last two issues are so intricately linked that it is difficult to deal with them as discrete entities;[11] therefore, we will discuss the two together. Due to the intense interest in this subject through the centuries we cannot hope to do justice to the scope of the scholarly material here, but will limit our discussion to the most popular theories.[12]

The Source and OT Background of Jesus' Proclamation

We will begin with what is, relatively speaking, the easiest of the three questions about these verses: what passage of Scripture is cited in v. 38? These words as quoted do not exactly match any extant Scripture passage either in the MT or the LXX, and so commentators have been frustrated in their search for an answer. Since no direct equivalent to Jesus' words can be found, it has been proposed that he is not quoting a particular passage, but rather calling up the general image of water as a source of life that is found throughout Jewish history, thought and literature. There are many such

---

11. Knapp, "Messianic," 113.

12. The following is a non-exhaustive list of sources which discuss the exegetical issues of this passage: Balabanski, "Let Anyone," 132–39; Beasley-Murray, *John*, 112–17; Brown, *Gospel*, 1.319–29; Daise, "Texture," 687–99; Fee, "Once More," 116–18; Freed, *Quotations*, 21–38; Hodges, "Rivers," 239–48; Jones, *Symbol*, 150–57; Keener, 1.721–30; Kilpatrick, "Punctuation," 340–42; Knapp, "Messianic"; Kuhn, "St. John," 63–65; Lightfoot, *St. John's Gospel*, 183–86; Marcus, "Rivers," 328–30; Menken, "Origin," 160–75; Smith, *John*, 174–76. Naturally the exegetical difficulties are also a topic of discussion in most commentaries on the passage.

connections that can be made. Some have found a correlation between Jesus' words and the water that Moses brought from the rock (Ex 17:1–7; Num 20:1–13; also Ps 78:15–16, 20; Isa 48:21), which is also associated with the flask in which the water from Siloam was carried at the Tabernacles water festival. This event would almost certainly have been on the minds of the people during this feast since Sukkoth had such deep connections with the traditions of their Jewish ancestors in the wilderness (Neh 9:15–20).

However, there are many other passages that may be associated with this statement by allusion. The mention of flowing water, particularly if one believes it to originate with Jesus, may have triggered memories of Ezekiel 47:1–12 where the healing waters flow from the temple in Jerusalem to revitalize the surrounding landscape. Earlier in the Gospel the narrator explicitly equated Jesus' body with the Jerusalem Temple (2:21). In Jeremiah Yahweh rebukes his people for abandoning him "the spring of living water" (Jer 2:13; 17:13) and Jer 17:13 states that those who turn away from the "spring of living water" [the Lord] will be "written in the dust."[13] Additionally, by inviting people to come and drink from him Jesus echoes the words of Yahweh in Isaiah 55:1: "Come, all you who are thirsty, come to the waters," and also recalls Isaiah 12:3, the verse that was traditionally recited when the waters were drawn from the Pool of Siloam at the Sukkoth water festival—"With joy you will draw water from the wells of salvation." Any or all of these verses may have been in the mind of Jesus (and the author) when he made his declaration. So, in this particular case it is best to view the words "as the Scripture has said" (καθὼς εἶπεν ἡ γραφή) as directing the hearer's minds to the larger constellation of previous stream/river imagery in the OT rather than as a rigid formula signifying the utterance of a direct Scriptural quotation.

The Punctuation of 7:37–38 and the Source of the Water in v. 38

Since the issues of the proper way to punctuate vv. 37–38 and the identity of the person from whose belly the water will flow are so intricately related we shall discuss the two together.

---

13. This phrase has a remarkable echo in the story of the woman caught in adultery, which immediately follows this passage, where Jesus writes in the dirt (8:6b, 8). Indeed, the Jeremiah reference may be the basis upon which the *pericope adulterae* was positioned where it is in John's Gospel, which is clearly not original to the text.

There is a long-standing debate over the proper punctuation and, hence, the proper interpretation, of vv. 37–38. The arguments fall traditionally into two camps, those who hold to punctuation which implies that the streams of water flow from the believer, and scholars who argue for an alternate punctuation which allows for Christ himself to be the source. They break down as follows:

> Interpretation A (Traditional):
> If anyone thirst, let him come to me and drink.
> He who believes in me, as the Scripture has said, streams of living water shall flow from within him [the believer].
>
> Interpretation B:
>
> If anyone thirst let him come to me; and let him drink who believes in me.
>
> As the Scripture has said, streams of living water shall flow from within him [usually interpreted as Christ].

The punctuation difference comes down to either placing a comma after πρός με and a period after εἰς ἐμέ, or placing a period after πινέτω and a comma after εἰς ἐμέ. This affects the relationship of "ὁ πιστεύων εἰς ἐμέ" to the rest of the verse and therefore impacts the interpretation of vv. 37–38. Is it intended to be the beginning of the new clause and the person about whom the Scripture has spoken (A), which makes καθὼς εἶπεν ἡ γραφή a nominative absolute referring to ὁ πιστεύων εἰς ἐμέ? Or, should ὁ πιστεύων εἰς ἐμέ be seen as in parallel to the person who thirsts and not necessarily related to the source of the water (B)? The "traditional" or "Eastern" interpretation (A) was supported by Origen and most of the Eastern Fathers.[14] Modern commentators who favor this reading include Barrett, Bernard, Cortes, and Lightfoot. It represents the primary reading of most English translations including the KJV, NIV and NASB. The best textual argument for this punctuation is that it is found in p[66] from the 2nd century. One grammatical argument in its favor is that it makes the participle ὁ πιστεύων ("he who believes") the head of a new construction (a pattern found 41

---

14. Brown suggests the reason for the Eastern fathers' insistence on this interpretation was theological rather than exegetical. Because the water in vv. 37–38 is directly equated with the Spirit in v. 39, they would be hesitant to see the waters as flowing from Christ due to the controversy over the procession of the Holy Spirit in the Trinity. If the water and Spirit were equated and the water proceeded from Jesus, then the Spirit would be said to proceed from Jesus as well. Therefore, they were possibly theologically inclined away from the christological interpretation. Brown, *Gospel*, 1.329.

times elsewhere in John), rather than tacking it on to the previous conditional sentence (a practice not elsewhere seen in John).[15]

However, interpretation B is of equal (or possibly greater) antiquity, going back at least to Justin in the 2nd century. Other early support is found in Tertullian, Cyprian, and Irenaeus. Modern scholars who accept this Western or "christological" interpretation include: Brown, Boismard, Braun, Bultmann, Dodd, Hoskyns, Jeremias, Macgregor, Mollat, Stanley. It has gained critical support in recent years, as is indicated by its inclusion as the primary punctuation in the text of the NRSV translation (see below). The following arguments may be advanced for the christological interpretation: (1) it creates poetic parallelism in the first two lines: the thirsty man in line one comes to Jesus, and the believer in line two drinks from Jesus. Viewing this as a chiasm would bring it in line with Johannine style elsewhere; (2) The idea that water will flow from Jesus is supported by 19:34, where it comes from his side; (3) Another Johannine work,[16] Rev 22:1, shows a river of living water flowing from the throne of God and of the Lamb (i.e., Christ); (4) According to 7:39 the water is the Spirit, and for John it is Jesus who gives the Spirit (19:30;[17] 20:22).

The traditional understanding (A) assumes that v. 38b—"As the Scriptures have said, 'Out of his belly shall flow rivers of living water'"—represents the direct words of Christ, with the editor's comment beginning in v. 39. If this supposition is true, then it seems unlikely that ἐκ τῆς κοιλίας αὐτοῦ could refer to Jesus' own belly since that would require an unnatural change from the first person pronoun ἐμέ to the third αὐτοῦ. It would be out of character for Jesus to refer to himself in the third person even if he were directly quoting from the Scripture, which it appears he is not. Instead, it is assumed that he is referring to "the believer," who is the most natural antecedent in of the word αὐτοῦ in this context.

Conversely, scholars who argue for interpretation B referring to Christ as the source of waters often do so on the assumption that v. 38b is an aside by the editor and not the words of Christ himself. In this theory the words of Christ end with καὶ πινέτω ὁ πιστεύων εἰς ἐμέ ("let him drink who believes

---

15. Brown, *Gospel*, 1.329.

16. A discussion of the authorship of Revelation is outside the scope of this work. But we believe that regardless of the actual hand(s) that composed the book it was clearly influenced by Johannine theology, imagery and language and therefore can be considered "Johannine" even if it did not originate with the same person/people who composed the Gospel of John.

17. Coloe, "Raising," 56.

in me"). Everything after that, including v. 38b and 39, is from the editor. Adopting this punctuation allows for more flexibility in the interpretation of αὐτοῦ in v. 38b. If the "quotation" is not directly spoken by Christ but, rather, a scriptural application by the narrator to clarify Jesus' comment about the source of living water, then the αὐτοῦ may be seen as referring to Christ (although this understanding of the word is not required, as we will see below). These are the two most popular views about the punctuation and interpretation of this passage.

However, a third reading is offered in the NRSV translation which essentially adopts the punctuation of view B with the understanding of view A. It reads: "Let anyone who is thirsty come to me, and let the one who believes in me drink. As the scripture has said, 'Out of *the believer's* heart shall flow rivers of living water'" (7:37b–38, emphasis added). This represents an interesting attempt to combine the two views listed above. It allows the interpreter to assume the punctuation which seems more consonant with Johannine style (Punctuation B) and still assert that the αὐτοῦ in the citation refers to the believer rather than Christ (Interpretation A), which to some seems a more natural reading within the Johannine theology. In this view, v. 38b could come from either Jesus or the editor as both would have referred to the believer in the third person.

Despite centuries of work by the world's best scholars on this subject a consensus about which of these interpretations is best has never been reached, and it seems that historical critical methods of examination have left the debate at a stalemate.[18] Jones summarizes the situation well: "Absolute certainty about which of these readings to consider the most reliable is unattainable because each one makes both good sense and Johannine sense."[19] This is where literary, narrative and intertextual methods may shed light on an issue that cannot be completely clarified through more traditional means. Brown, for one, does attempt something of a literary understanding of this passage by comparing it to other water passages in the Gospel.[20] However, his conclusion that the christological interpretation (B) must be correct because there is no parallel in John for the idea of living water flowing from the believer ignores or overlooks what happens in chapter 4 between Jesus and the woman of Samaria. Specifically, it doesn't deal with 4:14 where Jesus says that the living water he will give will become

---

18. Fee, "Once More," 116.
19. Jones, *Symbol*, 153.
20. Brown, *Gospel*, 1.320–21.

The Water from Jesus' Side

"within you" (meaning the woman, and all readers by extension) a spring of living water welling up to eternal life.

Brown dismisses any reading of this verse that interprets the believer, the one in whom the fountain of living water dwells, as a source of water for others. Jesus is the only source, in his view; the believer is simply on the receiving end. And in a literal sense he is correct; Jesus does not directly state anything about what happens to the water that "wells up" in the believer. However, to dismiss the notion that those who receive living water also go on to become conduits of it to others ignores *the rest of the story in chapter 4*. The first thing the woman of Samaria does after receiving the "water" from Jesus is to go and share that water with her fellow villagers. Yes, she brings them to Jesus to receive it, but in a sense she also has shared it with them herself. The water Jesus provides flows through her to those around them. This does not make her the ultimate source of the water; Brown is quite right about that. However, it does make her a secondary source, a conduit, through which the water flows from the original fountain (Christ) to those around him.

Therefore, Brown's theory should be rejected, as should any understanding of 7:37–39 which does not make room for water flowing from the believer in some fashion. There is other support for this idea in John, and, furthermore, in OT imagery as well (see section on the OT background of this passage below). More importantly, it fits well with the author's penchant for ambiguity in language and in his desire to bring diverse metaphors into a larger, coherent image. Indeed, we would propose that the author of the Gospel deliberately left the antecedent of αὐτοῦ ambiguous. As we have seen, the author elsewhere intentionally uses ambiguity in language to force the reader to bring together two divergent ideas into a coherent whole. The same thing may be happening here, only this time the ambiguity occurs in the punctuation and grammar rather than in language.

This understanding helps us see the ambiguous statement of Jesus in 7:37–38 more clearly. The interpreter does not have to choose between two options for the source of the rivers of living water; Jesus, the original source, grants this water to those who believe who, in turn, become another source of this water. This interpretation is echoed in the editorial comment of v. 39, which equates the water with the Spirit "which believers in him were to receive; for as yet there was no Spirit." Even the Spirit would be a gift, originating from Jesus and handed down to his disciples who would then also be sources.[21]

Previously in the Gospel we have seen examples of water coming both from Christ and from the believer. But these are just two halves of an incomplete image. In 7:37–39 the author brings these two halves together to form a whole: Christ's picture of the waters as pouring forth in rivers from the believer. This does not, of course, indicate that the believer is the origin of the water, but that the believer is a mediator of it to others. The ultimate origin remains the One whom the Meribah rock and the Feast foreshadowed—the Messiah. The words of Jesus thus foresee the believer as an intermediate source through whom the living waters will flow.

One might object to this understanding saying that the author surely does not intend to have the subject of the drinking also be the source of the out-flowing waters. However, if one adopts an understanding of the believer as the conduit through which water flows from Christ to others, this picture works. The believer is *at the same time* a drinker and a channel; as the believer receives, so does the believer give.

Identity Issues in 7:1–39

The question of Jesus' identity in John 7 is not only brought up by his proclamation in 7:37–39, but is a recurring theme throughout the entire Tabernacles narrative. Chapter 7 begins with the narrator informing the audience that Jesus is now avoiding Judea because there were those among the Jewish authorities who wanted to kill him. However, the approaching Festival of Tabernacles creates something of a dilemma for him. As one of the yearly festivals which all Jewish males were expected to attend, Jesus would be forced to make his way to Jerusalem. Indeed, his brothers urge him to go up to the festival with them so that his disciples might see his miracles (7:3): "No one who wants to become a public figure acts in secret. Since you are doing these things, show yourself to the world" (v. 4). But Jesus is uninterested in becoming a public figure, not because he doesn't

---

21. The problem with this view is how to harmonize it with John 20:22, where Jesus breathes the Spirit on his disciples. Was the Spirit given twice? However, see Coloe's argument for 19:30 "[Jesus] bowed his head and gave up his spirit" meaning that Jesus "handed over" or "handed down" his spirit. She makes a distinction between the "constitutive" gift of the spirit from the cross, "drawing believers into Jesus' own divine Sonship" and the later "ministerial" function which focuses on the disciples' relationship to the world. Coloe, "Raising," 56; cf. also Heil, *Blood and Water*.

want to be known, but because the timing is not right (vv. 6, 8). He knows his identity will eventually be revealed, but wants it to be on the Father's timetable, not anyone else's (cf. 2:4).

When he does eventually go to the feast, he does so incognito (v. 10). The Jewish authorities are on the lookout for him, knowing he must show himself in Jerusalem eventually (v. 11). Once again we are told that the crowds are divided on the issue of Jesus' character, with some believing he was a good man, and others saying he misled the people (v. 12). So, the story begins with Jesus being both hidden (unidentifiable from a physical standpoint) and misunderstood (improperly identified in terms of his character). This beginning must be seen in stark contrasting irony to the act that Jesus takes in 7:37–39 where he very publicly presents himself for all to see and clearly proclaims his identity utilizing the imagery of the festival.

Halfway through the festival Jesus comes out of hiding and starts teaching in the Temple. As a result of his statements there, the issue of his identity is once again raised by the crowd. At first they marvel that he is speaking so openly since the Jews are seeking to kill him, and also express surprise that the Jews have not yet confronted him. This causes some to believe that the Jews had concluded he really was the Christ (vv. 25–26). However, some in the crowd are doubtful because, "we know where this man is from; when the Christ comes, no one will know where he is from." This reads as supreme irony in light of Jesus' earlier efforts to avoid detection while in Jerusalem. He answers this charge by agreeing that, yes, they do know him and know where he is from. However, in another instance of misunderstanding, Jesus is talking about having come from the Father, while the crowd was referring to his hometown (vv. 28–29). As a result of this statement, they (either crowd or the authorities, it is unclear) "sought to seize him but no one laid a hand on him because his time had not yet come" (v. 30). This is the second reminder in the passage that the revelation of Jesus' identity will come, but only when the Father wills (cf. v. 8). However, some did believe in his identity as the Christ (v. 31).

As a result of the murmurings of the crowds, perhaps as an attempt to avoid disquiet at the festival, the Jewish authorities send troops from the Temple guard to arrest Jesus (v. 32). This prompts more discourse from Jesus on his identity; this time, however, the focus is not on where he is from, but where he is going: "Jesus said, 'I am with you for only a short time, and then I go to the one who sent me. You will look for me, but you will not find me; and where I am, you cannot come'" (vv. 33–34). Again the statement about looking for him and not finding him must be viewed as ironic in light of his earlier disguise to avoid detection by the authorities. And, as before, this announcement prompts confusion among the listeners. They try to interpret him very literally, wondering where in the world he could go where no one would find him (vv. 35–36). This, then, is apparently what prompts Jesus to stand up on the "last and greatest day of the festival" and make his much-studied proclamation.

We must pause for a moment to consider the timing of Jesus' action. Which day is being referred to as the "last, the greatest day" of the feast? Was it the 7th day, the day in which the water ritual was enacted seven times instead of just one? Or does it refer to the extra day, the solemn day that was appended to the end of the feast in which the water ritual was not performed? For our purposes it makes little difference. Either way it is clear that Jesus was borrowing imagery from the water libation festival (and later from the image of the lamps which were left burning in the courtyard—8:12) to talk about his identity and purpose in the world. Establishing which of the days of the festival he chose to do this is not integral to this understanding. However, there certainly is more poetic and dramatic impact if one views Jesus as making his proclamation on the 7th day, as that was the day the priest drew water and brought it to the altar 7 different times. This was the climax of the entire festival and it would be particularly fitting (and, no doubt, especially shocking to his audience) for Jesus to choose that very moment to declare his position as the giver of the true "living" water. However, the idea of Jesus offering his "living" water on the last day, the one day in which the water ritual was not re-enacted at the temple, also has a certain amount of symbolic potential.

Jesus' intention in making his proclamation is to clarify his identity, thereby answering some of the questions proposed by the crowds about him. That he waits to do this until the day of the water festival is significant: he needed to put the statement of his identity within a context that his Jewish audience could understand. By bringing himself into alignment with what the Jews already understood about Yahweh and his role in protecting and preserving their ancestors in the wilderness, Jesus invites his audience to shift that understanding and identification to himself. We've already examined the Scriptural background of his invitation, which echoes that of Yahweh to his people in Isaiah 55:1. As we have detailed elsewhere, the Jews saw Yahweh himself as the one and only master of the waters, both the waters of the seas and oceans, and of springs, rivers and streams. Having control over these entities, even metaphorically, would equate one with Yahweh.

That some of the crowd understood his meaning is clear from their reaction. Some merely proclaimed him as a prophet (v. 40), but others maintained that he was the Christ (v. 41). This once again prompted a debate about his origin. The Christ did not come from Galilee, but from Bethlehem, from the line of David, some argued (vv. 41b-42). This is another example of supreme irony: Jesus was born in the city of David and only raised in Galilee. But, of course, the crowd doesn't know this, another instance of the Christ being "hidden" in plain sight. The pericope ends with the people "divided because of Jesus" (v. 43), the same state they are often in after an instance of Jesus' self-revelation in the Gospel (cf. 9:16, 10:19).

So, the issue of identity is a very important part of this entire passage. It is the theme which anchors the irony of the section: people think they know who Jesus is because they know where he is from, but they don't really know where he is from, nor do they know his true origin from the Father and therefore don't know his true identity. Likewise, they assume that Jesus couldn't possibly go somewhere that they couldn't find him when in reality he had been travelling incognito among them for several days. The water imagery is intricately and inextricably linked to this revelation of identity. It is confusion over his identity that prompts Jesus to make the statement about rivers of living water. Likewise, it is only after Jesus' water-related statement that some in the crowd begin to understand who he truly is, even though that belief is still tentative. For an understanding of how this statement gives insight into his true identity, we must review the Jewish background of the water image in this passage, which we will do later in this chapter.

Section Summary

In his proclamation at the Feast of Tabernacles, Jesus employs ancient language, images and connections that were deeply ingrained into the minds of his Jewish audience as being related to the person and character of Yahweh. When Jesus appropriates this language to refer to himself, he is making a profound statement about his role in God's salvific plan. He himself is the eschatological blessing long promised, foreseen by the prophets, come in the here and now. He is the one who, like Yahweh in the OT, will pour out the spirit like water on those who believe in him. He is the one who will make this water/spirit flow from himself through all believers. However, God's plan is not complete, and will only be finished with Jesus' death, a message that is surely present in the flow of water from Jesus' side on the cross (19:34). So, in many ways 7:37–39 can be seen as the prelude to the final and ultimate revelation of Christ's true identity in the Gospel. Here we see most clearly, through the use of water imagery, the pivotal importance of Jesus to God's goal of salvation of the entire world. However, that actual salvation will not be finally and fully completed until Jesus' glorification on the cross, which is, not coincidentally, the place in the narrative where the next and final water image appears.

"HE WHO SAW THIS HAS TESTIFIED SO THAT YOU ALSO MAY BELIEVE": BLOOD AND WATER FROM JESUS' SIDE (JOHN 19:31–39)

Preliminary Discussion

As Jesus is dying on the cross the Johannine narrative relates an event contained nowhere else in the Gospels. John 19:34 tells us that "one of the soldiers pierced his [Jesus'] side with a spear, and at once blood and water came out." The inclusion of this detail in the Johannine account of the crucifixion has been the cause of much scholarly debate and discussion. Why was it included in this Gospel, especially as it is not found in the Synoptic accounts? What does it mean on the levels of history, narrative and theology? These are some of the questions we will address in this next section. But first, we will delineate the identity motif as it appears in John's passion narrative.

Issues of Identity in the Passion Narrative

It should not be surprising to even the most casual reader of the Gospel up to this point that the narrative of Jesus' arrest and crucifixion centers on issues of identity. Indeed, the revelation of Christ's true identity as the Son of God through his moment of glorification on the cross is what the entire Gospel narrative has been leading up to from the very beginning.

As is typical in Johannine water narratives, issues of identity, particularly Christ's identity, are at the forefront of the narrative of Jesus' arrest, trial and crucifixion beginning in 18:1. When Judas comes with the detachment of soldiers and Jewish authorities to arrest Jesus in an olive grove on the other side of the Kidron valley (18:1–3), they are careful to be sure they are arresting the correct man. Jesus, with characteristic Johannine foresight, knows they are looking for him, but asks them anyway who they seek. They respond that they are looking for Jesus of Nazareth (vv. 4–5). His simple answer "I am he" elicits a dramatic response from the group: "they stepped back and fell to the ground." This reaction is likely the result of Jesus' use of the theophanic "I am" (ἐγώ εἰμί). This scene then repeats itself. Once again Jesus asks who they want, and they respond "Jesus of Nazareth." Whereupon Jesus once again declares himself with ἐγώ εἰμί (vv. 7–8).

This two-fold questioning and double answering of the authorities' question incorporating the phrase ἐγώ εἰμί is reminiscent of the very first scene of the Gospel, when the Jews send priests and Levites from Jerusalem to grill John the Baptist on his identity and purpose (1:19–23). When they ask John point blank if he is the expected Messiah, he replies that he is not (Ἐγὼ οὐκ εἰμὶ ὁ Χριστός). Then they press him on whether he claims to be Elijah or another prophetic forerunner of the Messiah and he again denies it. The fact that in this scene the questioned (Jesus) now becomes the inquisitor—he asks all the questions; the authorities merely answer—is wonderfully ironic, particularly in light of John the Baptist's statements about the one who comes after him being greater than he. In both of these scenes the accused openly and freely admits his own identity (1:20; 18:5–8). The soldiers then arrest Jesus.

Jesus is then taken to Annas, but we are given no details about what transpires there (18:12–14). Instead, the scene switches to another instance of identity questioning—one which turns out very differently than the ones discussed above. In 18:15–18, Peter, who is following behind Jesus, is outside the high priest's house waiting for Jesus to emerge. While entering the courtyard he is recognized by the doorkeeper who asks him, "You are not one of his disciples, are you?" Peter's denial in v. 17 stands in stark contrast to the previous statements of both Jesus and John the Baptist. The Baptist "did not deny, but freely confessed" that he was not the Messiah in 1:20–21. Jesus freely and boldly claims his identity in 18:4–8. Peter also says that he "is not" something (as John did) but is being deceptive rather than truthful. He will be questioned about his identity two other times (vv. 25–27) and will twice again hide who he truly is. These scenes do not directly impact the revelation of Christ's identity throughout the passion narrative, but serve as a foil for the character of Jesus, who boldly reveals his true identity even though he knows it means death.

The next part of the Johannine Passion narrative that focuses on Jesus' identity begins in 18:28. Here Jesus is finally brought to Pilate after questioning by Annas (vv. 19–24) and a trip to Caiaphas, which is not recounted (vv. 24, 28). Pilate seems particularly eager to get down to the issue of Jesus' identity. After all, the only charge the Jews have to bring against him that might possibly persuade Pilate to punish Jesus under Roman law, which would allow for him to be executed, is his claim to be the King of the Jews (vv. 30–33). In this scene Jesus does openly confess to being a king (18:37) after prodding by Pilate. This is in contrast to Jesus' responses during his trials in the Synoptic Gospels. In Matt 27:11–12; Mark 15:2–5; Luke 23:3, 9, Jesus responds to his inquisitors' questions only by agreeing with the epithet "King of the Jews" that they bestow on him. He does not actually utter the words himself, and, in fact, gives no other answer at all. However, in John he responds to Pilate's question about whether he is the king of the Jews by saying, "You say that I am a king. For this I was born, and for this I came into the world, to testify to the truth. Everyone who belongs to the truth listens to my voice" (18:37). Although he does not use the title to refer to himself, he owns it and takes care to explicate its meaning. This is in keeping with the Johannine practice of revealing rather than hiding Jesus' identity.

After this Pilate makes an unsuccessful attempt to convince the crowds that Jesus is not worthy of punishment (18:38) and devises an ingenious plan to release him to the crowds as part of a traditional Passover amnesty for one Jewish prisoner. But the crowds demand Barabbas instead (vv. 39–40). At this Pilate allows Jesus to be flogged (19:1), probably hoping that this would be sufficient to get the crowds to calm down, for after this event he once again tries to convince them that Jesus is innocent and not worthy of death (19:4–6). During the flogging the soldiers in charge of Jesus mock him and his claim to be king by making him don a purple "robe" and a crown of thorns (19:2–3). This reads as highly ironic to those who understand Jesus' true identity as king not just of the Jews, but of the all people.

During his second attempt to release Jesus to the crowd, Pilate has Jesus stand before them and presents him saying, "Here is the man." This announcement also must be read against the background of the rest of the Gospel. Up until this point Jesus, while happy in certain situations to reveal his true identity and nature to individual persons or small groups, has generally tried to keep a low profile when it came to revealing himself in public. We have already seen how in chapter 7 Jesus travels to and through Jerusalem incognito in order that he will not be arrested by the Jews. In chapter 2, at the wedding in Cana, he insisted to his mother that the proper time for a full revelation of his identity had not yet come, so she should not expect such. In both chapter 5 and 9 Jesus performs healing miracles, but immediately thereafter disappears, causing consternation to the Jewish authorities who want to know who he is and by what authority he heals.

In light of this tendency of Jesus to reveal himself only to certain people, and only at the time appointed by the Father, this very public presentation of him by Pilate is significant. It may be seen as the beginning of the final and full revelation of Jesus' identity that will come through his death and glorification on the cross. The climax of this revelation will come at the moment on the cross when water and blood flow from the wound in his side.

Interpretation of the Water and Blood from Jesus' Side

The Fourth Gospel is the only account which relates the incident of the water and blood from Jesus' side on the cross. This leads to the natural question of why John felt the story to be important, as he clearly does from the emphasis he places on it. One possible explanation for the inclusion of this event is that it verifies that Jesus truly did die. In the light of both contemporary and later suggestions that Jesus didn't actually rise from the dead because he never physically died, this might be seen as an important concern of the evangelist. But how does this action succeed in verifying the death?

Some have suggested that when the soldier thrust the lance into Jesus' side he aimed for the heart, with the purpose of mortally wounding Jesus just to ensure that he would actually die quickly, since death by crucifixion could take days.[22] However, there are problems with this theory, mainly the fact that Jesus is already observed to be dead in v. 33. If the soldiers already saw that he was dead, the stated reason that they don't break his legs as they did the other victims', then why would the man find it necessary to deliver the coup de grace, as it were?[23] The other, and more likely, explana-

22. Brown, *Gospel*, 2.935.
23. Brown, *Death*, 2.1177

tion for what is happening here is that the soldier intended to simply prod Jesus to detect signs of movement. In the process he became overzealous and actually pierced the skin. Evidence seems to indicate that this might have been a common practice among Roman execution squads to verify a person's death.[24] The verb νύσσω can mean "to prod" as well as "to plunge."[25]

For the last 200 years medical professionals have attempted to explain both what caused Jesus' death on the cross,[26] as well as how blood and water could have flowed out of his body after death.[27] However, this approach has been justly criticized for attempting to extract physical details of Jesus' torture and death from a narrative that does not provide such material. The description of Jesus' crucifixion is extraordinarily terse in both John and the Synoptics, consisting of only a few words, no more than a dispassionate statement of fact (Matt 27:35; Mk 15:24; Lk 23:33; Jn 19:23). A little more can be ascertained from studying outside evidence of the method of execution by crucifixion as practiced by the Romans, but even there the data is somewhat scanty. Most importantly, though, these doctors have been criticized, by Brown among others, for failing to recognize that the narratives of Jesus' crucifixion are written for primarily theological, not physiological, reasons; one cannot expect to be able to come to an adequate conclusion about physical matters because the Gospel writers themselves were not particularly concerned with them.[28] The Gospel writers were not concerned with *how* Jesus died so much as *why* he died and *what* that death meant.

This is nowhere made clearer than in John's account of the crucifixion, particularly at the point of the blood and water flowing from Jesus'

---

24. Cf. Quintilian, *Declamationes maiores* 6.9; also Brown, *Death*, 2.1177.

25. The Vulgate and Peshitta have the verb as "opened" probably a result of the misreading of ηνυζεν for ηνοιζεν. This reading may also be influenced by the words of Zechariah 13:1: "On that day a fountain shall be opened (נִפְתָּח) for the house of David and the inhabitants of Jerusalem, to cleanse them from sin and impurity." Cf. Brown, *Death*, 2.1177, n. 91.

26. Some of the more prominent examples from the 20th century include Barbet, *Doctor*; Ball and Leese, "Physical," 248; Edwards, Gabel and Hosmer, "Physical Death," 1455–63; also see the criticism of this approach (especially as applied by Edwards, Wesley and Hosmer) in Smith, "Autopsy," 14–15.

27. The best and most comprehensive overview of the material published up to 1975 can be found in Wilkinson, "Incident," 149–72; also see Brown, *Death*, 2.1088–92.

28. Brown describes most of those who have attempted to examine the issue from a medical standpoint as "doctors who did not stick to their trade and let a literalist understanding of the Gospel accounts influence their judgments on the physical cause of Jesus' death" (*Death*, 2.1092).

side. This event is apparently so extraordinary, so unbelievable, that the narrator feels it necessary to interrupt the story to add: "He who saw this has testified so that you also may believe. His testimony is true, and he knows that he tells the truth" (19:35). In other words, John interprets these events, particularly the flowing of water and blood from Christ's dead body, as incredibly unusual, perhaps even miraculous. This would seem, then, to undermine any attempt to make a physical explanation for the blood and water because it clearly is beyond the range of human comprehension. Brown sums it up best: "Even though that testimony pertains primarily to the theological import of the blood and water, it would scarcely have been invoked if what is described was normal or easily explicable."[29]

The author has clearly chosen to focus on the theological import of this event and so we will investigate possible meanings for the blood and the water from Jesus' side within this context. There are several possible theological purposes for the flow of blood and water. First of all, it has been suggested that it is intended as a symbol of Jesus' divinity. In ancient Greek folklore and religion gods and goddesses were believed to have running through their veins a different substance than mere humans—a mixture of blood and water sometimes called *ichor*. When they were wounded in battle this substance would flow from wounds in the place of blood.[30] Indeed, in some legends secreting blood instead of *ichor* was a sign of one's humanity.[31] Could John possibly be using this symbolism to signify Jesus' role as God? It is certainly not impossible that readers well-versed in Hellenistic traditions may have caught a hint of this connection; but as Brown points out it seems unlikely that this is John's main purpose as he has never relied on "blatant pagan imagery" anywhere else in the Gospel to describe Jesus.[32]

A popular theory suggests that John includes this bit of imagery as a deliberate counter to gnostic philosophies which denied the true humanity of Christ and/or taught that he did not really die.[33] This theory is usually based on gnostic writings and teachings from the 2nd century. However, there is little evidence that such teachings were prevalent in the last half of the first-century; at best there may have been proto-gnostic ideas beginning

---

29. Ibid., 2.1179.
30. Homer, *Iliad*, 5.340ff.
31. Plutarch, *Moralia* 180e.
32. Brown, *Death*, 2.1180.
33. Ibid., 2.1181.

to take form.[34] There certainly do seem to be gnostic misconceptions behind the vehement assertion of Jesus' humanity in 1 John 5:6-8: "This is the one who came by water and blood, Jesus Christ, not with the water only but with the water and the blood. And the Spirit is the one that testifies, for the Spirit is the truth. There are three that testify: the Spirit and the water and the blood, and these three agree." However, it may be better to see this passage as a later interpretation of the meaning of the blood and water, one that is not antithetical to the Evangelist's ideas, but a necessary corrective for those who failed to understand its significance in the Gospel.[35] In the John 19 account the author seems more concerned with depth of faith, as indicated by the insistence on eyewitness testimony in 19:35, than in correction of any particular theological error.

One other natural way of reading the meaning of the blood and water is to see them as indicating that Jesus has fulfilled the requirements of the Passover sacrifice. An understanding of the blood as representing atonement comes, of course, from the Jewish sacrificial system which required a blood sacrifice for the expiation of certain sins.[36] In the Gospel of John, however, very intentional links are made between Jesus' death and the sacrifice of the Passover lamb: the entire passion narrative is molded to emphasize this role. This is the explanation for the shifting of the time of Jesus' death from the day of the Passover itself to the day before the Passover, the day of Preparation when the lambs were slaughtered. It is also the reason behind several minor tweaks John makes to the Passion narrative including the use of a hyssop branch by the soldiers to administer the wine to Jesus (19:29), and the inclusion of the Scripture quotations after the piercing of his side (19:36-37).

Water, of course, also has the ability to cleanse from impurities in Jewish law and practice.[37] And purification issues have already occupied a place in John's Passion narrative. Concern for ritual purity seems to underlie the Jewish leaders' insistence that Jesus' body be removed from the cross before the sun set (19:31). According to the law anyone hung on a tree must be taken down before nightfall and buried for they were considered to be under a curse and remaining overnight would defile the land (Deut.

---

34. Keener, *Gospel*, 161ff.

35. Miguens, "Tres Testigos," 74-94; Witherington, "Waters of Birth," 155-60.

36. Grigsby, "Cross, 51-80."

37. Lev 1:9, 13; 8:6, 21; 11:32; 14:8-9, 52; 15:5-27; 16:4, 24, 26, 28; 17:15; 22:6; Num 8:7; 19:7-21; 31:23.

21:22–23). Jesus' body remaining on the "tree" overnight, then, would be a source of defilement.

Connections between water, purification, and Jesus' death were established early in the Gospel. John's practice of baptizing with water directed people to the Lamb of God who would take away the sin of the world (John 1:29–34). The sign at Cana foreshadowed the 'hour' of Jesus' passion, when purification would be accomplished through the revelation of his glory (2:1–11). Jesus washed his disciples' feet in anticipation of the cleansing that he would provide through his death (13:1–11). Given these connections, it is appropriate to see the water flowing from Jesus' side as a way of conveying the purifying aspect of his death. To some, the body of Jesus was a source of defilement, but in the eyes of the evangelist, the crucified Christ is a source of cleansing from sin, another Johannine irony; Jesus' body, which under normal human circumstances would have been considered unclean and therefore defiled, in reality cleanses itself from impurity by the means of the water flowing out from it. Therefore, seeing the blood and the water in 19:34 as representative of the cleansing from sin that comes to all through Christ's death is certainly not inappropriate, either within the context of Jewish theology or the previous understandings in the Gospel of John.

However, this is not the only way to understand these symbols. Indeed the tradition of reading the water and blood as representative of the sacraments of Eucharist and Baptism is related to their ability to provide purification. After all, baptism is connected to the idea of cleansing from sin or impurity in much of Christian thought, and is certainly the primary understanding of baptism in the Synoptics.[38] However, one must recall that in the Fourth Gospel baptism serves a very different purpose, as we discussed in chapter 3 above. John's baptism, and later that of Jesus, are not said to be efficacious for the forgiveness of sins, but rather serve a revelatory function (1:31; 3:27–35). In this Gospel baptism is never connected directly to the idea of the forgiveness of sins or cleansing from impurity, nor is water. Therefore, although later Christian interpretation may see the water in 19:34 as representative of baptism, this does not seem to be a natural interpretation in the Johannine context. However, seeing the water from the side of Jesus as revelatory in some way of his identity, a function we have seen water serve elsewhere in the Gospel, is a valid interpretation. This

---

38. Matt 3:6, 11; Mark 1:4–5; Luke 3:3.

is where the connection between water and Spirit in the Gospel reaches its climax and its ultimate purpose.

Interpreting the blood as a reference to the Eucharist is perhaps less problematic within the Johannine context than the water. In 6:54–56 Jesus exhorted his disciples to drink his blood (and eat his flesh) in order to receive eternal life. However, outside of this passage there are no other references to blood in the Gospel except at 19:34. Indeed, the fact that the symbol appears only here and in the Eucharistic passage of chapter 6 might seem rather to strengthen the Eucharistic interpretation of the blood from the cross. It is probably best, however, to see the Eucharistic connection as secondary, one that might well have been implied by the author and inferred by the community to whom he was writing, but which is not of primary importance for the interpretation at the narrative level of the story.[39]

To this point we have surveyed possible explanations for the blood and the water together from Jesus' side. We have yet to examine the possible connotations of the water alone. Unshackled from the blood image, the water still has plenty of significance. Indeed, given that water has been such a prevalent motif in the Gospel to this point, it would not be unfair to say that it has far more meaning alone than does the blood. Since the water which Jesus declared would flow from him (and/or the believer) in the last day has been directly connected with the Spirit already in this Gospel (7:39), water flowing from the side of Jesus at his death is an especially evocative image. Within the context of the Gospel, it is clear that this is intended to be the climax of the water motif. The living water which Jesus alone can give, which will flow out of him and through all those who believe, which represents the Spirit, is now literally released at the moment of Jesus' death. The imagery could hardly be any clearer: Jesus' death provides the Spirit.

Rivers of Living Water in Previous Jewish Literature

Although we have highlighted above certain OT verses that are the most similar to Jesus' Tabernacles statement in both image and language, the proclamation should also be understood against the larger background of the water image in relation to Yahweh that recurs frequently in the OT, especially in the Psalms and the writings of the prophets. Isaiah, whose work has clearly influenced Johannine theology and language,[40] employs

---

39. Cf. Brown, *Gospel*, 2.952; Schnackenburg, *Gospel*, 3.291

40. Cf. Dahms, "Isaiah," 78–88; Griffiths, "Deutero-Isaiah," 355–60; Ronning,

some of the best examples of this imagery. Most often the prophet portrays water, particularly water that gives life, as flowing from Yahweh. In Is 30:25 the Lord is the one who makes brooks run with water from the high hills and mountains. In 27:3 Yahweh is pictured as a gardener tenderly watering his precious vineyard. Both Isaiah 43:20 and 44:3 call up the image of the Lord's provision of streams of water in the dry and dusty wilderness. Then, there is the well-known parallel to this passage found in Isaiah 55:1: "Ho, everyone who thirsts, come to the waters" with the waters representing Yahweh (cf. 55:5–6).

However, there are also hints of persons who follow Yahweh serving as a conduit for this water. In 58:11 the one who is continually guided by the Lord is compared to a spring whose waters never fail. That the Lord, and not the person, is the ultimate source of these waters is made clear in the verse when we are told that "the Lord will guide you continually, and satisfy your needs in parched places." It is only as a result of the quenching of this thirst that the believer is then able to be a spring of water and "a well-watered garden." In Is 32:2 Yahweh's appointed king, the one who rules in righteousness and justice, is said to be like streams of water in a dry place. Later in that chapter the author compares the spreading of falsehood or error concerning the Lord by fools to the withholding of water from a thirsty person (32:6). This image equates "water" with God's truth and assumes the godly person as the supplier of this kind of water. So, while there is no strict verbal equivalent to Jesus' statement in the Jewish Scriptures, the image of water flowing from the provision of Yahweh was certainly not new to the Jews whom Jesus was addressing. Indeed, Jesus' setting himself up as the one who provides water to the thirsty would have been understood by the Jewish crowds as a profound statement about his identity and relationship to Yahweh, the ultimate source of water in the OT. However, there also is evidence of the one who believes in the Lord being an intermediate source of living water as well. This, then, establishes Jewish precedent for our argument above that the water spoken of in 7:37–39 can flow out of Christ through the believer, and therefore be said to originate from both at the same time.

The image of water from Jesus' side also has strong connections to previous Jewish metaphors concerning the coming of the new eschatological age foretold by the prophets, which Jesus' ministry has been inaugurating

---

"Targum," 247–78; Sawyer, "Gospel," 39–43; Swancutt, "Hungers," 218–51; Williams, "Isaiah," 101–16; Young, "Relation," 215–33.

all throughout the Gospel. One of the most natural connections the Jewish audience might make between both Jesus' statement in 7:37–39 and the flow of water from his side in 19:34 is with the vision of the end times in Ezekiel 47:1–12. Here the prophet is shown a river flowing from the temple in Jerusalem which brings healing to the dry, dead landscape and vegetation and makes salty waters fresh. Earlier in the Gospel the narrator made an explicit connection between Jesus' body and the Jerusalem temple (2:21). The flow of water from Jesus is an indication that the new age of blessing foretold by the prophets was beginning as a result of Jesus' ministry and death. This new age was not something relegated to the distant future, as it was to the people of Ezekiel's day, but was here now. As a result of Jesus' sacrifice humanity could realize this glorious coming kingdom right now. This seems to be the most natural reading of the flow of water from Jesus within both the Gospel and the greater Jewish context.

A similar image is found in Zechariah 14:8 which pictures living waters flowing in two streams out of Jerusalem at the end of the age. However, the parallels extend far beyond this single verse. Indeed, all of Zechariah chapter 14 seems to have particular resonance with Jesus' statement in 7:37–38 and its surrounding context. Zechariah speaks of the "day of the Lord" when the nations will rally against Jerusalem and the Lord will come in power to win victory and reign supreme. The key elements in the prophecy are these: Jerusalem will be occupied by *alien forces* (14:1–2); *the Lord will appear* and fight on Israel's behalf (14:3); he will "*stand* upon the *Mount of Olives*, east of Jerusalem" and provide an avenue of escape for His people (14:4–7). On that day *living water* will flow out from Jerusalem; the Lord will be King over the whole earth (14:8–9a) and the surviving nations will celebrate *Tabernacles* in Jerusalem (14:16–19). Each of the crucial elements of this prophecy play a part in Jesus' appearance at the feast of Tabernacles. At that time Jerusalem was indeed under *alien occupation* (as it had been for several hundred years); Christ *appeared* (midweek and unexpectedly) at *Tabernacles* to offer Himself on the behalf of the faithful; Jesus *stood* and promised *living water* and then retired to the *Mount of Olives*. The striking similarities between these two passages also support the idea that John is framing the water from Jesus (both metaphorical and literal) as concrete evidence that the Messianic Kingdom foretold by the prophets has now arrived in his person.

CONCLUSIONS

Jesus' speech at the Feast of Tabernacles and the water and blood from his side at the cross represent the climax of the water motif in the Gospel. Jesus' statement foreshadows the literal occurrence that takes place on the cross. At that point several things take place symbolically: the Spirit is released and "poured out" on all people; the cleansing for sins, represented previously by the blood of the sacrificial lamb and also by ritual water purifications, now has taken place once for all and never need be repeated; and God's eschatological kingdom, foretold by the latter prophets, is inaugurated, symbolized by the water flowing from the temple-body of Christ. Most importantly, Jesus is finally and fully revealed as the agent for all of these things—the true Son of the Father, and, most importantly, God himself incarnate.

Chapter 7

Summary and Conclusions

SUMMARY

The Gospel of John contains some of the most sophisticated usage of symbolism and imagery found anywhere in the Bible. These devices are not intended only as artistic embellishment, but carry a large portion of the Gospel's theological and spiritual significance.[1] Water is one of the most frequently recurring motifs, particularly in the first half of the book. It is clear from our survey, and that of many others, that this motif is not the result of chance or happenstance. Certainly water would be expected to make an appearance at some point in the Gospel because it is such an important everyday substance of life for anyone in any time—and especially for those in ancient Palestine where it was relatively scarce. However, the way the various instances of water in the Gospel (both figurative and literal) are structured to relate to one another, play off one another, and slowly build to a climax, as well as their intricate weaving into the theological message of the book, shows that the author was quite intentional in his use and placement of the water image.

The first appearance of water in the Gospel is found in the narrative of John's baptism in chapter 1. Here, the author establishes the significance of water in the Gospel and gives us a key to interpreting it throughout: water serves a revelatory function in relationship to Jesus. John plainly states that

1. Culpepper, *Anatomy*, 181.

Summary and Conclusions

he baptizes only so "that he [the one coming after him] may be revealed to Israel" (1:31). Never does he indicate that his baptism is efficacious in any other way or for any other person. Moreover, his baptism is inferior to that which the one coming after him will give because it is not administered with the spirit. Only the one coming after him will be able to bestow this gift. Therefore, once his baptism has revealed this "coming one" as Jesus, John no longer has any meaning or purpose in terms of the narrative. This becomes clear in 3:22–36 when John's disciples complain that more and more people are going to Jesus for baptism instead of John. John, however, is neither confused nor concerned: this is how it should be, for Jesus' baptism administers the spirit while John's does not. He is merely the best man at the wedding whose importance is eclipsed by the bridegroom when he makes his arrival.

Starting, then, with this understanding of the purpose of the water motif in the Gospel as revealing something about Jesus we note that Jesus' identity as Son of the Father, the Son of God, is revealed in every major narrative which involves water. Indeed, several of these stories heavily feature the theme of Jesus' identity, be it his earthly human identity, or his "true" identity as God's son, or both. At the wedding at Cana in chapter 2 Jesus turns large pots of water into wine and as a result "reveal[s] his glory" and his disciples come to "believe" in him for the first time (2:11).

Jesus' conversation with his mother early in the passage becomes the interpretive key to understanding what exactly Jesus is revealing about himself and why it is only the disciples who are said to believe. Through this act Jesus not only shows himself to be a miracle worker—that alone would not reveal his true nature—but to be the one who can manipulate and control the waters of the earth to do his bidding, something only God does in Jewish Scripture. He connects himself with the God of the Old Testament by performing a miracle that, on one level, could be seen as a recreation of one of Yahweh's great miracles, the turning of the Nile River to blood. This sign on Yahweh's part had the express stated purpose of making the people believe that "the Lord—the God of their Fathers—has appeared to you" (Ex 4:5). Jesus' repetition of this miracle, albeit on a smaller scale, would have carried a pointed message to the disciples that Jesus was no mere itinerate rabbi or wandering miracle worker: he was actually Yahweh himself standing in their midst.

In chapter 4, the water motif becomes far less subtle as it takes center stage in a conversation between Jesus and a Samaritan woman. There, against the backdrop of a well, and with blatant water language, Jesus reveals himself to the woman as the Messiah—the *taheb* of Samaritan belief—for whom she had been patiently waiting. Jesus' true identity is to some extent symbolized in the "living water" that he offers to give the woman. Just as baptism apart from the spirit was useless, so also was water without the Christ. Only he could supply the "living water"—the water of spiritual cleansing and renewal—that the woman so badly needed, and he was only capable of doing this because of his special relationship to the Father. Not only does the ability to impart this water make Jesus special, the water itself gains its significance and potency from the fact that it is given by Jesus. Apart from him it would be useless, like the forgotten water jar the woman leaves behind her at the well.

We encounter another example of water that is impotent when not associated with Jesus in John 5. Here, a handicapped man desires healing, but is unable to get into the Pool of Bethesda in time. Instead of helping him into the pool ahead of the others, which is what the man envisions when Jesus offers to help, Jesus simply heals the man on his own without the use of the water. Jesus can provide healing water, as it were, from himself, without needing to resort to waters of the earth. Later, in chapter 9, we read a story with some very similar elements: a blind man is healed after Jesus tells him to wash in the Pool of Siloam. The waters of Siloam were publicly available and widely used by the average person in Jerusalem. They had no special healing capabilities on their own, as Bethesda apparently did. These waters gain all of their potency and significance from their association with the person of Jesus, the one who was "sent" to do the work of the Father and who then "sent" the man to the Pool. After each of these healings a debate erupts between the man who was healed and Jewish authorities because the healings had taken place on a Sabbath. In the course of these discussions, Jesus' identity—both his earthly personality and his "true" identity as the Son of God—come under scrutiny. In the end, Jesus' ability to administer healing through water—either figurative or literal—is what causes some to believe that he is from God.

The climax of the metaphorical water motif in the Gospel comes as Jesus stands up among the worshippers at the Feast of Tabernacles and appropriates the imagery of the water ritual to himself (7:37–39). By declaring that rivers of living water will flow out of him and out of those who believe in him, Jesus equates himself with Yahweh, the one and only source of water in Jewish history and belief. Jesus is the spring of living water which was rejected by the people (Jer 2:13; 7:13). He is both the giver of the water, and the means by which it is given, the rock in the wilderness out of which those life-giving waters flow (quite literally when we get to 19:34). He is the provider of the drink that will fill the thirsty one who comes to the waters (Isa 55:1). But more than just the source of spiritual nourishment and cleansing, Jesus also is the sole dispenser of the spirit, which the water represents (7:39), a role elsewhere reserved specifically for Yahweh (cf. 3:34; Isa 4:4; 32:15; 44:3; 63:11; Ezek 36:27; 39:29; Joel 2:28–29; Zech 12:10).

If this proclamation is the climax of the metaphorical water in the Gospel, the recurrence of literal water in the Gospel reaches its high point at the moment of Jesus' death on the cross where water flows together with blood from his side. That the author believes this to have truly occurred is obvious from his insistence on the reliability of the eyewitness testimony to the same. However, that doesn't mean the water doesn't have symbolic significance. Whatever the reason for the soldier prodding Jesus' side and whatever the explanation for the flow of water, the event was recorded in the Gospel primarily for theological rather than historical purposes. Here was a palpable, physical representation of the water symbol: literal water flowing out of the body of Jesus. What had heretofore been metaphorical was now made real, much in the same way that the Father, Yahweh, whom no one had ever seen except the Son (1:18), had now been made visible in fleshly human form in Jesus.

As this survey has shown throughout, the significance of Jesus' relationship to the various forms of water in the Gospel is based on and modeled after Yahweh's relationship with water in the OT. We have reviewed Yahweh's role in manipulating the waters of the תהום to bring about the creation of the world. The ability to control the waters of the cosmos, or the deep, was considered one of the hallmarks of a true deity in the ANE, as is attested in cosmologies and cosmogonies of various people groups. In these belief systems, the creator god often had to defeat the watery chaos monster in order to bring about the earth and the cosmos. However, in the Genesis creation narratives Yahweh does not do battle with such a figure because he is never challenged by anyone. Indeed the fearsome chaos monsters Leviathan and Rahab are completely tamed by Yahweh's might and rendered as powerless as a baby.

God also shows his power to direct the waters of the earth when necessary for his purposes. In the time of Noah Yahweh effects a complete cosmic cataclysm, which is accomplished by undoing all that he previously did in creation. The waters held captive above and below the earth are let loose, allowed to triumph over the passive and helpless terrain. This great flood is then abated at God's command as well. Because Yahweh was the creator of the universe and the one who contained the waters at creation, he is free to release or withhold them as he sees fit. It is only because of his manipulation of the waters at creation that God has control over the waters of the earth.

Much later in history the Israelites get the opportunity to witness firsthand God's control of the waters of the earth at the Sea of Reeds. Again, it is because God designed the water systems of the earth that he is able to control them to do his bidding. In this case, he manipulates the water to provide a glorious victory for his people, and for himself, over the Egyptians. After this event, Yahweh's reputation as the God of the waters was forever cemented. From that point on Yahweh's identity was intimately connected to his abilities to control the waters.

This very identification came into question in the minds of the Israelites, however, not long thereafter. In the wilderness they arrived at Meribah where there was no water to drink. This precipitated a crisis of faith that was, at least partly, based on the Israelite's understanding of God as the one who provides the waters. If Yahweh was with them, as they believed he was, and Yahweh was the sole provider of water, then why did they have no water? Had they displeased him in such a way that he had left them? As if to answer this question, Yahweh decisively provides them with streams of water from a rock. Yes, Yahweh was still the God of the waters; they had only to trust him.

This last event became an especially evocative recurring image in Israelite consciousness. The prophets and poets often refer to the Lord's provision of water in the wilderness and springs in the desert in their litany of praises to Yahweh. It especially speaks to those who feel that Yahweh has abandoned them in a vast, dry wasteland. It seems natural, then, that the later prophets pick up on this image to represent the expected blessings of Yahweh at the end times. Steams of water will flow, not from just any rock in the wilderness, but from the rock at the very center of Jerusalem, from the temple mount itself, bringing life and regeneration to everything it touches (Ezek 47:1–9; Zech 14:8). This stream also promises cleansing to those who partake of the waters (Zech 13:1). That this image was a powerful one in the Johannine community's interpretation of Jesus is clear from its later appearance as the culminating image of the book of Revelation (Rev 22:1–2).

Summary and Conclusions

This repeated connection between God and his relationship to the waters of the universe and the earth was so strong in the Israelite imagination that it became an intimate part of who God was in their minds. His identity was inseparable from his ability to control the waters.

Building on this foundation, the Fourth Evangelist cleverly and often subtly weaves water imagery into passages of the Gospel where important revelations of Jesus' character and identity are paramount. In 2:1–11 it is a miracle involving the transformation of water which first gives his disciples a hint of his true nature. In 4:4–26 the woman at Samaria doesn't know who Jesus is, and only comes to understand him as the Messiah as a result of Jesus' water language. The water that he offers her is efficacious and desirable only because it comes from him. His identity as the Son of God is what enables him to provide her with water that will allow her to never thirst again. Apart from him it would be just as useless as that of Jacob's well. In chapters 5 and 9 it is a miracle based partly on the use (or neglect) of water that leads to serious debates among the Jewish officials about who Jesus is. At the Pool of Bethesda Jesus makes a profound statement about his identity when he heals a man in the midst of a healing shrine, possibly one dedicated to another god, and without the benefit of the sacred water and its alleged powers. What other gods were only capable of doing through the special waters of a shrine, Jesus could do based solely on the water contained within himself.

The Tabernacles narrative in chapter 7 is filled with the motif of Jesus' identity. He goes to Jerusalem for the festival in disguise for fear that he will be arrested. The crowds in Jerusalem talk about Jesus, look for him, and debate his character (7:12–13). Even when Jesus begins teaching in the temple courts people are not completely sure who he is. They wonder why, if this was the man the authorities were seeking, he had not yet been arrested. Had the authorities determined that he was really the Messiah after all? (7:25–26). They are incredulous at this prospect as they knew where he was from, yet no one was supposed to know where the Messiah came from (7:27). The people are ironically correct about Jesus' true identity as the Messiah, but they don't know it.

The crowds are still divided and confused when Jesus steps up to address them against the backdrop of the water festival at Tabernacles. Here, at a time where he needs to reveal his true identity unambiguously and in a way that all will understand, Jesus calls once again upon water imagery, specifically imagery of the water that was provided from the rock in the wilderness. His choice is not coincidental. One of the clearest signs of a deity's nature in the ancient world, and a fundamental part of Yahweh's identity in Jewish thought, was the ability to provide water. The Jews in the crowd could hardly have misunderstood Jesus' intent: he was announcing himself to be one and the same with the person of Yahweh.

By the end of the Gospel, with the last water image in 19:34, the character of Jesus has become thoroughly fused with that of the Lord of the Old Testament, Yahweh himself. He has controlled waters and given water, both metaphorical and literal. His special relationship with water has played a role in identifying him as the Son of God to major characters in the story and his water miracles have served as catalyst for debates about this same identity.

CONCLUSIONS

Given that Yahweh's relationship with water is so critical to his identity in the Old Testament tradition, it is not particularly surprising that one of the Evangelists of the New Testament would pick up on this connection and use it in his depiction of Jesus. After all, in creating their portraits, the Evangelists were concerned to reveal Jesus as more than a mere man: they wanted to emphasize his deity. He was man, but he was also God incarnate. This is an especially important theme for John, whose purpose in writing is to convince people that Jesus is the Son of God (20:31).

What is surprising, however, is the lack of attention this topic has received in examinations of the water imagery of John. Previous studies have focused on the connections between water imagery and eschatology, pneumatology, and even ecclesiology.[2] Water certainly figures in each of these in the Gospel, but the true focus of Johannine water imagery is Christology: it is to Jesus and his identity that the water imagery most often and most significantly points. Therefore, this study has sought to fill this gap by providing the first integrative and comprehensive look at how the identity motif of the Gospel, the foremost concern of the evangelist, interacts with water imagery and symbolism, long and widely noted as one of the most significant literary elements of the work.

Jesus was sent by God, but he was not a separate being or entity as previous messengers had been: he was one and the same with the God of Israel. By virtue of his deity Jesus became active not only in the events that

---

2. See literature review in chapter 1.

Summary and Conclusions

occurred during his time on earth, but also in all the previous salvific acts of Yahweh and those that would occur in the future. This is underlined by the various Old Testament water echoes that can be heard in John's text: Jesus was at the same time the God who helped rescue Israel at the Reed Sea and the water which would pour out from the temple at the end times. In John's view, history truly does find its center in Jesus. The past and the future are both present in some real sense in his person. Jesus is also, paradoxically, both the giver of water and, at times, the water itself. This is an echo of the way God is portrayed in the OT—he is the powerful master of the water, but at other times he is described as "the fountain of living waters." The message in the Gospel is clear for those familiar with previous Jewish thought: Jesus is the source of waters and is able to make it do his bidding because he is in reality God, the one who has controlled the waters from the beginning of time.

The author of the Fourth Gospel chose this most fundamental characteristic of Yahweh as an entrée for Jesus into the divine identity because it was such a familiar image and foundational to so much of Israelite history and theology. It was a way to get Jesus in "on the ground floor" so to speak of God's work in the world. If Jesus is the Word which was with God "in the beginning" at creation (1:1–4), then he naturally would be expected have power over the waters of the universe as Yahweh did. Jesus was there with Yahweh when he manipulated the waves of the תהום; he was responsible for the great deluge in the time of Noah; and he was powerfully at work right alongside the Father in the parting of the Sea of Reeds and the providing water in the wilderness. In Christ the people of God were witnessing for the first time the fleshly manifestation of Yahweh in their midst. God became a man and walked among them (John 1:14). This is, at its very core, the important message of the water imagery of the Gospel.

Bibliography

Adan, David. "The 'Fountain of Siloam' and 'Solomon's Pool' in First-Century C.E. Jerusalem." *Israel Exploration Journal* 29 (1979) 92–100.
Aichele, George and Gary A. Phillips. "Introduction: Exegesis, Eisegesis, Intergesis." *Semeia* 69/70 (1995) 7.
Allen, Leslie C. *Psalms 101–150*. Word Biblical Commentary 21. Waco, TX: Word, 1983.
Allison, Dale C. *Jesus of Nazareth: Millenarian Prophet*. Minneapolis: Fortress, 1998.
Alter, Robert. *The Art of Biblical Narrative*. New York: Basic, 1981.
———. *Genesis: Translation and Commentary*. New York: Norton, 1996.
Anderson, Paul N. *The Christology of the Fourth Gospel: Its Unity and Disunity in Light of John 6*. Wissenschaftliche Untersuchungen zum Neuen Testament. Second Series 78. Tübingen: Mohr Siebeck, 1996.
Ashton, John. *Understanding the Fourth Gospel*. Oxford: Clarendon , 1991.
Asiedu-Peprah, Martin. *Johannine Sabbath Conflicts as Juridical Controversy*. Tübingen: Mohr, 2001.
Avalos, Hector. *Illness and Health Care in the Ancient Near East: The Role of the Temple in Greece, Mesopotamia, and Israel*. Harvard Semitic Museum Publications 54. Atlanta: Scholars, 1995.
Balabanski, Victoria. "'Let anyone who is thirsty come to me': John 7:37–38 in dialogue with Josephus and the archeology of aqueducts." *Lutheran Theological Journal* 39:2–3 (2005) 132–39.
Ball, R.O., and K. Leese, "Physical Cause of the Death of Jesus." *Expository Times* 83 (1971–72).
Barbet, P. *A Doctor at Calvary*. New York: Kenedy, 1953.
Barclay, William. *The Gospel of St. John*. St. Andrews: St. Andrews Press, 1955.
Barrett, C. K. *The Gospel According to St. John*. 2nd ed. Philadelphia: Westminster, 1978.
Bauckham, Richard. *God Crucified: Monotheism and Christology in the New Testament*. Grand Rapids: Eerdmans, 1999. Reprinted as part 1 of *Jesus and the God of Israel: God Crucified and Other Studies on the New Testament's Christology of Divine Identity* (Grand Rapids: Eerdmans, 2008).
Bertrand, Daniel Alain. *Le baptême de Jésus: Histoire de l'exégèse aux deux premiers siècle*. Tübingen: Mohr, 1973.
Beasley-Murray, George R. *Baptism in the New Testament*. London: Macmillan, 1962.
———. *John*. Word Biblical Commentary 36. 2nd ed. Nashville: Thomas Nelson, 1999.
———. "John 3:3,5: Baptism, Spirit and the Kingdom." *Expository Times* 97:6 (March 1986) 167–70.

Bibliography

Bernard, J.H. *A Critical and Exegetical Commentary on the Gospel According to St. John.* International Critical Commentary. 2 vols. Edinburgh: T. & T. Clark, 1928.

Bird, Chad. *Water: A Theme Throughout Scripture.* St. Louis: Concordia, 2004.

Bonneau, N. R. "The Woman at the Well: John 4 and Genesis 24." *The Bible Today* 67 (1973) 1252–59.

Borg, Marcus J. *Jesus: A New Vision.* 2nd ed. San Francisco: Harper, 1991.

Bostock, D. Gerald. "Jesus as the New Elisha." *Expository Times* 92:2 (1980) 39–41.

Brant, JoAnn A. "Husband Hunting: Characterization and Narrative Art in the Gospel of John." *Biblical Interpretation* 4:2 (June 1996) 205–23.

Brodie, Thomas L. "Jesus as the New Elisha: Cracking the Code." *Expository Times* 93:2 (1981) 39–42.

Broer, Ingo. "Knowledge of Palestine in the Fourth Gospel." In *Jesus in the Johannine Tradition*, edited by R. Fortna and T. Thatcher, 83–90. Louisville: Westminster John Knox, 2001.

Brown, Raymond E. *The Gospel According to John.* Anchor Bible Commentary 29. 2nd ed. 2 vols. Garden City, NY: Doubleday, 2000.

Brown, Tricia G. *Spirit in the Writings of John.* Journal for the Study of the New Testament Supplement Series 253. New York: T. & T. Clark, 2003.

Bruce, F. F. *The Gospel of John: Introduction, Exposition and Notes.* Grand Rapids: Eerdmans, 1983.

Brunson, Andrew C. *Psalm 118 in the Gospel of John: An Intertextual Study of the New Exodus Pattern in the Theology of John.* Wissenschaftliche Untersuchungen zum Neuen Testament. Second Series 158. Tübingen: Mohr Siebeck, 2003.

Bultmann, Rudolf. *The Gospel of John: A Commentary.* Translated by G. R. Beasley-Murray. Philadelphia: Westminster, 1971.

Burge, Gary M. "Revisiting the Johannine Water Motif: Jesus, Ritual Purification and the Pool of Siloam in John 9." Paper presented at the annual meeting of Society of Biblical Literature. New Orleans, November 22, 2009.

Burrows, M. "The Conduit of the Upper Pool." *Zeitschrift für die Alttestamentliche Wissenschaft* 10 (1958) 221–27.

Caird, G. B. *The Language and Imagery of the Bible.* 2nd edition. Grand Rapids: Eerdmans, 1997.

Carmichael, C. M. "Marriage and the Samaritan Woman." *New Testament Studies* 26 (1980) 332–46.

Carson, D. A. *The Gospel According to John.* Grand Rapids: Eerdmans, 1991.

———. "Understanding Misunderstandings in the Fourth Gospel." *Tyndale Bulletin* 33 (1982) 59–92.

Carter, Warren. *John: Storyteller, Interpreter, Evangelist.* Peabody, MA: Hendrickson, 2006.

Cassuto, Umberto. *A Commentary on the Book of Exodus.* Translated by I. Abrahams. Jerusalem: Magnes, 1967.

Ceresko, Anthony R. "The Identity of 'the blind and the lame' in 2 Samuel 5:8b." *Catholic Biblical Quarterly* 63:1 (Jan 2001) 23–30.

Chadwick, Charles. *Symbolism.* London: Methuen, 1971.

Charlesworth, James H. *The Old Testament Pseudepigrapha, Volume 1: Apocalyptic Literature and Testaments.* Anchor Yale Bible Reference Library. New Haven: Yale University Press, 1983.

Clifford, Richard J. *Proverbs.* Old Testament Library. Louisville, KY: Westminster John Knox, 1999.

BIBLIOGRAPHY

Coloe, Mary. "Raising the Johannine Temple (John 19:19–37)." *Australian Biblical Review* 48 (2000) 47–58.

Cooper, Karl T. "The Best Wine: John 2:1–11." *Westminster Theological Journal* 41:2 (Spring 1979) 364–80.

Craigie, Peter C. *Psalms 1–50*. Word Biblical Commentary 19. Waco, TX: Word, 1983.

Croatto, J. Severino. "La epifanía bautismal del cordero pascual: estructura literaria y teología de Juan 1:19–34." *Cuadernos de teología* 6:3 (1983) 33–46.

Cross, Frank Moore. *Canaanite Myth and Hebrew Epic: Essays in the History of the Religion of Israel*. Cambridge: Harvard University Press, 1973.

Cross, Frank Moore. "The 'Olden Gods' in Ancient Near Eastern Creation Myths and in Israel." *From Epic to Canon: History and Literature in Ancient Israel*. Baltimore: Johns Hopkins University Press, 1998.

Crossan, John Dominic. *The Historical Jesus: The Life of a Mediterranean Jewish Peasant*. Edinburgh: T. & T. Clark, 1991.

Cullmann, Oscar. "Der johanneische Gebrauch doppeldeutigen Ausdrücke also Schlüssel zum Verständnis des vierten Evangeliums." *Theologische Zeitschrift* 4 (1948) 360–72.

Cullmann, Oscar. *Early Christian Worship*. London: SCM, 1962.

Culpepper, R. Alan. *Anatomy of the Fourth Gospel: A Study in Literary Design*. Philadelphia: Fortress, 1983.

Culpepper, R. Alan. "John 5:1–18: A Sample of Narrative Critical Commentary." In *The Gospel of John as Literature*. Edited by Mark W.G. Stibbe. New Testament Tools and Studies 17. Leiden: Brill, 1993.

———. "The Theology of the Gospel of John." *Review and Expositor* 85 (1988) 417–32.

Dahms, John V. "Isaiah 55:11 and the Gospel of John." *Evangelical Quarterly* 53 (April-June, 1981) 78–88.

Dahood, Mitchell. *Psalms II: 51–100*. Anchor Bible. Garden City, NY: Doubleday, 1983.

Daise, Michael A. "'If anyone thirsts, let that one come to me and drink': the literary texture of John 7:37b-38a." *Journal of Biblical Literature* 122:4 (2003) 687–99

Davies, W. D. *The Gospel and the Land: Early Christianity and Jewish Territorial Doctrine*. Berkeley: University of California Press, 1974.

Day, John. *God's Conflict with the Dragon and the Sea: Echoes of a Canaanite Myth in the Old Testament*. University of Cambridge Oriental Publications 35. Cambridge: Cambridge University Press, 1985.

Deeks, David. "The Structure of the Fourth Gospel." *New Testament Studies* 15 (1968–69) 107–28.

Dennis, John A. *Jesus' Death and the Gathering of True Israel: The Johannine Appropriation of Restoration Theology in the Light of John 11.47–52*. Wissenschaftliche Untersuchungen zum Neuen Testament. Second Series 217. Tübingen: Mohr Siebeck, 2006.

Derrett, J. Duncan M. *Law in the New Testament*. Eugene, OR: Wipf & Stock, 2005. First published 1970 by Darton, Longman & Todd.

———. "The Samaritan Woman's Purity (John 4:4–52)." *Evangelical Quarterly* 60:4 (1988) 291–98.

———. "Water into Wine." *Biblische Zeitschrift Neue Folge* 7 (1963) 84–93.

Dibelius, Martin. *Die Formgeschichte des Evangeliums*. 2nd edition. Tübingen: Mohr, 1933.

Dodd, C.H. *Interpretation of the Fourth Gospel*. Cambridge: Cambridge University Press, 1953.

Dods, Marcus. *The Gospel of St. John*. New York: Armstrong, 1905.

Bibliography

Dube, Musa W. "Toward a Post-Colonial Feminist Interpretation of the Bible." In *Reading the Bible as Women: Perspectives from Africa, Asia, and Latin America*, edited by Phyllis A. Bird, Katharine Doob Sakenfeld, and Sharon H. Ringe. *Semeia* 78 (1997) 11–26.

Dunn, James D.G. *Jesus Remembered*. Grand Rapids: Eerdmans, 2003.

Durham, John I. *Exodus*. Word Biblical Commentary 3; Waco, TX: Word, 1987.

Edwards, William D., Wesley J. Gabel, and Floyd E. Hosmer. "On the Physical Death of Jesus Christ." *Journal of the American Medical Association* 255 (March 21, 1986) 1455–63.

Elitzur, Yoel. "The Siloam Pool—'Solomon's Pool'—Was a Swimming Pool." *Palestine Exploration Quarterly* 140:1 (2008) 17–25.

Enz, J. J. "The Book of Exodus as Literary Type for the Gospel of John." *Journal of Biblical Literature* 76 (1957) 208–15.

Eslinger, L. "The Wooing of the Woman at the Well: Jesus, the Reader and Reader-Response Criticism." In *The Gospel of John as Literature*, edited by M. W. G. Stibbe, 165–82. London: Brill, 1993.

Farmer, Craig S. "Changing Images of the Samaritan Woman in Early Reformed Commentaries on John." *Church History* 65:3 (Sept 1996) 365–75.

Fee, Gordon D. "Once More—John 7:37–39." *Expository Times* 89:4 (1978) 116–18.

Ferguson, Everett. *Baptism in the Early Church: History, Theology and Liturgy in the First Five Centuries*. Grand Rapids: Eerdmans, 2009.

Finch, W. O. "The Interpretation of St. John 5:6." *Studia Evangelica IV*. Edited by F. L. Cross. Berline: Akademie-Verlage, 1968.

Findlay, J. A. *The Fourth Gospel: An Expository Commentary*. London: Epworth, 1956.

Flemington, W. F. *The New Testament Doctrine of Baptism*. London: SPCK, 1948.

Fowler, R. "Born of Water and the Spirit (Jn. 3:5)." *Expository Times* 82 (1971) 159.

Freed, Edwin D. *OT Quotations in the Gospel of John*. Leiden: Brill, 1965.

Freedman, William. "The Literary Motif: A Definition and Evaluation." *Novel* 4 (1971) 123–31.

Funk, R.W. *A Credible Jesus: Fragments of a Vision*. Santa Rosa, CA: Polebridge, 2002.

Glasson, T. Francis. "Exodus Typology in the Fourth Gospel." *Journal of Biblical Literature* 81 (1962) 329–42.

Glasson, T. Francis. *Moses in the Fourth Gospel*. London: SCM, 1963.

Green, Alberto R.W. *The Storm God in the Ancient Near East*. Biblical and Judaic Studies from the University of California San Diego 8. Winona Lake, IN: Eisenbrauns, 2003.

Griffiths, David R. "Deutero-Isaiah and the Fourth Gospel: Some Points of Comparison." *Expository Times* 65:12 (1954) 355–60.

Grigsby, Bruce H. "The Cross as an Expiatory Sacrifice in the Fourth Gospel." *Journal for the Study of the New Testament* 15 (1982) 51–80.

Gunkel, Hermann, and Heinrich Zimmern. *Creation and Chaos in the Primeval Era and the Eschaton: a Religio-Historical Study of Genesis 1 and Revelation 12*. Translated by K. William Whitney Jr. Grand Rapids: Eerdmans, 2006. Translation of *Schöpfung und Chaos in Urzeit und Endzeit: eine religionsgeschichtliche Untersuchung über Gen 1 und Ap Joh 12*. Göttingen: Vandenhoeck und Ruprecht, 1895.

Habel, Norman C. *The Book of Job: A Commentary*. Old Testament Library. Philadelphia: Westminster Press, 1985.

Haenchen, Ernst. *The Gospel of John*. Hermeneia. Vol. 1. Minneapolis: Augsburg Fortress, 1988.

BIBLIOGRAPHY

Hamid-Khani, Saeed. *Revelation and Concealment of Christ: A Theological Inquiry into the Elusive Language of the Fourth Gospel.* Wissenschaftliche Untersuchungen zum Neuen Testament. Second Series 120. Tubingen: Mohr Siebeck, 2000.

Hamilton, Victor P. *The Book of Genesis Chapters 1-17.* New International Commentary on the Old Testament. Grand Rapids: Eerdmans, 1990.

Harstine, Stan. *Moses as a Character in the Fourth Gospel: A Study of Ancient Reading Techniques.* New York: Sheffield Academic, 2002.

Hasel, Gerhard F., and Michael G. Hasel. "The Hebrew Term 'ed in Gen 2,6 and its Connection in Ancient Near Eastern Literature." *Zeitschrift für die Alttestamentliche Wissenschaft* 112:3 (2000) 321–40.

Hays, Richard B. *Echoes of Scripture in the Letters of Paul.* New Haven: Yale University Press, 1989.

Heidel, Alexander. *The Babylonian Genesis: The Story of Creation.* 2nd ed. Chicago: University of Chicago Press, 1951.

Heil, John Paul. *Blood and Water: The Death and Resurrection of Jesus in John 18-21.* Catholic Biblical Quarterly Manuscript Series 27. Washington, DC: Catholic Biblical Association of America, 1995.

Hodges, Zane Clark. "Rivers of Living Water: John 7:37–39." *Bibliotheca Sacra* 136 (July-Sept 1979) 239–48.

———. "Water and Spirit—John 3:5." *Bibliotheca Sacra* 135:539 (July-Sept 1978) 206–20.

Hollander, John. *The Figure of Echo: A Mode of Allusion in Milton and After.* Berkeley: University of California Press, 1981.

Holm-Nielsen, Svend. "Did Joab Climb 'Warren's Shaft'?" In *History and Traditions of Early Israel: Studies Presented to Eduard Nielsen,* edited by A. Lemaire and B. Otzen, 38–49. Leiden: Brill, 1993.

Hyatt, J. P. *Exodus.* New Century Bible. Grand Rapids: Eerdmans, 1971.

Hylen, Susan. *Allusion and Meaning in John 6.* Berlin: DeGruyter, 2005.

Issar, Arie. "The Evolution of the Ancient Water System in the Region of Jerusalem." *Israel Exploration Journal* 26 (1976) 130–36.

Janzen, J. Gerald. *Exodus.* Westminster Bible Commentary. Louisville: Westminster John Knox, 1997.

Jones, Larry Paul. *The Symbol of Water in the Gospel of John.* Journal for the Study of the New Testament Supplement Series 145. Sheffield: Sheffield Academic Press, 1997.

Kaiser, Otto. *Isaiah 1-12: A Commentary.* Old Testament Library. Philadelphia: Westminster Press, 1972.

Keener, Craig. S. *The Gospel of John: A Commentary.* 2 vols. Peabody, MA: Hendrickson, 2003.

Keck, Leander E. "Derivation as Destiny: 'Of-ness' in Johannine Christology, Anthropology and Soteriology." In *Exploring the Gospel of John,* edited by R. Alan Culpepper and C. Clifton Black, 274–88. Louisville: Westminster John Knox, 1996.

Kilpatrick, George Dunbar. "Punctuation of John 7:37–38." *Journal of Theological Studies* 11:2 (1960) 340–42.

Kim, Jean K. "A Korean Feminist Reading of John 4:1–42." In *Reading the Bible as Women : Perspectives from Africa, Asia, and Latin America,* edited by Phyllis A. Bird, Katharine Doob Sakenfeld, and Sharon H. Ringe. *Semeia* 78 (1997) 109–19.

Kim, Stephen S. "The Christological and Eschatological Significance of Jesus' Passover Signs in John 6." *Biblioteca Sacra* 164:655 (July-Sept 2007) 307–22.

Bibliography

Kleven, Terence. "Up the Waterspout: How David's General Joab Got Inside Jerusalem." *Biblical Archaeology Review* 20:4 (July 1994) 34–35.

Knapp, Henry M. "The Messianic Water Which Gives Life to the World." *Horizons in Biblical Theology* 19:2 (1997) 109–122.

Koester, Craig R. *Symbolism in the Fourth Gospel: Meaning, Mystery, Community*. Minneapolis: Fortress, 1995.

Kraus, Hans-Joachim. *Psalms 60–150: A Commentary*. Translated by H. C. Oswald. Minneapolis: Augsburg Fortress, 1989.

Kristeva, Julia. "Word, Dialogue and Novel." In *Séméiotiké: Recherches pour une sémanalyse*, 64–91. Paris: Le Sevil, 1969.

Kubina, Veronica. *Die Gottesreden im Buche Hiob*. New York: Herder, 1979.

Kuhn, K. H. "St. John 7:37–8." *New Testament Studies* 4:1 (1957) 63–65.

Labuschagne, C. J. *The Incomparability of Yahweh in the Old Testament*. Leiden: Brill, 1966.

Lee, Dorothy A. *The Symbolic Narratives of the Fourth Gospel: The Interplay of Form and Meaning*. Journal for the Study of the New Testament Supplement Series 95. Sheffield: JSOT Press, 1994.

Leroy, H. *Ratsel und Missverstandnis: Ein Beitrag zur Formgeschichte des Johannesevangelisums*. Bonn: Hanstein, 1966.

Lierman, John. "The Mosaic Pattern of John's Christology." In *Challenging Perspectives on the Gospel of John*, edited by John Lierman, 210–32. WUNT 2/219. Tübingen: Mohr Siebeck, 2006.

Lightfoot, R.H. *St. John's Gospel: A Commentary*. London: Oxford University Press, 1956.

Lincoln, Andrew T. *The Gospel According to St. John*. Black's New Testament Commentary 4. London: Continuum, 2005.

Lindars, Barnabas. *The Gospel of John*. New Century Bible. Grand Rapids: Eerdmans, 1982.

Little, Edmund. *Echoes of the Old Testament in the Wine of Cana in Galilee (John 2:1–11) and The Multiplication of the Loaves and Fish (John 6:1–15) Towards an Appreciation*. Cahiers de la Revue Biblique 4. Paris: Gabalda, 1998.

MacRae, George W. "Meaning and Evolution of the Feast of Tabernacles." *Catholic Biblical Quarterly* 22:3 (July 1960) 251–76.

Malina, Bruce J., and Richard L. Rohrbaugh. *Social-Science Commentary on the Gospel of John*. Minneapolis: Fortress, 1998.

Malina, Bruce J. *The New Testament World: Insights from Cultural Anthropology*. Louisville: Westminster John Knox Press, 2001.

Marcus, Joel. "Rivers of Living Water from Jesus' Belly (John 7:38)." *Journal of Biblical Literature* 117:2 (1998) 328–30.

Mayer, Allan. "Elijah and Elisha in John's Signs Source." *Expository Times* 99:6 (1988) 171–73.

McCabe, Robert V. "The Meaning of 'Born of Water and the Spirit' in John 3:5." *Detroit Baptist Seminary Journal* 4 (Fall 1999) 85–107.

McCarter, P. Kyle. *II Samuel*. Anchor Bible. New York: Doubleday, 1984.

Meir, J. P. *A Marginal Jew: Rethinking the Historical Jesus*. 3 vols. New York: Doubleday, 1991–2001.

Menken, Martinus J. J. "The Christology of the Fourth Gospel: A Survey of Recent Research." Pages 292–320 in *From Jesus to John: Essays on Jesus and New Testament Christology in Honor of Marinus de Jonge*. Edited by Martinus de Boer. Journal for the Study of the New Testament Supplement Series 84. Sheffield: JSOT Press, 1993.

———. "The Origin of the Old Testament Quotation in John 7:38." *Novum Testamentum* 38:2 (1996) 160–75.
Metzger, Bruce M. *A Textual Commentary on the Greek New Testament*. 3rd edition. New York: UBS, 1971.
Meyers, Carol. *Exodus*. New York: Cambridge University Press, 2005.
Miguens, Manuel. "Tres Testigos: Espiritu, Agua, Sangre." *Liber annuus Studii biblici Franciscani* 22 (1972) 74–94.
Mlakuzhyil, George. *The Christocentric Literary Structure of the Fourth Gospel*. Analecta Biblica 117. Rome: Pontifical University Press, 1987.
Morris, Leon. *The Gospel According to John*. New International Commentary on the New Testament. Grand Rapids: Eerdmans, 1971.
Morton, J. R. "Christ's Diagnosis of Disease at Bethesda." *Expository Times* 33 (1921–22) 424–25.
Mowinckel, Sigmund. *He That Cometh*. Translated by G. W. Anderson. Nashville: Abingdon, 1954.
Moyise, Steven. "Intertextuality and the Study of the Old Testament in the New Testament." in *The Old Testament in the New Testament: Essays in Honour of J. L. North*. Edited by S. Moyise. JSNTSS 189. Sheffield: Sheffield Academic, 2000.
Murphy, Roland E. *Proverbs*. Word Biblical Commentary 22. Thomas Nelson: Nashville, 1998.
Neyrey, Jerome H. *The Gospel of John*. New Cambridge Bible Commentary. New York: Cambridge University Press, 2007.
———. "Jacob Traditions and the Interpretation of John 4:10–26." *Catholic Biblical Quarterly* 41 (1979) 419–37.
Ng, Wai-yee. *Water Symbolism in John: An Eschatological Interpretation*. New York: Peter Lang, 2001.
O'Day, Gail R., and Susan E. Hylen. *John*. Westminster Bible Companion. Louisville, KY: Westminster John Knox, 2006.
———. "Narrative Mode and Theological Claim: A Study in the Fourth Gospel." *Journal of Biblical Literature* 105:4 (Dec 1986) 657–68.
Painter, John. *John: Witness and Theologian*. 2nd ed. London: SPCK, 1979.
Pamment, Margaret. "John 3:5: 'Unless One Is Born of Water and the Spirit, He Cannot Enter the Kingdom of God.'" *Novum Testamentum* 25 (1983) 189.
Poirier, John C. "David's 'Hatred' for the Lame and the Blind (2 Sam 5:8a)." *Palestine Exploration Quarterly* 138:1 (2006) 27–33.
Pope, Marvin H. *Job: Introduction, Translation and Notes*. Anchor Bible 15. 3rd ed. Garden City, NY: Doubleday, 1973.
Porter, Stanley E. "The Use of the Old Testament in the New Testament: A Brief Comment on Method and Terminology." In *Early Christian Interpretation of the Scriptures of Israel: Investigations and Proposals*, edited by C. A. Evans and J. A. Sanders, 79–96. Sheffield: Sheffield Academic, 1997.
Potterie, Ignace de la. "Naître de l'eau et naître de l'Esprit.": le texte baptismal de Jn 3:5." *Sciences ecclésiastiques* 14:3 (Oct–Dec 1962) 417–43.
Propp, William H. *Exodus 1–18*. Anchor Bible 2. Doubleday: New York, 1999.
Pyle, William T. "Understanding the Misunderstanding Sequences in the Gospel of John." *Faith and Mission* 11.2 (1994) 26–47.
Richard, Earl. "Expressions of Double Meaning and Their Function in the Gospel of John." *New Testament Studies* 31 (1985) 96–112.

Bibliography

Ridderbos, Herman. *The Gospel of John: A Theological Commentary.* Translated by J. Vriend. Grand Rapids: Eerdmans, 1997.

Ronning, John L. "The Targum of Isaiah and the Johannine Literature." *Westminster Theological Journal* 69:2 (2007) 247-78.

Ross, Allen P. *Recalling the Hope of Glory: Biblical Worship from the Garden to the New Creation.* Grand Rapids: Kregel, 2006.

Rowold, H. L. "The Theology of Creation in the Yahweh Speeches of the Book of Job as a Solution to the Problem Posed by the Book." PhD diss., Concordia Seminary in Exile, 1977.

Safrai, S. "The Temple." pages in *The Jewish People in the First Century: Historical Geography, Political History, Social, Cultural and Religious Life and Institutions,* edited by S. Safrai and M. Stern, 865-907. 2 vols. Philadelphia: Fortress, 1976.

Sailhamer, John H. *The Pentateuch as Narrative: A Biblical-Theological Commentary.* Grand Rapids: Zondervan, 1992.

Sanders, E. P. *The Historical Figure of Jesus.* London: Allen Lane, 1993.

Sandnes, Karl Olav. "Whence and Whither: A Narrative Perspective on the Birth *anothen.*" *Biblica* 86:2 (2005) 153-73.

Sawyer, John F. "The Gospel According to Isaiah." *Expository Times* 113:2 (Nov 2001) 39-43.

Schaefer, Konrad. *Psalms.* Berit Olam: Studies in Hebrew Narrative and Poetry. Edited by David W. Cotter. Collegeville, MN: Liturgical, 2001.

Schapdick, Stefan. "Religious Authority Re-Evaluated: The Character of Moses in the Fourth Gospel." In *Moses in Biblical and Extra-Biblical Traditions,* edited by A. Graupner and M. Wolter, 181-210. Berlin: De Gruyter, 2007.

Schnackenburg, Rudolf. *Baptism in the Thought of St. Paul.* Translated by G. R. Beasley-Murray. New York: Herder & Herder, 1964.

——— . *The Gospel According to John.* 3 vols. Translated by K. Smyth. New York: Herder & Herder, 1968.

Schüssler Fiorenza, Elizabeth. *Jesus and the Politics of Interpretation.* New York: Continuum, 2000.

Scott, R. B. Y. *Proverbs/Ecclesiastes.* Anchor Bible 18. Doubleday: New York, 1965.

——— . "Wisdom in Creation: the '*āmôn* of Proverbs viii:30a." *Vetus Testamentum* 10 (1960) 213-23.

Shaheen, Naseeb. "The Siloam End of Hezekiah's Tunnel." *Palestine Exploration Quarterly* 109 (1977) 107-12.

Shanks, Hershel. "The Siloam Pool: Where Jesus Healed the Blind Man." *Biblical Archaeology Review* 31 (Sept-Oct 2005) 16-23.

Smith, D. E. "Autopsy of an Autopsy: Biblical Illiteracy Among Medical Doctors." *Weststar Magazine* 1.2 (1987) 3-6, 14-15.

Smith, D. Moody. *John.* Abingdon New Testament Commentary. Nashville: Abingdon, 1999.

Söding, Thomas. "Wiedergeburt aus Wasser und Geist: Anmerkungen zur Symbolsprache des Johannesevangeliums am Beispiel des Nikodemusgesprächs (Joh 3,1-21)." Pages in *Metaphorik und Mythos im Neuen Testament,* edited by Karl Kertelge, 168-219. Freiburg: Herder, 1990.

Spaulding, Mary B. *Commemorative Identities: Jewish Social Memory and the Johannine Feast of Booths.* Library of New Testament Studies 396. New York: T. & T. Clark, 2009.

Bibliography

Spencer, Franklin Scott. "'You Just Don't Understand' (Or Do You?) Jesus, Women and Conversation in the Fourth Gospel." In Vol. 1 of *A Feminist Companion to John*, edited by Amy-Jill Levine and Marianne Blickenstaff, 15–47. Sheffield: Sheffield Academic, 2003. Reprinted as chapter 4 in Franklin Scott Spencer, *Dancing Girls, Loose Ladies and Women of the Cloth: The Women in Jesus' Life* (New York: Continuum, 2004).

Spriggs, D. G. "Meaning of 'Water' in John 3:5." *Expository Times* 85 (1974) 149–50.

Staley, J. L. "Stumbling in the Dark, Reaching for the Light: Reading Character in John 5 and 9." *Semeia* 53 (1991) 55–80.

Sukenik, Yadin. *The Art of Warfare in Biblical Lands*. New York, 1963.

Swancutt, Diana M. "Hungers Assuaged by the Bread from Heaven: 'Eating Jesus' as Isaian Call to Belief: the Confluence of Isaiah 55 and Psalm 78(77) in John 6:22–71." In *Early Christian Interpretations of the Scriptures of Israel*, edited by Craig A. Evans and James A. Sanders, 218–51. Sheffield: Sheffield Academic, 1997.

Talbert, C. H. *Reading John: A Literary and Theological Commentary*. New York: Crossroad, 1992.

Thatcher, Tom. "The Sabbath Trick: Unstable Irony in the Fourth Gospel." *Journal for the Study of the New Testament* 76 (1999) 53–77.

Theissen, Gerd, and Annette Mertz. *The Historical Jesus: A Comprehensive Guide*. Translated by J. Bowden. London: SCM, 1998.

Thomas, John Christopher. "'Stop Sinning Lest Something Worse Come Upon You': The Man at the Pool in John 5." *Journal for the Study of the New Testament* 59:1 (Sept 1995) 3–20.

Thompson, Marianne Meye. "Word of God, Messiah of Israel, Savior of the World: Learning the Identity of Jesus from the Gospel of John." In *Seeking the Identity of Jesus: A Pilgrimage*, edited by B. R. Gaventa and R. B. Hays, 166–79. Grand Rapids: Eerdmans, 2008.

Tillich, Paul. "The Religious Symbol." In *Symbolism in Religion and Literature*, edited by Rollo May, 71–82. New York: George Braziller, 1960.

Tsumura, David T. *Creation and Destruction: A Reappraisal of the* Chaoskampf *Theory in the Old Testament*. Winona Lake, IN: Eisenbrauns, 2005.

———. *The Earth and the Waters in Genesis 1 and 2: A Linguistic Investigation*. Journal for the Study of the Old Testament Supplement Series 83. Sheffield: Sheffield Academic, 1989.

Vermes, Geza. *The Authentic Gospel of Jesus*. London: Penguin, 2004.

Waetjen, Herman C. *The Gospel of the Beloved Disciple: A Work in Two Editions*. New York: Continuum, 2005.

Wagner, G. *Pauline Baptism and the Pagan Mysteries*. Translated by J. P. Smith. Edinburgh: Olive & Boyd, 1967.

Wahlde, Urban von. "The Pool of Siloam: The Importance of the New Discoveries for Our Understanding of Ritual Immersion in Late Second Temple Judaism and the Gospel of John." In *Jesus, John and History*, vol. 2, *Aspects of Historicity in the Fourth Gospel*, edited by P. Anderson, F. Just, and T. Thatcher, 155–74. Atlanta: SBL, 2009.

Waltke, Bruce K. *The Book of Proverbs: Chapters 1–15*. New International Commentary on the Old Testament. Grand Rapids: Eerdmans, 2004.

Walton, John H. "Creation in Gen 1:1—2:3 and the Ancient Near East: Order Out of Disorder after *Chaoskampf*." *Calvin Theological Journal* 43 (2008) 48–63.

Bibliography

Watson, Rebecca S. *Chaos Uncreated: A Reassessment of the Theme of "Chaos" in the Hebrew Bible*. Beihefte zur Zeitschrift für die Alttestamentliche Wissenschaft 341. Berlin: deGruyter, 2005.

Watson, W. G. E. *Classical Hebrew Poetry*. Journal for the Study of the Old Testament Supplement Series 26. Sheffield: JSOT, 1986.

Wead, David W. *Literary Devices in John's Gospel*. Basel: Friedrich Reinhardt, 1970.

Wenham, Gordon J. *Genesis 1–15*. Word Biblical Commentary 1. Waco: Word, 1987.

Wensinck, A.J. *The Ocean in the Literature of the Western Semites*. Wiesbaden: Sändig, 1918. Repr., 1968.

Westcott, B.F. *The Gospel According to John*. London: John Murray, 1892.

Westermann, Claus. *Genesis: A Commentary*. 3 vols. Translated by J. J. Scullion. Minneapolis: Augsburg, 1984–1986.

———. *Isaiah 40–66*. Old Testament Library. London: SCM, 1969.

Wheelwright, Philip. *Metaphor and Reality*. Bloomington: Indiana University Press, 1962.

Wilkinson, John. "The Incident of the Blood and Water in John 19:34." *Scottish Journal of Theology* 28:2 (1975) 149–72.

Williams, Catrin H. "Isaiah in John's Gospel." In *Isaiah in the New Testament*, edited by S. Moyise and M. J. J. Menken, 101–116. London: T. & T. Clark, 2005.

Witherington, Ben. *The Jesus Quest: The Third Search for the Jew of Nazareth*. 2nd ed. Downers Grove, IL: InterVarsity, 1997.

———. "The Waters of Birth: John 3:5 and 1 John 5:6–8." *New Testament Studies* 35:1 (Jan 1989) 155–60.

Witkamp, L. Th. "The Use of Traditions in John 5:1–18." *Journal for the Study of the New Testament* 25 (1985) 19–47.

Wright, N. T. *Jesus and the Victory of God*. London: SPCK, 1996.

Young, Franklin W. "Study of the Relation of Isaiah to the Fourth Gospel." *Zeitschrift für die neutestamentliche Wissenschaft und die Kunde der älteren Kirche* 46:3–4 (1955) 215–33.

www.ingramcontent.com/pod-product-compliance
Lightning Source LLC
Chambersburg PA
CBHW052059230426
43662CB00036B/1694